Mastering
Customer relations

Macmillan Master Series

Accounting	Geography
Accounting Skills	German
Advanced English Language	German 2
Advanced English Literature	Global Information Systems
Advanced Pure Mathematics	Human Resource Management
Arabic	Information Technology
Banking	Internet
Basic Management	Italian
Biology	Italian 2
British Politics	Java
Business Administration	Marketing
Business Communication	Mathematics
C Programming	Microsoft Office
C++ Programming	Microsoft Windows, Novell NetWare and
Chemistry	UNIX
COBOL Programming	Modern British History
Communication	Modern European History
Computer Studies	Modern US History
Counselling Skills	Modern World History
Customer Relations	Networks
Database Design	Organisational Behaviour
Delphi Programming	Pascal and Delphi Programming
Desktop Publishing	Philosophy
Economic and Social History	Photography
Economics	Physics
Electrical Engineering	Psychology
Electronic and Electrical Calculations	Shakespeare
Electronics	Social Welfare
English Grammar	Sociology
English Language	Spanish
English Literature	Spanish 2
Fashion Buying and Merchandising	Statistics
Fashion Styling	Systems Analysis and Design
French	Visual Basic
French 2	World Religions

Macmillan Master Series
Series Standing Order ISBN 0–333–69343–4
(outside North America only)

You can receive future titles in this series as they are published by placing a standing order. Please contact your bookseller or, in case of difficulty, write to us at the address below with your name and address, the title of the series and the ISBN quoted above.

Customer Services Department, Macmillan Distribution Ltd
Houndmills, Basingstoke, Hampshire RG21 6XS, England

Mastering
Customer relations

Roger I. Cartwright, MA

Business Series Editor
Richard Pettinger

First published 2000 by
MACMILLAN PRESS LTD
Houndmills, Basingstoke, Hampshire RG21 6XS
and London
Companies and representatives
throughout the world

ISBN 0–333–80159–8

A catalogue record for this book is available
from the British Library.

This book is printed on paper suitable for recycling and
made from fully managed and sustained forest sources.

10   9   8   7   6   5   4   3   2   1
09   08   07   06   05   04   03   02   01   00

Printed in Great Britain by
Creative Print & Design (Wales) Ltd, Ebbw Vale

Contents

◪ Preface

It is hard to find an organisation that could exist without customers. When Tom Peters and Robert Waterman (1982) introduced the phrase 'Close to the customer' they were articulating a belief that had been gaining ground for a number of years, i.e. successful organisations listened to and cared about their customers.

The above statement may seem self-evident and it is true that many organisations have long paid lip service to customer relationships. However it is still possible to find may organisations that do not practise the concepts of customer relations that will be put forward in this book. All too often organisations act in an arrogant and couldn't care less manner with their customers. This is evidenced by the continuing success of television programmes such as BBC's *Watchdog* and ITV's *We can work it out*, where examples are shown of customers being treated in a dreadful manner often by organisations which are household names.

In 1997, George Green and myself published *In Charge of Customer Satisfaction*, a text designed to support the UK levels 2 and 3 customer service National and Scottish Vocational Qualifications. We had no problem at all in finding many examples of bad customer service to go alongside those organisations that were exemplars of the art of looking after their customers. That book was designed for those who were in work and thus able to influence their organisation's attitude to the customer. This book is designed to be complementary to that volume and to be used not only by those in work but also by those who are studying prior to entering work, or indeed as has been the pattern in the 1990s, studying before re-entering the world of work.

A point that has been made by many of those working in the customer relations field and one that is reiterated in this book is that it does not matter whether a person is working in the front office (as described by Clutterbuck *et al.*, 1993) and dealing directly with the external customer or in the back office and perhaps never meeting the final customer – everybody in an organisation is part of the customer value chain. Training in customer care etc. should be a priority for all employees, regardless of their position within the organisation.

More and more qualifications in business administration and management at ordinary level/standard grade and above require a knowledge of customer relations and customer service. Within the frameworks for Scottish Qualification Authority (SQA) Higher National Certificates and Diplomas (HNC/D) customer care is one of the most frequently chosen options, showing that students recognise the importance of the subject within the field of commerce.

The fields of customer relations, customer service and customer care draw their subject matter from a variety of sources. Operations management, quality management, psychology and retailing all contribute to the area of study we call customer relations. To study this important component of the business world this book blends the conceptual with the practical. The various components of customer relations are considered from a conceptual point of view in order to provide a theoretical underpinning which is then overlaid with practical examples and case studies.

The examples, which are all from the real world, feature a wide variety of organisations and sectors together with real people. Retailing, entertainment, tourism, the public sector including prisons and even politicians have all been used to illustrate the concepts required for effective customer relations.

Chapter 10 provides a series of case studies on real organisations (or individuals) that will allow the reader to contrast and compare attitudes to customer relations. There have been many case studies on retail operations published and therefore this book looks at some different areas drawing on interviews and observations with an entertainer (actually a comedy magician) whose customers are called an audience, a tourist attraction, a cinema, a cruise line, a public sector organisation that may well be a grudge purchase (a term covered in the early parts of this book) for many, namely the Scottish Prison Service, and lastly another possible grudge purchase in the form of a politician. In the latter case the customers are called electors and constituents. Whether they are an audience, a tour party, colleagues or constituents, they are customers first and foremost and the most important relationship any organisation can have is the one with its customers.

Four of the case studies are set in organisations/individuals based in Scotland but often operating much further afield. The simple reason for this is that the author lives and works in Scotland and has thus been able to observe the chosen operations at close hand over a period of time.

This book is designed to take you on a journey through what is one of the (if not the prime) objectives of all organisations, understanding and responding to the needs and wants of those organisations' customers. It is customers who pay the wages and provide the dividends to shareholders in the private sector, it is customers that provide the tax income and votes required for the public sector and it is customers that provide the charitable donations that provide the *raison d'être* for the voluntary sector. As will be shown in Chapter 1, the boundaries between these sectors have become very blurred and that chapter will explore the status of customer relations as applied to not-for-profit organisations in addition to those types of organisation where success is measured in terms of profit.

It is likely that there will be two main categories of people using this book:

- Those undertaking studies for which customer relations forms part of the framework for a qualification
- Those interested in developing their customer relations' skills at work.

Whilst this book has been written primarily for the former group, the two aims are not mutually exclusive and in good customer relations' tradition the needs and wants of both types of reader have been considered and addressed.

When I first began, with George Green, to look at customer service, we were told that it was all common sense. That was 50% correct. It all made sense, unfortunately it was not as common as many people believed. Our research led us to ten very simple rules that were published in *In Charge of Customer Satisfaction* (1997, Blackwell). These are repeated below as they form the basis for any study of customer relations:

THE 10 GOLDEN RULES OF CUSTOMER CARE
(Cartwright & Green, 1997, with permission)

1. IT COSTS FAR MORE TO GAIN A NEW CUSTOMER THAN IT DOES TO RETAIN AN EXISTING ONE
2. UNLESS YOU RECOVER THE SITUATION QUICKLY, A LOST CUSTOMER WILL BE LOST FOR EVER
3. DISSATISFIED CUSTOMERS HAVE FAR MORE FRIENDS THAN SATISFIED ONES
4. THE CUSTOMER ISN'T ALWAYS RIGHT, BUT HOW YOU TELL THEM THAT THEY'RE WRONG CAN MAKE ALL THE DIFFERENCE AND ULTIMATELY THEY DO PAY YOUR WAGES
5. WELCOME COMPLAINTS – THEY ALLOW FOR RECOVERY
6. IN A FREE MARKET ECONOMY NEVER FORGET THAT THE CUSTOMER HAS A CHOICE
7. TREAT INTERNAL CUSTOMERS AS YOU WOULD EXTERNAL ONES
8. YOU MUST LISTEN TO THE CUSTOMER TO FIND OUT WHAT THEY WANT
9. IF YOU DON'T BELIEVE, HOW CAN YOU EXPECT THE CUSTOMER TO?
10. IF YOU DON'T LOOK AFTER YOUR CUSTOMERS, SOMEBODY ELSE WILL.

Simple rules but ones that every organisation would do well to follow.

At the end of each of Chapters 1–9 are a series of questions that will allow you to reflect on the subject matter.

At the end of the book there is a Bibliography where you can find details of all the sources quoted.

Acknowledgements

Grateful thanks for assistance in the preparation of this book are due to:

Highland Distillers
The Scottish Prison Service
Caledonian Cinemas
Princess Cruises
Hal Malquardt
Roseanna Cunningham MP, MSP
George Green
Richard Pettinger
and not forgetting my wife, June, for the illustrations of body language and Sue Macfarlane, of Perth College, for her patience when my word processing skills let me down.

Every effort has been made to trace copyright holders, but if any have been inadvertently overlooked the publishers will be pleased to make the necessary arrangements at the first opportunity.

▮ Introduction

The importance of customer service – Goods and services – Competition and market share – Changing attitudes of customers – Satisfaction and delight – Public and private sectors – Customer service and the bottom line – The customer accumulator – Lifetime value of the customer – Customer led v product driven – Value added – Customer service at the centre of an organisation's objectives – Typologies of organisations – Grudge purchases

The question of why customer service is so important should be relatively simple to answer – no customers, no work, no income and no jobs. However, given that there is still a great deal of poor customer service to be found then the situation must be more complex.

To explore this it is necessary to examine the nature of the relationships between customers and suppliers, which is the main focus of this book.

Customer relations is more than just providing excellent service and care at the point of a transaction. Relationships, by the very meaning of the word, have a temporal span – they have a beginning, a middle and unfortunately an end over a span of time. Relationships also need effort in establishing them and there are vital maintenance functions. The thrust of this book will be to provide an understanding of those relationships and the methods with which they can be made positive and beneficial to all the parties in the relationship. Relationship is a neutral word: relationships can be either good or bad, we can love or hate but these extremes are still just relationships. It is a good relationship that every organisation should seek with its customers, not just a relationship *per se.*

Goods and services

Goods are something that somebody provides for somebody else; another word for this is PRODUCT. Traditional thinking held that goods were tangible products, i.e. ones that you could hold in your hand or at least touch, such as watches, foodstuffs, motor cars etc. Services were considered as intangible products, i.e. ones that could be experienced but not seen or touched directly, such as health care or financial services. In the context of this book all of the above are products and service is what surrounds them. Service is the way they are promoted, delivered and looked after by the supplier.

In this way everything that somebody provides for someone can be defined as a product. The nature of the transaction is that A has something that B wants and in order to acquire it B has to make a purchase in some form or another.

Purchases do not have to be made with money although this is the normal commercial method. All money is a common commodity that is accepted by a number of parties. B might pay for the goods in money, but could pay in affection or barter. Where A provides something for B with no form of exchange whatsoever is known as altruism, which happens less frequently than we might wish to imagine. A parent wishing to quiet a child might buy it a toy. That is a straightforward transaction; the parent wants peace and quiet and buys it with a product, in this case a toy. The value of the toy is recognised by both the child and the parent. The child pays for the toy (perhaps subconsciously) with quietened behaviour. The danger in this scenario is that the child realises that its noisy behaviour has produced a toy and thus the temptation is to be noisy again in order to obtain another toy – sometimes this works, often it doesn't. Eric Berne (1964) and Thomas Harris (1970) have both examined the way human transactions can be described in terms of payment with positive or negative strokes in just the same way as people buy their everyday commodities.

There are two major reasons for an acceptance of poor customer service:

- No choice
- Attitudes.

If the customer has no choice or relatively few choices and wants the product then they may have little alternative but to accept poor service. What is clear is that a situation of no choice has a relatively short life cycle. Monopolies, situations where one organisation provides the sole source of supply, are legislated against in the UK, the USA and many other countries. Governments have realised that a lack of choice leads to dissatisfied consumers and dissatisfied consumers can display their frustration through the ballot box. Organisations, whilst espousing the ideal of competition publicly, often try to achieve as near a monopoly situation as possible. For the supplier a monopoly is the ideal situation as it gives total control of the market and prices. For the customer, as much choice as possible without destroying the market is ideal. Competition usually means lower prices and higher quality. It is important that there is some form of control of competition. All organisations need a critical mass of customers to survive. Too many organisations chasing the same number of customers could lead to a situation where the market is so divided between them that no organisation actually has enough customers to survive. To illustrate this mathematically, suppose that the total market for a product is 1000 customers and that to survive an organisation must have 200 customers. If there were 5 organisations, all selling at the same price and the same quality then the chances are they would each have the required 200 customers (see Figure 1.1).

If a sixth organisation joins the market then either they will fail very early on because they attract no customers or they will (more likely) attract some customers from the original five (see Figure 1.2).

We now have a situation where no organisation has enough customers to be viable. What is likely to happen over time is that the market will expand as

Organisation	Customers	Market Share
A	200	20%
B	200	20%
C	200	20%
D	200	20%
E	200	20%

Figure 1.1   The initial market.

Organisation	Customers	Market Share
A	180	18%
B	180	18%
C	180	18%
D	180	18%
E	180	18%
F	100	10%

Figure 1.2   The market with one new member.

Organisation	Customers	Market Share
A (+ B + F)	700	47%
C (+ E)	500	33%
D	300	20%

Figure 1.3   The market after 3 years.

organisations create demand and that there will be mergers and take-overs. In three years' time the market may have expanded to 1500 customers and the position of the organisations may look like that shown in Figure 1.3.

Organisation *D* now looks ripe for a take-over leaving the customer with only two choices. Competition can remove choice almost as easily as it creates it. For legislators the aim of competition is to widen the market and create choice, for organisations it is to remove the competition and gain as much market share as possible. Market share is an important indicator of an organisation's success as it is one of the aspects of performance given considerable prominence by investors.

Customers seem to be best served by organisations that are either big enough to offer such economies of scale so as to be able to compete on price or small enough to offer a personal, exclusive service. Supermarkets have developed rapidly in the UK as have the smaller, more specialised food shops and delicatessens. It has been the middle of the size range organisations that have been squeezed, in many cases out of business.

Changing attitudes of customers

It was John Wannamaker, a Philadelphia Department store owner who, in the 1860s coined the immortal phrase 'the customer is always right'. (Popular belief in the UK ascribes the remark to John Sainsbury and perhaps there is nothing wrong with two different groups claiming ownership in this instance!) The retail trade, dependent as it was and remains on good face-to-face, continuing relationships with customers, was far quicker to pick up on this concept. By the early 1900s the steamship companies taking immigrants from Europe to North America had upgraded their immigrant or 'steerage' accommodation considerably. As Davie (1986) has pointed out, this was less as a result of official rules on the transportation of immigrants and more to do with a realisation that there was profit to be made in attracting the immigrant trade and that those who went out steerage might, having done well in the New World, make visits home using second or even first class. If they were impressed by the steerage accommodation, they might well book themselves and their families in higher priced cabins for visits to their ancestral homes.

As competition has increased, so the suppliers of goods and services for profit have had to 'woo' their customers. The ability to travel, brought about firstly by the railways and then by the motor car and the aeroplane, has increased the distance that customers are able to go in order to fulfil their require-ments. Village and even city centre shops have found it difficult to compete with supermarkets situated on the outskirts of town, especially when those supermarkets provide good parking facilities, buses in some cases for those without cars and even petrol pumps. As will be shown in Chapter 4, even loyalty has a price and customers have been looking further and further afield not just for the lowest prices but for enhanced service and facilities. The latest such developments include not only a supermarket but other retail outlets, bringing them into line with the mall developments in the USA. Large shopping malls such as the Arndale and Trafford Centres in the Manchester area, Meadowhall in Sheffield, the Metro Centre on Tyneside and Thurrock in Essex are regional in nature but more and more local malls have been developed providing one-stop shopping, mainly for the motor car owner.

Customers are becoming used to choice and quality. Other sectors of busi-ness have been slower to respond to the more sophisticated customer. Today's customer challenges and wants to know the why and not just the how. The medical and legal professions, local and national government, newly privatised industries and education have all been required to become more responsive to the needs of their customers.

The 20th Century saw the development of huge organisations. Prior to the industrial revolution of the 19th Century, organisations were small, limited as they were by the lack of effective means of transport. Small organisations find it much easier to remain close to their customer base; this is much more difficult for a larger organisation.

The development of improved communication systems after World War II, in particular the telephone and television, helped bring about a consumer revolution. It became much easier for consumers to exchange information and the development of commercial broadcasting, firstly in the United States and then in the UK, meant that viewers were exposed to increasing amounts of advertising. Customers were becoming much more aware of the choices open to them.

In 1965 a young US lawyer and freelance political consultant named Ralph Nader published a book entitled *Unsafe at any Speed* (Nader, 1965) in which he attacked the lack of concern for consumer safety amongst the US automobile industry (Celsi, 1991). Ralph Nader's efforts, which many have described as a crusade, grew to encompass not only the safety of motor vehicles but also many other areas of interest to US consumers from sport to nuclear power. Nader and his 'Raiders' (as he and his seven associates were known) became feared by corporate America and, as Celsi (1991) reports, he became 'the nation's self-appointed consumer advocate'. Nader's work led to the US Congress setting up the Consumer Protection Agency in 1970. As Celsi points out, the 1960s were a time of social revolution in Western society, the music of Bob Dylan and others fuelling the revolutionary fervour of a generation of teenagers and young adults. Civil Rights was a huge issue in the USA and Nader's consumer revolution fitted neatly into the pattern. For too long the huge corporations had been able to operate in a manner that assumed that they knew what the customer wanted. The consumers began to fight back and demanded quality and service. The signs had been there for some time. Just after World War II, Ford designers had developed what they believed would be the best automobile they had ever produced, the Ford Edsell named after Henry Ford's son. Unfortunately they never consulted the potential customers and whilst the vehicle might have been technologically advanced, it did not meet the needs of the customer and very few were sold (Cartwright & Green, 1997). Such charges were levelled against the UK aircraft industry after World War II. It produced the aircraft it was happy with, the Brabazon, the VC10 and the Concord, but not those required by the airlines. Even the famous Comet was not a commercial success, being eclipsed by the Boeing 707 and the Douglas DC8 (Eddy *et al.*, 1976). Similar charges were levelled by the airline industry against Boeing in the 1980s, charges that resulted in both discussions and collaborations with airlines not only in the construction but in the initial design stages of the Boeing 777 (Sabbach, 1995).

In the UK, Nader's work was followed closely. Even before he became a household name on both sides of the Atlantic, the Consumers' Association was founded in 1957 and began publication of the magazine *Which?*. The magazine tested products and provided an independent guide to consumers. As will be shown in Chapter 6, the UK government set up an Office of Fair Trading in response to the growing sophistication of customers.

In 1982, Tom Peters and Bob Waterman published *In Search of Excellence*, their study of successful US companies, and made the point that closeness to the customer and active listening to customers were key attributes for successful companies (Peters & Waterman, 1982). A similar study in the UK by Goldsmith and Clutterbuck drew remarkably similar conclusions – the *Winning Streak* (as they entitled it) for the successful UK company was closely related to the care given to effective customer relations (Clutterbuck & Goldsmith, 1983).

The social revolution of the 1960s has led to a much more questioning customer base. Doctors and lawyers now find that their customers ask questions and demand excellent service – questioning a doctor used to be unheard of. Dissatisfied customers are much more likely to resort to litigation (see Chapter 6) if their problems cannot be resolved and the major television channels have espoused the cause of the consumer. In the UK the BBC consumer affairs programme *Watchdog* and the ITV series *We can work it out* attract excellent viewing figures and have provided embarrassing moments for those companies that have failed to respond to legitimate customer complaints.

When Boeing introduced the 747 'Jumbo' in 1969, they enabled the British to begin to visit the USA in large numbers; Florida has become a major outbound destination for British holidaymakers. The British were able to see at first hand how the US retail, hospitality and entertainment industries treated their customers and that has led to a revolution in service standards in the UK. The USA has had a tremendous influence on British customer relations. Not every US company gets it right first time, every time, but there has been a greater awareness of the need to delight the customer (a term that will be covered further in the next chapter) and as British customers have experienced the US standards of service, so they have returned demanding the same standards at home.

Satisfaction and delight

Many, many organisations can satisfy their customers. It is only those few that are prepared to really put the customer at the centre of their operations that are able to truly delight the customer. Satisfaction is better than dissatisfaction but even the use of the word in English suggests that there is far more that could be done. Satisfaction is only a step on the road to delight. Chapter 4 will consider customer loyalty and it is not satisfaction but delight that secures long-term loyalty. In emotive terms satisfaction is what the customer expects, delight is what provides a warm glow. Delight, from the customer's point of view, could be described as receiving more than the minimum expected added value. Delighting a customer actually adds added value to the relationship between the supplier and the customer.

Public and private sectors

The importance of good customer relations was first realised by those areas of the private sector that had immediate, face-to-face contact with paying customers, such as the retail, hotel, transportation and entertainment sectors. Today all private companies who rely on profit (see later) need to be conversant with the factors that lead to good customer relations. In the public sector, comprising more monopolistic situations, it might be thought that customer service is less important. However customers are also voters and thus the customer is able to express an opinion (albeit only every few years) on the standard of service received from the public sector. Most sections of the public sector have now developed customer care programmes and the necessary training for staff. As funding from central government has been targeted to follow the individual, so local government, the education service and the National Health Service have seen, perhaps more transparently, the value of the individual to their growth and budgets. Whilst such organisations do not measure success by profits, government has begun to apply strict performance targets and monies are contingent on achieving those targets, one of which is invariably customer satisfaction. Definitions of customers (see Chapter 2) are perhaps harder in the public sector but the subject of customer relations is equally relevant across all sectors.

Customer service and the bottom line

Market share, as stated earlier, is one of the aspects of an organisation's performance given considerable weight by investors. This is obviously only a factor with private, for-profit organisations but it is an important one as the effect of a drop in market share on investor confidence can be quite dramatic.

The effect of a loss of customers to a rival is not an arithmetic progression but follows what may be described as the 'customer accumulator', as follows. Imagine a situation where there are two shops in a town and each has 100 customers initially. For the purpose of this exercise it is assumed that the total customer base will remain at 200. The effect of shop B gaining 1, 2, 10, 25 and 50 customers off shop A is examined in Figure 1.4.

Shop A has lost half its customers but it is now three times smaller and thus perhaps three times less attractive to investors than shop B. If we assume for the exercise that each customer generates £10 of profit, the effect of this on profit is shown in Figure 1.5.

Not only is shop B now three times bigger in terms of market share, it is three times more profitable and the comparison of profitability is a key ratio in deciding the relative strength and success of organisations.

One of the most useful definitions of an effective organisation is:

Shop A Customers	Shop A Market share	Shop B Customers	Shop B Market share	Numerical difference B − A	Relative size of B compared to A
100	50%	100	50%	0	equal
99	49.5%	101	50.5%	2	1.02
98	49%	102	51%	4	1.04
90	44%	110	56%	20	1.2
75	37.5%	125	62.5%	50	1.6
50	25%	150	75%	100	3

Figure 1.4   The customer accumulator.

Shop A Customers	Shop A Profit	Shop B Customers	Shop B Profit
100	£1000	100	£1000
99	£990	101	£1010
98	£980	102	£1020
90	£900	110	£1100
75	£750	125	£1250
50	£500	150	£1500

Figure 1.5   The effect of the customer accumulator on profit.

one that listens to its customers and then meets their needs at an acceptable cost to both parties

It is easy to meet the needs of customers if cost is not an issue but in the real world there are always costs. To provide any kind of product or service always involves a series of costs, which can include:

- materials
- staff
- overheads
- time.

Every product requires raw materials and even a purely service organisation needs stationery, postage etc. Staff are one of the biggest costs most organisations have to bear. In the public sector and in service industries the staffing budget may be 75%–80% of the overall budget, a considerable proportion. Organisations, even the smallest, need to consider the costs of electricity, telephones, heating, premises, maintenance and perhaps marketing. Time forms what is known as an opportunity cost. Time is finite. The time spent doing one thing is time that is not available for another.

The costs of the organisation need to be less than the price that a customer is prepared to pay either directly or indirectly for the products and services of that organisation. In the private sector the difference between the total costs to the organisation and the total amount collected from customers in whatever form is profit. In the public sector it is the difference between a budget surplus and a budget deficit.

Private sector organisations that depend on profit eventually go out of business if their costs outweigh the payments received. Public sector organisations either have to cut services or receive a subsidy from the taxpayer.

Accountants use a term 'cost of sales' as part of the accountancy procedure for companies. This book introduces the term 'cost of service'. Cost of sales is easy to calculate as the company can easily calculate the costs that are directly associated with selling their product. Cost of service is less easy to calculate as only part of the cost is directly measurable, but it is just as important.

To illustrate the concept, imagine two customers entering a showroom to purchase a new motor car. One, who is 25, has £10,000 to spend and the other who is 65 has £18,000 available. Now imagine you are the salesperson, which of these customers is the most important to you, i.e. if you have only a finite amount of time and limited discounts to offer – which one has priority?

This is not an easy question to answer and the first thing that needs to be considered is the concept of the lifetime value of the customer.

Lifetime value of the customer

It is clear that the 65-year-old customer has more money to spend, or have they? They have at this moment in time but consider not only this purchase but also their future purchases. At the age of 65 they might buy three more new cars, probably trading down slightly each time. To simplify matters, assume that each car costs £18,000, i.e. that inflation against a slight trading down leads to an identical price.

The younger customer will possibly buy ten new cars during their motoring career, trading up for at least seven of the purchases. This leads to the situation shown in Figure 1.6.

The older customer may have more money initially but neglecting the younger one could cost dearly.

It is no coincidence that banks and building societies target students as potential account holders. Although they are likely to be very short of money whilst at college or university, statistics show that they are likely to earn higher than average salaries later on and, as people are very reluctant to change their bank or building society account, they will become good lifetime customers.

It has been calculated (Cartwright & Green, 1997) that an average person spends in a lifetime over £150,000 on motor cars, £25,000–£50,000 on holidays and no less than £100,000 in the supermarket. No wonder that loyalty schemes abound in the supermarket industry. A dissatisfied customer does not leave £30 of groceries at the till, if they never come back then £100,000 of business, according to the accumulator model introduced earlier, goes to a competitor, boosting their market position.

In the case of the motor car sale, both customers may be of equal importance. Time spent with the younger customer may be repaid with a lifetime of business. Remembering the *Golden Rules of Customer Care* (Cartwright and Green, 1997), quoted in the Preface, if the older customer is also satisfied, then they may well advise their family and friends to buy their vehicles from the same dealership.

It is, of course easy for the salesman to sell a vehicle to either of the customers. All they need to do is provide plenty of optional extras at no cost and to lower the price! However the organisation can only sell at a profit if it is to remain in business. There are occasions when organisations may sell a particular product at a loss in order to attract customers to buy other products and such *loss leaders* have been a feature of supermarket operations for some time. This strategy can

Purchases	Customer A 25 years	Customer B 65 years
Vehicle	£10,000	£18,000
Vehicle	£12,000	£18,000
Vehicle	£15,000	£18,000
Vehicle	£17,000	
Vehicle	£20,000	
Vehicle	£22,000	
Vehicle	£25,000	
Vehicle	£23,000	
Vehicle	£21,000	
Vehicle	£20,000	
TOTAL	£185,000	£54,000

Figure 1.6 Lifetime value.

only be successful, however, if the loss leader stimulates sales of profitable products.

Economists use a model known as a supply and demand curve (see Chapter 3) to show the relationship between the number of items a seller will produce for sale at a given price and the number of customers who will buy at that price.

If, after taking all the costs into consideration, a supplier can produce 100 items for sale at £50 each and there are at least 100 customers who will pay £50 each, the project will at least break even. If only 40 customers are prepared to pay that much, 10 items will remain unsold. Simplistically there are only two options then left to the supplier, either reduce the price because it may be that 150 people would buy at £45 or try to stimulate the market, a concept that will be considered in Chapter 3. The vital point is that there is a price below which a supplier cannot drop however much the customer may want to pay less.

What any supplier can offer is a good relationship with the customer – indeed such a relationship may not cost much in terms of money or time. There are however real costs associated with an excellent relationship. Nevertheless these costs of service are nearly always recouped by repeat business.

In the case of our car buyers, time spent listening to them will not be wasted. Listening to the customer provides vital information about their requirements. Remember the definition of an effective organisation given earlier in this chapter:

one that listens to its customers and then meets their needs at an acceptable cost to both parties

It is vital to listen carefully to the customer, not only at the time of their first transaction with you but throughout the lifetime of the relationship – which is how organisations can not only meet the requirements of their customers but also can anticipate them. Being proactive can lead to much better relationships than being merely reactive.

Customer driven v product led

There are two extremes to a relationship with the customer and indeed to marketing as a whole. An organisation which adopts a **product led approach**, develops products and systems that are suited to the organisation. Henry Ford expressed this approach well in the 1920s when he offered customers a Model T Ford in 'any colour as long as it's black'. Such an approach can work in a situation where there is no competition and demand exceeds supply. Modern vehicle manufacturers, having listened to their customers, develop a whole range of variations and options around the same model and are thus able to adopt a much more **customer driven** (excuse the pun) approach. It may be cheaper to produce only one basic model but the modern customer has shown that they wish to make choices. Indeed in the motor vehicle industry, yesterday's options rapidly become today's standard features. Power steering, air-conditioning, CD players etc. were once highly priced options or only standard on the most expensive top of the range products. In the 2000s they are standard on many medium priced products. The customers had expressed a preference for these items through their purchasing decisions and the more proactive manufacturers made proactive decisions to offer their mainstream products with such features. Such features may also form part of the cost of service – offering the customer more will probably cost more but it will generate more income!

It is not only in terms of the features of physical products that a customer driven approach is manifested. Service features such as opening times, new means of communications and even the provision of disabled and mother-and-child parking spaces demonstrate a commitment to putting the needs of the customer before those of the organisation, reflecting the *Golden Rule* (see Preface) that it is the customer and the customer alone that directly or indirectly pays the bills and wages of any organisation.

Many organisations claim that they put the customer at the centre of their operations but experience shows that this is sometimes a false belief. Chapter 4 on customer loyalty will show that customers may exhibit loyalty only because they have no choice and Chapter 8, which introduces the concept of Organisational Body Language (OBL), first described by Cartwright and Green in 1997, will demonstrate how the real messages that organisations give out to their customers may well be in conflict with statements of intent.

Value added

Chapter 3 considers the concept of value for money but this is an appropriate place to think about how customers place a value on goods and services. In the motor car sale example earlier in this chapter it is interesting to consider how the cost of the £10,000 model would have been built up. If the customer had the time and skills they could, perhaps, have bought the various components of the vehicle themselves and assembled them. Indeed, it is possible to buy kits for cars, boats and even aircraft and houses and do just that. Furthermore kits are nearly always cheaper. (It should be noted at this point that a newspaper survey in September 1999 discovered that if one tried to build a car from the spare parts supplied by the manufacturer it could cost up to three times more than buying it ready built. This does not negate what has been said above, as spare parts are an area where a manufacturer can make extra revenue and the price charged does not always indicate the cost to the manufacturer.) Why don't more people take this approach and save themselves money? The answer is simple; most people do not have either the skills or more importantly the time to do so. It is convenience that forms part of the price. Indeed, as will be shown in the next chapter, Kotler (1980) changed the PLACE component of the marketing mix to CONVENIENCE to reflect the importance that modern society attaches to convenience. A component of the cost of any product/service, including our vehicle example, must reflect the perceived value that the customer places on the skills of those producing the product/service and time saved by the customer in purchasing it rather than doing it themselves. Not only could we build our own cars but we could make our clothes, erect our own homes and even carry out legal tasks such as drawing up our own last will and testament and carrying out the conveyencing of property. Time is an opportunity cost and the value of the time is greater than the price charged for the skills and time of those delivering the product/service.

Each step of the process of delivering a product/service, be it building a vehicle or processing a loan or dealing with a planning application, carries a skill/time cost and a monetary amount of added value that the customer is prepared to pay. This is known as a value chain with the costs of the product building up at each step together with a contribution to the added value. The costs of each step of a process consist of a series of factors:

cost of raw materials

+

labour

+

contribution to the overheads of the organisation

+

extra costs (marketing, distribution etc.)

+

costs of ongoing servicing etc.

+

added value to the customer

As profit was defined earlier as the difference between the total costs of the product/service and the price paid, it is easy to see that added value and profit are closely linked.

Customer service at the centre of an organisation's objectives

There are four basic typologies of organisations, defined by ownership and prime function (for-profit and not-for-profit as the terms are generally understood) as shown in Figure 1.7.

	Public ownership	Private ownership
For-profit	Nationalised industry	Commercial organisations
Not-for-profit	National/local government	Voluntary sector

Figure 1.7   Typologies of organisations.

In terms of size, the current position in the UK is that the for-profit/private ownership and the not-for-profit/public ownership sectors are in fact by far the biggest components in terms of economic activity. The former includes the majority of all commercial activities and the latter the entire public sector including national and local government, the National Health Service, education and the armed forces. Prior to the 1980s, the for-profit/public ownership sector was very large and contained some huge monopoly or near monopoly organisations. These included the steel, coal, gas, electricity and ship building industries, railways, British Airways and other nationalised concerns. Under privatisation they have moved into the for-profit/private ownership quadrant.

In the next chapter the somewhat complex question of 'who is the customer?' is considered. What it is important to realise is that every organisation has customers and that unless those customers are placed at the centre of an organisation's objectives they may go elsewhere. Even in a monopoly situation the customer still has the right to not partake of the product or service. Monopolies rarely last for ever and as soon as there is some form of choice, some customers will be lost. If the relationship with the customer has not been at the centre of the organisation's objectives then there is a danger that there will be exodus rather than just leakage of customers.

Managers are taught that objectives should always be written in SMART criteria, i.e. they should be:

Specific
Measurable
Agreed
Realistic
Timely (that is, with deadlines and timescales attached)

This book suggests that SMART should be amended to C-SMART with the all-important CUSTOMER DRIVEN being the most important.

The Ford Edsell mentioned earlier met all of the SMART criteria: there was a SPECIFIC project, the outputs were MEASURABLE, all of the Ford executives AGREED to the project, it was REALISTIC and it was built on TIME. Unfortunately it was product led and not CUSTOMER DRIVEN. If only that had been the main objective, much investment would not have been wasted.

Grudge purchases

It is easy to consider customer relations in terms of the products and services customers actually enjoy – motor cars, clothes, holidays etc. This book will make much of repeat business as an indicator of good customer relations. Not all organisations however wish to use repeat business as an indicator. Surgeons do not want the patient back and the police have a reduction in repeat business as an indicator. We all need hospitals and police stations but they are not something that we actively want to partake in. It is, therefore, more problematic to consider those products and services that people actually need but begrudge paying for. Insurance is a classic grudge purchase. It is necessary but the costs are often resented. Indeed if somebody has to claim it is because something has gone terribly wrong. Hospital and dental treatment are other examples of grudge purchases, as are home maintenance and essential public services such as prisons and the police force. It might also be considered that undertakers fall into this category – despite the fact that we will all need their services one day, few of us wish to admit it. Astute marketing by the funeral industry has managed to convince a growing number of people to pre-pay for their own funeral; perhaps this is the ultimate grudge purchase! Even where payment is not direct and the services are funded through taxation there may still be a resentment to pay. The managers and staff of such organisations have a much more difficult task in developing a meaningful relationship with their customers, most of whom may be very reluctant partakers of the product or service. Many doctors' surgeries, dental practices and local/national government offices have become much more customer friendly with appointments being made where possible to suit patients and clients rather than the organisation. Even politicians have come to realise that they too may be a grudge purchase but that repeat business is very, very important to them. Two of the case studies in Chapter 10 relate to grudge purchases and it is obvious that the strategies the organisation needs to employ, in many cases to avoid repeat business, will be different from those used by the vast majority of organisations which see repeat business as an important performance indicator.

Whilst this book does not intend to be a treatise on selling, those involved with sales make the point that it is important to sell benefits not products. Even grudge purchases have benefits. Insurance can ease worries, life assurance can allow a person to look after his or her loved ones, dental care can ensure fewer fillings etc. By concentrating on the benefits a customer can be convinced of the importance of what is in fact a grudge purchase.

Summary

This chapter has considered why customer service is so important, and the changing attitudes of customers within both the public and private sectors. The move towards a customer centred approach within organisations, together with the effect of customer service on the bottom line and value added, were explored, followed by the link between customer service and overall objectives and the difficulties posed by grudge purchases.

Terms introduced

- Bottom line
- C-SMART criteria
- Customer accumulator
- Customer driven
- Delighting the customer
- Effective organisations

- Goods and services
- Grudge purchases
- Lifetime value of the customer
- Market share
- Monopoly
- Organisational objectives
- Product
- Product led
- Public and private sectors
- Repeat business
- SMART criteria
- Value added

QUESTIONS

1. Explain how the customer accumulator shows the importance of retaining an organisation's customer base and how losing just a few customers to a competitor can have a dramatic effect on the relative positions.
2. In what ways will a product led organisation differ from one which is customer driven? Why should monopolies still develop good customer relations even when they have no competitors?
3. Explain, using examples, what is meant by the term grudge purchase. What effects can this have on an organisation delivering such a product or service?

☑ **2** Who is the customer?

Needs and wants – Motivation – Value and customer chains – Internal and external customers – Marketing mix – Core and supplementary products – Branding – Competition – Listening to the customer – Market research – Focus groups – AIDA – Differentiation and segmentation – Delighting the customer

For those working in a retail or direct service environment, 'Who is the customer?' may appear an easy question – it is the person who is served. However, as this chapter will show, the true picture is more complex yet still easily understood. What will be introduced here is the concept of a customer chain, each member of which has their own wants and needs. For the enterprise to be a success, all of the members of the chain need to be at least satisfied and preferably delighted. This concept is analogous to the value chain introduced in the previous chapter.

In Chapter 1 the distinction between satisfied and delighted customers was introduced and it is now necessary to consider the differences between needs and wants, two concepts that are frequently confused and sometimes treated as synonymous, which they are not.

A *need* is something that we cannot do without; a *want* is the method by which we would like the need to be satisfied – in many ways a want is a need with added value.

Abraham Maslow (1970) suggested that needs were hierarchical in nature and that a need can only be truly satisfied when the ones below it have been dealt with. Maslow proposed that human beings have five levels of needs, as depicted in Figure 2.1.

Maslow's concept was that humans (and other animals) would put physiological needs – food, water etc. – before safety, which comes before belonging. Esteem needs are only met when the needs up to and including belonging have been met, and self-actualisation only becomes a motivator when all other needs have been fulfilled. The Maslow model has some inconsistencies, it fails to explain how an artist or poet can starve in an attic whilst working on their masterpiece – the model postulates that such self-actualisation should not take precedent over physiological needs. It does however explain the risks that animals will take to obtain food and water even in the face of apparent danger. A human equivalent is that of sailors who have been shipwrecked and have taken to the lifeboats drinking seawater which can be fatal because the need for water (physiological) overrides that for safety. Note that in the version used in this book, the top of the hierarchy is truncated as there will always be that which is unobtainable.

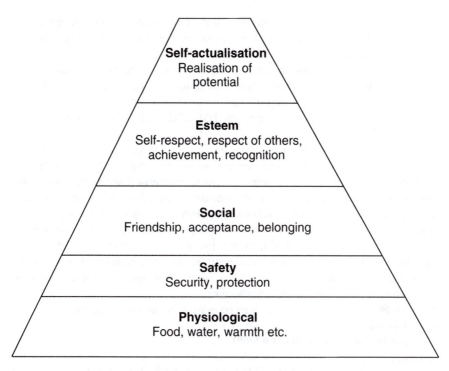

Figure 2.1   Maslow's hierarchy of needs.

Maslow's hierarchy is useful in that it allows us to distinguish between levels of needs. In respect of human beings, physiological and safety can be described as LOWER LEVEL or BASIC needs, belonging as a MIDDLE LEVEL need, and esteem and self-actualisation as HIGHER LEVEL needs. The role of any supplier of goods or services is *at a minimum* to satisfy the respective need.

Thus a baker, in selling bread in a village outlet, is satisfying the lowest or most basic need. Whilst bread may seem a mundane, everyday product, it receives many mentions in religious texts testifying to its importance as not only a food but a symbol of basic human needs, and bread has achieved political significance when its price has risen and rioting has broken out! That is a PRIMARY need.

There is also a need to be able to purchase the bread in safety and convenience, what can be described as a SECONDARY need, and a baker should ensure that their shop is attractive and that the purchaser feels safe and comfortable in it. Later in this book there will be a consideration of the effects of quality, price, convenience etc. However, for the moment take some time to consider whether a purchaser is more motivated to buy bread that is more expensive at a place that is perceived as being safer or more convenient (in this context it would be fair to consider that having to undertake a vehicle journey might entail more risks to one's safety than walking around the corner) than one where the bread is much cheaper.

Given that man is a social animal, there might also be a TERTIARY need of some recognition of belonging. Physiologists are beginning to recognise that there is a social as well as a commercial aspect to shopping. 'Shopping therapy' may have started as a gag from comedians but it is possible that there is a serious side to the concept.

Herzberg (1962), writing in the context of work, concluded that there were factors which led to satisfaction and thus motivated people, he termed these MOTIVATORS, and those which did not motivate but led to dissatisfaction and thus demotivation, which he named HYGIENE FACTORS. His results are summarised in Figure 2.2.

This research showed that recognition and achievement are important motivators and whilst Herzberg was primarily concerned with motivation at work, there are important lessons for those concerned with customer care. Achievement and recognition can be considered both from the point of view of the customer, who may receive satisfaction from the achievement of an excellent product or service and normally relishes recognition even if it is the use of his or her name in a transaction, and from the point of view of the person delivering customer service, who should be more motivated when a satisfactory transaction is concluded than when there is a dissatisfied customer. Recognition of good service nearly always reinforces that service.

Based on the above, a customer can be defined in simple terms as:

one for whom you satisfy a need

It should also be obvious that needs are very basic and it is wants that grow in importance once basic needs are satisfied.

Unfortunately many people believe that the definition above is enough and that all that is required is to satisfy a customer's needs. If you only want to see the customer once, that may be true but most organisations want to retain their customers.

Later in this book the concept of customer loyalty will be considered. Whilst there are exceptions, once an organisation has an external customer (the difference between internal and external customers will be considered later in this chapter) they normally wish to retain that customer be it an individual or another company. There are exceptions: the Prison Service do not want their

MOTIVATORS, presence of which leads to satisfaction	HYGIENE FACTORS, absence of which leads to dissatisfaction
ACHIEVEMENT RECOGNITION WORK ISSUES RESPONSIBILITY ADVANCEMENT GROWTH	POLICY & ADMINISTRATION SUPERVISION RELATIONSHIPS WORK ENVIRONMENT SALARY PERSONAL LIFE STATUS SECURITY

Figure 2.2   Summary of Herzberg's findings.

clients back but they do wish to retain the confidence of society; the police; parts of the Health Service etc. also do not want cured patients back and may take steps through preventative medicine to actually reduce the number of potential customers.

If you are starving, a meal, any meal, will suffice to satisfy your basic physiological need for food. Once the means (usually money) exist to choose how the need is satisfied, then it is wants that are important: 'I need lunch, I want a steak and French fries!'

It used to be thought that customers had to be satisfied but in today's competitive world satisfaction is not enough – in order to retain customers they need to be delighted. Needs can be satisfied but to delight a customer it is necessary to understand their wants.

In modern society basic needs are satisfied using money and money has to be earned, giving rise to what may be termed a FACILITORY need (a new term first introduced in this book).

In order to earn money, large numbers of people *need* to travel to work (they have little or no choice) and thus transportation is a facilitory need in order to fulfil basic needs. Their preference for transportation forms their wants; they may want a motor car or for environmental or cost reason prefer to travel on public transport. Put succinctly, they do not need a motor car but they do need transportation in order to gain the money to fulfil the basic needs of food and shelter etc.

Chapter 3 will consider how to delight the customer but for the moment, the earlier definition of a customer can be refined to:

one for whom you satisfy a need and who you delight in respect of their wants

The value chain and the customer chain

It is your child's birthday and sitting proudly in their bedroom is a new computer system bought from a major retailing chain. In this section it is intended to use the above simple but familiar scenario to demonstrate the importance of firstly the **VALUE** and then the **CUSTOMER CHAIN**.

A modern home computer system consists of a number of components manufactured mainly from metal and plastic. The total cost of the metal and plastic is a very small proportion of what will have been paid for the system. What happens is that each step in the manufacturing, distribution and retailing process adds value to those bits of metal and plastic. The individual value of the materials in a memory chip may be only a few pence whilst the value of the completed chip is many times that (even though prices fell steadily throughout the 1990s). In assembling those components, value was added to them. At each stage of the assembly process, the part completed system is potentially worth more than at the preceding stage. Those who are interested in the more esoteric motor cars, boats or even aircraft know that it is possible to buy a kit of parts, a part-assembled kit or a completed product each costing more than the other to reflect the value that has been added during the various assembly processes.

By the end of assembly a diverse set of metals, plastics etc. will have become a coherent computer system which the manufacturer/assembler can then sell to a retailer at a profit.

Profit according to accountancy practice is the situation where the book value of a company is greater at the end of an accounting period than at the beginning (Cartwright *et al.*, 1998b). That book value includes the worth of buildings, machinery, stock, cash held and monies owed. Thus it is possible to be in profit but to have no cash to pay bills. For the purposes of this chapter, profit can be defined as the:

added value left when all the costs have been taken into account

As such this definition reinforces the concepts introduced in the previous chapter.

When the computer leaves the factory for the retailers it will have incurred direct costs relating to the materials and labour used and the indirect costs of heating, lighting, administration, marketing, packaging etc. apportioned to each unit. Provided it is passed at an added value price greater than these costs then a profit will have been made. Chapter 3 considers value for money and the ability of customers to judge whether the price charged is realistic – too high a price and it ceases to be added value and is perceived as a 'rip off'.

Retailers also add value to a product. In a later section of this chapter it will be shown how convenience is an important part of the marketing mix but in addition to convenience the retailer may offer extra services such as advice, after sales service and even (in the case of computers) training if required.

Each step in the chain 'adds value' and within each step there is a customer relationship. If you bought the computer you are clearly a customer of the retailer who is in turn a customer of the manufacturer/supplier. However, each step in the manufacturing process has a set of customer relationships. If to carry out their job a person in the factory needs a computer case delivered to their work station in a certain condition and by a certain time, then they are a customer of the person before them in the process; they are an INTERNAL CUSTOMER and quite clearly fit the definition of a customer given earlier, namely:

one for whom you satisfy a need and who you delight in respect of their wants

Anecdotal evidence suggests that the better the internal relationships are, so the likelihood of the external customer being delighted increases (Cartwright & Green, 1997).

One company that has recognised the importance of internal customer relations is Princess Cruises, the US operation of the British P&O Company. Passengers on their cruises are asked to submit the names of those who have given them excellent service with the view to an award. Whilst this is a laudable idea, passengers only come into contact with a minority of the ship's crew and thus the company have a parallel scheme whereby those crew members who interact with the passengers on a regular basis are able to nominate colleagues behind the scenes who have provided them with excellent service. A table steward can only provide the highest standard of service to a passenger if all those working unseen in the galley have provided the steward with a high standard of service, good food, cleaned plates etc. Princess Cruises are considered in more detail as a case study in Chapter 10.

Thus there are two main categories of customers – **INTERNAL** and **EXTERNAL** – and whilst the latter is important for the final profit, the former add value and have a vital role in quality. The value chain has a customer service chain running parallel to it.

In the computer purchase scenario introduced earlier, you bought the computer but gave it to your child as a birthday present – who was the customer, you or your child? It was your money that paid for it but it is your child who will (hopefully) be delighted with it. You may never use it. In this case you were a PURCHASER but your child was the END USER.

The customer chain can be represented as shown in Figure 2.3.

It is important to realise that the purchaser and the end user may not be one and the same but that there is likely to be considerable feedback between them and good customer care can double the potential for repeat business. The purchaser may come back again for something else but if the end user is delighted with what the purchaser has provided for them and the purchaser relays a good report on the service they received, then the end user may also become a purchaser.

It is presumed, in this scenario, that your child is delighted with the computer. However, if the child is dissatisfied then the retailer has probably lost a customer even if the service to you was good – you have become vicariously dissatisfied. One should not, perhaps, refer to the parent–child relationship as part of the customer chain but in the scenario examined that is precisely what it is (Cartwright & Green, 1997); your child is in effect your customer and if they are dissatisfied then so are you likely to be.

It is easy to see the relationship between internal and external customers and purchasers and end users in the retail and commercial segments of business but less easy to understand the customer relationships in other areas such as the public service. Who are the customers of the Prison Service, are they the prisoners or are they the taxpayers who pay for the service? Other areas of the public sector face the same dilemma and many use the term CLIENT for the end user to distinguish the users of a service from those who pay for it.

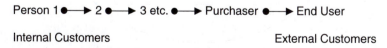

Person 1 ● ⟶ 2 ● ⟶ 3 etc. ● ⟶ Purchaser ● ⟶ End User

Internal Customers   External Customers

Figure 2.3   The customer chain.

The marketing mix

In the previous chapter the concept of customer driven and product led organisations was introduced. Product can be taken to mean both goods and services and is applicable across all sectors of activity. Those in manufacturing often have a very tangible product whilst the product for those in the service and public sectors may be more intangible as discussed in Chapter 1.

Core and supplementary products

Earlier in the chapter the difference between needs and wants was considered. Most products comprise two components: a core product that is designed to meet need requirements and often supplementary products that concentrate on the want element (Figure 2.4).

Most modern private motor vehicles are basically very similar. Any car purchased in the UK should be of acceptable quality and fit for the purpose for which it was intended. Many of the cars sold look very similar. Where there are differences is in the supplementary products that are attached to the core: power steering (rapidly becoming a part of the core product), extra safety features, air-conditioning, the sound system etc., and of particular importance in the context of this book, the after sales service offered. More and more buying decisions are being based on these supplementary components, especially service. It is no use in acquiring the car of your dreams if the company cannot look after you post purchase. Indeed it would not be in their interest not to offer

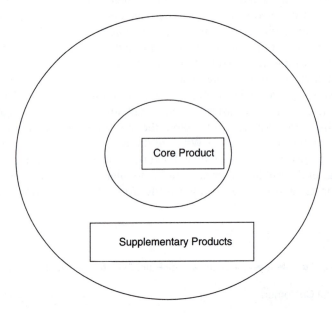

Core Product

Supplementary Products

Figure 2.4   Core and supplementary products.

excellent after sales service, as they will wish you to buy another of their vehicles in the future.

Consumer legislation in the UK is examined in Chapter 6, but as consumer protection has increased so the basic quality of products has followed suit and all products should satisfy the customer by law; what has become important is going beyond mere satisfaction and actually delighting the customer.

The *marketing mix* is a term introduced and refined by Kotler (1980) and in its original form comprised four ingredients:

- PRODUCT
- PRICE
- PROMOTION
- PLACE

These have been later refined by Kotler to:

- Customer Value
- Cost
- Communication
- Convenience

Both the original and revised terms will be considered side by side.

Product/customer value

In this chapter some of the factors relating to the product have been considered. Customers are not just buying a car, a television set etc. but the supplementary products that surround it, such as ambience, service and, of increasing importance, after sales service. As the goods and services supplied by different organisations become more and more alike, then it is the supplementaries that affect the final buying decision, as discussed earlier.

Products and services go through a life cycle from birth to decline and it is important for you to be aware of this life cycle in order to understand the behaviour of your customers.

Life cycles can be short, as in the fashion industry or some of the more esoteric products that appear, for example hula hoops or those linked to other products, Batman accessories, Power Rangers and the vast range of spin-offs from other films and TV series, or they may be very long – the Boeing 747 and Kit Kat chocolate bars being good examples.

Customer value

This is the term that Kotler uses instead of product. It reflects the fact that it is not the product *per se* that the customer buys or uses but what they perceive that product to be and how they value it. The Ford Edsell was a good product; technically, it just lacked customer value.

Price/cost

A 5-dollar bill, a £20 note or 100 rupee note have no intrinsic value, the value is that which the person using it ascribes to it.

How much is your home worth (a question that will be pursued in the next chapter)? Assuming that you own your home (if you don't then the answers relate to your landlord), there are a number of possible answers:

- How much you paid for it
- How much it would cost to rebuild it
- How much you could sell it for.

The last amount is the nearest to the truth; the value of any product or service is that which a customer is prepared to pay. A supplier may have the best product or service in the world, but if the price is deemed too high, then they will have few customers. Conversely, if the price is too low, questions may be asked about quality.

Price is what is charged for your product or service and all products and services have a price attached to them. In government it may be the taxpayer who provides the resources indirectly but nothing comes free.

The price is built up by looking at all the costs that go into the provision of the product or service: those which are fixed (i.e. the organisation would have to pay them whether they made one or a hundred items or serviced one or a hundred people), those that are variable (these include materials that are needed more of as more product is produced), overhead costs (heat, light, marketing and distribution), the desired level of profit and what the market will bear. The difference between the organisation's costs and the price the customer is prepared to pay represents the margin or profit.

For those working in the public sector, the word profit may not apply but profit is the added value that is received over and above costs. In situations where money does not change hands, profit could be considered in more subjective terms. For example, schools do not make a profit but they should add value; charities may see profit in terms of alleviating distress or saving lives; hospitals may be able to generate extra income to allow improved health care facilities to be installed. In balance sheet terms, a company has made a profit when it has more assets at the end of an accounting period than at the beginning. In educational terms, a school or college could have made a 'profit' if the pupils were more capable at the end of a term or a semester than at the beginning, Equating such ideas from the private sector into the public and voluntary sectors has proved difficult but it is not impossible given some lateral thinking.

Branding

Branding will be covered in more detail later in this chapter but at this point it is important to note that customers relate as much to brand names as to products. Brands make for customer loyalty and there is a perception that certain brands are of better quality and value than others are. All is not always as it seems. Many electrical items including TVs, radios and CD players are made generically, i.e. by one manufacturer, often in the Far East, and then branded by the suppliers with their own labels.

Brands can be so powerful that they will be kept even after a take-over. When Carnival Cruises took over Cunard in 1998, they not only kept the names of the ships but that of the company as well. Cunard had an excellent reputation and appealed to a different set of customers than the normal Carnival product.

Wherever a person works within an organisation, he or she needs to ensure that they know what products and services are available and how they are branded; as we shall see in the next section, staff can be one of an organisation's best advertisements.

Promotion/communication

Organisations spend large sums on advertising. If they have the right product at the right price, it is pointless if nobody knows about it. Promotion, including advertising, lets people know and, often just as important, keeps the product and service in their mind. Individuals working for organisations have two roles to play:

1. They need to know the promotions that their organisation has underway so that they anticipate customers' requests and queries.
2. The way they deal with customers can be an advertisement itself.

Most customers talk to their friends and colleagues and tell them about good and bad products and services. Personal recommendations are very important in purchase decisions.

Kotler prefers the term COMMUNICATION to PROMOTION because communication is a two-way process and allows customers to give you feedback. All interactions with customers, whether face-to-face, on the telephone or by letter, are communications and the way they are handled can promote the product or service and give signals about the type of organisation the customer is dealing with.

Place/convenience

Does your customer come to the organisation or does the organisation go to the customer? Not all transactions take place on the supplier's premises and recent years have seen a move towards making the provision of products and services convenient to the customer. New technologies including the INTERNET offer exciting prospects, especially for the delivery of services. With domestic video conferencing through WINDOWS on a PC, a whole range of consultancy opportunities in the health, financial advice and educational markets are being opened up. The use of new technologies and their application to customer care are considered in Chapter 7.

These ideas will be considered again in the next chapter which looks at quality and value for money.

Product and benefit

Modern selling techniques have shifted the emphasis away from the product or service and onto the benefits to the customer of acquiring that product or service. In describing the SCRS (Sales Control and Record System), Fenton (1984) makes a point of introducing the benefits straight away – it is not just a system that the customer is purchasing, it is a means of doing business. In a similar vein a car is not just an object but it is personal transportation, it is freedom, it may even be a method of expressing an image. Indeed image is a very important supplementary to a number of products, possession of which sends out a message regarding the customer's status.

Competitiveness

Unless there is only one supplier of a product or service, i.e. a monopoly situation, there is likely to be a degree of competition. More and more throughout the world the customer has a choice of apparently similar products and services. Political philosophies have encouraged competition even within the public sector in such areas as transportation, health care and even the provision of local government services.

There are four basic ways to compete:

- Price
- Quality
- Uniqueness
- Service.

Most people, unless they are very high up in the organisational hierarchy, have control over only the last – service.

Price competition

There are two ends of the price spectrum. A supplier can deal in large volumes and make a small margin on each (high volume/low margin) or can supply only a few units and make a large margin on each (low volume/high margin). Supermarkets are examples of the former and aircraft manufacturers of the latter. In the car industry, Ford is a high volume/low margin supplier and Morgan (who make sport's cars) represents the low volume/high margin end of the market.

Within any organisation's chosen part of the market it may decide to compete on price and be cheaper than anybody else. There is a danger to this position in that many customers equate quality with price, as will be shown in the next chapter. For that reason prices need to be set at a level that the customer expects for that particular quality of product; too cheap and the customer may wonder what is wrong.

Quality competitiveness

The next chapter centres on quality, which will be examined in depth. The Sale of Goods Act (1996), which is introduced in Chapter 6, lays down certain quality related criteria for products so there is a minimum below which no product should fall.

Chapter 3 will show that quality goes hand in hand with delighting the customer, i.e. providing more than just mere satisfaction, and more and more organisations are offering products of higher and higher physical quality. What can be improved is the quality of service, as will be shown later.

Uniqueness

In a global marketplace it is difficult for any product or service to maintain its total uniqueness for long. Many organisations aim therefore for a Unique Selling Point (USP) which can differentiate their offerings from those of the competition. This uniqueness may be an ingredient, an added extra, a particular service etc. Whilst the average employee may not be able to influence the USP, it is important that they know as much as possible about their own products and services.

Product knowledge has assumed an important status as customers become more sophisticated and knowledgeable. In the computer scenario used earlier in this chapter, one would expect the sales assistant to be able to advise on the appropriateness of the product and of its features and benefits. Cartwright & Green (1997) have pointed out that sales and future business have been lost because of a lack of product knowledge and many organisations now arrange rigorous product knowledge training for staff.

Substitutes

Even when there is a unique aspect to a product, Porter (1985) has pointed out that competition may come from unexpected quarters. The biggest competitor to the traditional airlines on the London to Paris route is not another airline but a railway through the Channel Tunnel, a development Porter refers to as the threat of substitution (see next chapter).

Service

Whilst the three areas of competition above may be mainly in the hands of senior staff, service is a function of everybody. Service can be described as the ultimate piece of added value; it may be what differentiates two seemingly identical products, services or suppliers. As disposable incomes in the Western world have risen since World War II, so has a desire for service both in the methods with which customers are treated and the convenience offered to them. As was stated earlier and as will be reinforced in the next chapter, convenience is an important aspect of service. The provision of parking spaces at out-of-town shopping centres, home shopping, cash dispensers and telephone banking are all aspects of convenience applied to a highly competitive environment.

For a further discussion on competitive advantage you are advised to read the works of Michael Porter (1980, 1985), the 'guru' of competitive advantage.

Listening to the customer

One way of recognising a product led organisation from one that is customer driven is that the former spends more time listening to itself whilst the latter listens to the customer.

As mentioned earlier it was John Wannamaker, a Philadelphia store owner who in 1869 termed the phrase 'the customer is always right' (Cartwright & Green, 1997). In many ways he did a disservice as the customer is not always right and often does not actually know what they need or want. If listening to the customer aids that customer in choosing a product or service that best suits their needs and wants then they are more likely to become a repeat customer. High pressure selling techniques may enable a sale to be made but the customer is likely to be dissatisfied if they have been sold something that does not meet their needs and wants and not only are they unlikely to make another purchase from the organisation, they may well tell their friends about their dissatisfaction.

Listening to the customer is an important part of market research (see later) but it can also be part of the informal component of customer care.

To achieve effective communications it is generally agreed that one should talk for 20% of the time and listen for the other 80%. However, many of those involved in sales seem to believe that they should do all the talking and that the customer should listen. A proper use of listening techniques and the proper type of questioning should ensure that the customer receives a product or service that meets their needs and wants and not what the salesperson believes that they should have.

Many organisations in the retail sector have adopted a 'meet and greet' approach to customers. The customer should be greeted as soon as they enter the premises. A laudable idea but one that can actually lose customers if it is not handled properly.

Take the simple question:

'Can I help you?'

This is an example of a closed question; there are really only two possible answers, 'yes' or 'no'. A more open question would be:

———

'How can I help you?'

A 'yes' or 'no' answer will not suffice.

Even the above question assumes that the customer wants to be helped. They may just be browsing or they may be at a part of the change cycle (see Chapter 8) where they wish to consider what they want privately. A better form of greeting may be not to ask a question but to say:

———

'Good morning/afternoon, if there is anything I can help with, please don't hesitate to ask.'

In this case the customer is not forced into making a response but their presence and thus their importance has been recognised and acknowledged.

A salesperson who is sensitive to their customers will note what they are looking at so as to be prepared to render assistance when it is required. In Chapter 8 there will be a more detailed consideration of communication and the important role of non-verbal communication, i.e. body language and the concept of Organisational Body Language (Cartwright & Green, 1997).

Peters & Waterman (1982) stressed the importance of being close to the customer and Chapter 8 will reinforce the importance of your relationship to the customer and the importance of listening in order to discover his or her actual needs and wants.

Assuming that you know better than the customer is a form of arrogance and arrogance can lose customers. You may know more about the product or service but it is important that you do not patronise the customer.

Market research

Market research is concerned with finding out about your customer, especially their lifestyle, needs and wants. Effective market research ensures that the products and services offered are those desired by the customer.

As the *Mechanical Engineering EDC* wrote in 1971 and as quoted in Wilmshurst (1978): 'One no longer seeks to make decisions solely on the basis of hunch or flair. One now seeks first the facts upon which the hunch, or flair can nourish itself'.

There are four areas in which organisations can use market research. For finding:

- About new services and products required by the customer
- Indications of the lifestyle trends of the customer base
- Information about the suitability and quality of current products and services
- Information about the perceptions of customers and potential customers in relation to the organisation and the organisation's competitors.

Effective market research is about asking the right questions of the right people so that only those hunches that meet customer requirements come to market.

The *Daily Telegraph* newspaper on a Saturday has a feature in its motoring pages entitled 'A good idea at the time'. To modern eyes some of the ideas seem very strange. What they have in common, however, is that they appear to have been somebody's hunch that was never properly researched with the potential customers. The tiny Sinclair C5 vehicle of the 1980s is another example of a wonderful idea that appears not to have been put to potential buyers first, as was the Ford Edsell mentioned in the previous chapter.

There are three 'rights' associated with market research:

- The RIGHT questions
- The RIGHT sample of customers/potential customers
- The RIGHT action following analysis.

Formulating research questions is a skill unto itself. If the researcher uses leading questions (where there is an indication of the answer required) there is a danger that bias may creep in. If the questions are too open then the subject may veer away from the issue at hand. Yes/No (known as dichotomous) questions can be very inflexible and may researchers prefer to present subjects with multiple choices.

Even if the questions are correct, there is little point in putting them to the wrong people. Effective market research requires a balanced sample of sufficient size to inform the decision-making process. It is important that the sample size (n) is not so small as to make the results unrepresentative. Adler (1969) makes the point that even a nation-wide survey in the UK will have a sample size of only 2000 and that it is rare for this to rise as high as 5000. This means that the members of the sample need to be chosen with great care if they are to represent a large population.

Whilst some surveys may wish to consider the total possible population (say of the UK), most are concerned with specific populations, such as the population that buy chocolate or drink beer, or drive motor cars etc.

In order to identify a population it may be necessary to approach a much bigger sample than required and ask some simple questions to see if the subject is part of the target population. If the research is into gardening equipment, then perhaps asking 'do you have a garden?' may, repeat *may*, allow the research to discard those who answer 'no'. It may be that some negative respondents are required – perhaps it would be useful to know why they do not have a garden. Approaching a large number of previously unknown people in this manner is known as random sampling. Where individuals can be targeted either as a result of a previous random sample or because their preferences are already known (perhaps they already form part of the customer base) is known as quota sampling. A supermarket sampling shoppers leaving the premises already knows that they are customers. To be effective in a case like this, previous qualitative analysis should have been carried out to ascertain a gender, age etc. profile. If it is known that 65 of the customers are female and that of those 40% are over 35, then the sample for the market research should replicate these proportions in order to provide a true picture of the customer base.

Much market research is conducted using questionnaires. These may be either sent to customers with, perhaps, an incentive for return (entry to a prize draw is a popular incentive), or conducted on the street or on the organisation's premises. The major downside to sending questionnaires to customers and especially potential customers is that the number of returns can be very low, giving a small sample size. If the returns are low, then this can give a very biased sample. Suppose an organisation wished for information about the quality of its products. It is likely that anybody dissatisfied with the product would be more likely to return the questionnaire and thus the sample might show a higher rate of dissatisfaction than was actually the case. Where questionnaires are used on a face-to-face basis, then care must be taken to ensure that there is a balanced sample. Package holiday companies often give out the customer satisfaction questionnaire on the return flight home, when there is little else for the customer to do. These questionnaires often contain extra questions relating to lifestyle, the answers to which can provide the organisation with added details of the customer's lifestyle and source of income, as such information is very valuable.

One problem with such an immediate customer satisfaction questionnaire is that it provides little time for the customer to reflect on the product/service and may be just a 'happiness sheet' coloured by immediate events and not truly indicative of the total experience.

Focus groups

Focus groups have become an interesting method of 'getting close to the customer' (Peters & Waterman, 1982). Supermarkets, political parties, car dealerships and bookshops have experimented with the idea of bringing a group of customers together for free and frank discussions. Careful chairing of such a group can provide much more detailed information than a questionnaire. The process also links those customers involved into the organisation, strengthening their loyalty. It goes without saying that the comments from such a focus group should always be taken seriously. Experience has shown that such a group can provide valuable information about products and the standard of service and can also give the organisation a useful sounding board for new ideas.

Getting people together in this way requires an input of resource from the organisation and time from the members of the group. That many people are prepared to give of their own time to provide information about an organisation with which their only relationship is that of a customer is indicative of how powerful customer loyalty, the subject of Chapter 4, can be.

Implementing research

Why do your customers choose a particular product and service? Customer behaviour often follows a pattern known as AIDA:

- ATTENTION
- INTEREST

- DESIRE
- ACTION.

In order to attract the customer's ATTENTION, he or she has to know about you and your products. This may be through advertising but it may also be through conversation with friends and colleagues. Once attention has been gained then, if the customer feels that the product or service is right for them, their INTEREST is stirred. Once somebody is interested they will try to find out more about what is on offer. If they still like what they see and hear, they will begin to DESIRE the product or service and that will produce ACTION to acquire it for themselves or their client.

From the customer service point of view there are two major problems associated with AIDA:

1. Stimulating demand for one product, service or even supplier tends to stimulate demand for similar offerings across the market. After the Gulf War in the early 1990s, British Airways introduced the 'World's Greatest Offer' in order to stimulate demand in a stagnant market. They stimulated demand for their own product but at the same time they also stimulated demand for their competitors' products. The same has happened with more mundane products. An effective advertising campaign for one brand of coffee tends to produce increases in sales for all coffee manufacturers. Provided you are supplying a good level of product and customer service, this will not be too much of a problem but you don't want to be stimulating your competitors' sales if they are likely to take trade from you. Once you have gained attention and interest, the person is likely to purchase so you must make sure that it is you that they purchase from. At the start of the home computer boom in the 1980s, Sinclair Electronics stimulated massive interest with their relatively cheap machines. Unfortunately they could not supply enough of them and purchasers had to go elsewhere and, once there, they stayed with the competition to the detriment and downfall of Sinclair.
2. It is very easy to lose a purchase at any stage. If, having gained attention, you are unable to fulfil the customer's need for information in the INTEREST stage, you risk losing him or her altogether. Bad service at any stage after gaining attention can mean a lost customer on a permanent basis. Treat every expression of INTEREST as potential DESIRE and eventual ACTION. The aim is to ensure that the ACTION is with you and not with a competitor. Everybody whether up front or behind the scenes has a part to play. DESIRE without fulfilment can fade quickly. This is known as 'Buyer's Regret' in the USA. Once the customer has made up their mind, the longer the wait between order and delivery, the greater the danger that they will have second thoughts. Even asking somebody to wait a few minutes whilst you go for further information or a sample can cause desire to fade and you may find them gone when you return. Never leave a customer waiting, provide them with something to read; keep them interested.

Market segmentation and differentiation

It is easy to talk about the car market or the holiday market but such generalisations obscure the complex nature of markets.

Segmentation

The car market consists of a number of market segments, for example:

- The family car market
- The sport's car market
- The business user
- The luxury car market etc.

Each of these markets has its own set of customers. Whilst the basic need for transportation may be common to all segments, the manner by which this need is fulfilled – the wants – may be very different. Cost is more important in the family car market than for luxury cars; speed may be an important want in the sport's car market but of little concern to the business user.

The car manufacturers are very aware of the importance of appealing to chosen market segments. The larger companies will try to appeal to as many segments as possible whilst smaller manufacturers, Morgan is a good example, may target their production at just one segment.

The holiday market is also split into a whole series of segments and even the segments themselves are differentiated. Ward (1998) has split the cruise holiday market into Standard, Premium and Luxury sections and Cartwright & Baird (1999) have added another section – niche cruising to Ward's categories. The companies in the industry have arranged their operations to take account of the various segments, in many cases using branding.

Branding

Branding allows organisations to offer a series of similar products to different market segments, often at different prices. To illustrate branding, an example is taken from the cruise industry – probably the fastest growing commercial operation in the UK in the late 20th and early 21st Centuries.

Carnival Cruises, the largest cruise company in the world, consists of a series of brands, each targeted at different segments of the market. Cartwright & Baird (1999) in their study of the cruise industry postulated that within the customer base there were in fact customers whose motivation for taking a cruise differed. Their work is summarised below (with permission), the typologies being:

- Party goer
- Relaxer
- Enthusiast
- Stroller

- Seeker
- Explorer
- Dipper.

For the purposes of clarity they referred to each characteristic as though it existed in isolation, although, of course, the characteristics do not exist in isolation but are acted on one with another. For many cruisers it was the cruise itself, i.e. the shipboard experience, that was the major motivator although all of the sample used by Cartwright & Baird agreed to some extent with McCannell (1973) in that they wanted some authenticity in the place they visited but perhaps not too much, especially if it involved confronting poverty.

Party goer

The Party goer is on a cruise for the activities and nightlife. They are likely to be happiest on a ship that has the latest in entertainment features, a lively casino and plenty of organised activities. For the Party goer, cruises that resemble the atmosphere of the traditional UK holiday camp may well appeal. By definition the Party goer is gregarious by nature and will therefore be less concerned at the higher density often associated with high-activity, intensive destination oriented vessels.

Relaxer

The Relaxer will not object to days spent at sea and may well only venture ashore briefly on port days. The Relaxer is on the cruise to unwind and whilst he or she may well take in a degree of the action at night, the daytime is likely to find him or her lying on a sun lounger and devouring the ship's library.

Relaxation has associations with a degree of solitude and thus the Relaxer is likely to be less comfortable with high-density vessels where private space may be at a premium.

Enthusiast

The Enthusiast is addicted to cruising. The itinerary is not important, the ship may not be a major priority but a cruise is. Dickinson & Vladimir (1997) refer to people being addicted to cruising.

One distinction noted between UK and North American cruisers who fit into this category is the higher degree of company loyalty amongst the former. Despite the fact that virtually all of the major cruise companies are accessible to both markets, UK cruisers interviewed were three times more likely to stick with one company for the majority of their cruises than their North American counterparts.

The Enthusiasts spoken to were very knowledgeable about the industry and the cruise companies use this enthusiasm through their various loyalty schemes to ensure that the cruisers feel part of the family and thus cruising with somebody else becomes less a commercial decision and more an act of treachery!

Stroller

Strollers were those who originally 'strolled' the Boulevards of Paris in the late 19th Century (Benjamin, 1973) both seeing and as importantly being seen. Cruising is still one vacation where dressing up can be important. Whilst many of the newer entrants to the market stress the informality of their operation, it was found that the opportunity to dress for dinner was welcomed by many cruisers. It gives the opportunity to escape from normality and to experience a perception of a glamorous yesteryear. Whilst Cartwright & Baird did not find anybody who only went on cruises in order to dress up, they did find a substantial number of both genders for whom a degree of formality was part of the attraction of cruising.

The cruise companies seem well aware of this as the following quotes show:

'. . . After 6pm, the atmosphere becomes a little dressier; long trousers for men and smart–casual for women. On gala evenings, everyone dresses up: ladies change into party dresses [sic], while many gentlemen bring out a dinner jacket'.

(Thomson 1998–99 Cruise Brochure, 1st edition)

'. . . If you have not been on a Princess cruise before you may be reassured to hear that the days when starched collars were *de rigeur* every night are long gone. During the day, classic resort wear is now the norm, and stylish casuals are fine for most evenings too.

In addition there are one or two semi-formal evenings (more on longer cruises) when everyone opts for something stylish with jacket and tie preferred for the men. And during every cruise there are two formal nights (up to four on longer cruises) when dressing up is half the fun, black tie or a dark suit adds an extra sense of occasion and glamorous outfits shimmer throughout the ship'.

(Princess 1999 Caribbean Brochure)

Seeker

The Seeker was not present to a great extent in our survey for the reason that most major cruise lines do not cater for this category. The Seeker is concerned with finding out a great deal about the area he or she visits and will wish to imbibe and try to become a part of the culture. In general, cruises are more suited to those who sample cultures (Dippers, to be covered later). Cruising does not give the time in any one place to really immerse oneself in the culture.

There are however a small number of cultural cruises on blue water as opposed to the river variety that may appeal to the Seeker. The specialist cruises offered by Swan Hellenic (P&O) on board the 12 000 GRT *Minerva* are characterised by itineraries that visit the more interesting places, often of antiquity, and the ship carries acknowledged experts in the fields related to the cruise destinations. Their lectures are delivered with considerable depth and knowledge and, interestingly, whilst the ship's library and lecture facilities are good, there is no casino or slot machines and only a maximum of 456 passengers.

It is only on low-density ships with itineraries very different from mainstream cruising that the Seeker will truly be comfortable, but more and more cruise companies are recognising that there is a little of the Seeker in many of their customers and are adding more interesting destinations and excursions to their traditional offerings.

Explorer

The Explorer wishes to see those places few have seen before. The growth in expedition cruising (to be considered in niche cruising, in Chapter 10) has made exploration ever more easier. The Explorer does not need shopping malls or West End shows, they are seeking different lifestyles (usually more primitive than their own) and the wildlife and scenery that exist in areas relatively untouched by man. The Explorer does not need lavishly equipped tenders to take them ashore, a zodiac inflatable landing in a small cove and depositing him or her on slippery rocks is what cruising is about for this type of person.

Dipper

The Dipper takes in the vast majority of the 7.6 million cruisers in 1996. A little bit of culture, a small taste of a different lifestyle and then back to the welcoming cultural bubble of the ship. The Dipper is truly the 'been there, seen that, experienced this and bought the T shirt'. The Dipper will be, in the main, satisfied with an explanatory leaflet, a briefing from the port lecturer and a tour of the highlights. One US couple on a two-week Mediterranean cruise managed to: ride on a gondola plus a visit to the Doge's Palace in Venice, visit the ruins of Ephesus in Turkey, see the Parthenon and the Acropolis in Athens, have a half day in Pompeii, a day in Rome and another day in Florence, shop in Cannes and have a two-hour city tour of Barcelona – all the time dipping in and out of the cultures they were visiting. They enjoyed it, they had great memories but admitted that they learnt little, saw only what the tour guide wanted them to see and were desperately tired at the end of the cruise – hardly relaxing!

Dickinson & Vladimir (1997) had a different set of categories more attuned to the US market. Their categories (which they called segments) and their descriptions were:

Restless baby boomers

Newcomers to cruising who may still be inhibited by cost and with an average age of 44 and an average US income of $58,000 (£36,500 – a very high UK salary). They are relatively inexperienced travellers and the authors see them as trying out various vacations.

Enthusiastic baby boomers

With an average age of 49 and slightly less wealthy with an average income of $55,000, they undertake (according to the authors) vacations for escape and relaxation although they enjoy activities and night life.

Consummate shoppers

These are people who shop around for the best value, which does not necessarily mean the cheapest. Average age 55 and average income $60,000.

Luxury seekers

Average age of 52 and a staggering average income (to UK eyes) of $95,000, they can afford the best and demand it. They are also amongst the more culturally aware.

Explorers

Well travelled with an average age of 64 and an average income of $81,000, these explorers are not looking for rest or pampering but for experiences.

Ship buffs

These could be equated with Cartwright & Baird's Enthusiasts. Dickinson & Vladimir found that they had an average age of 68 and an average income of $78,000. They were knowledgeable about ships, not because they were ship buffs *per se* but because they had cruised on so many.

In order to satisfy the needs and wants of as many of the above as possible, Carnival operate a series of different companies, each targeted at different needs and different price groups from the standard to the luxury, as shown in Figure 2.5.

By using a series of brands, Carnival itself, Cunard, Costa etc., the organisation is able to appeal to a very wide customer base both in terms of price and lifestyle.

Soap powders, chocolate bars, electrical goods are all branded. Many may be made by the same manufacturer but are designed to appeal to different segments of the market.

A recent phenomenon has been that of **generic products.** A manufacturer, say

	STANDARD	PREMIUM	LUXURY	NICHE
UK MARKET	Share in Airtours/ Direct Cruises	Cunard	Cunard	
N. AMERICAN MARKET	Carnival Costa	Holland America	Cunard Seabourne	Windstar
EUROPEAN MARKET	Costa			
FAR EAST MARKET	Plans with Hyundai abandoned 1998			

Figure 2.5   Branding of Carnival Cruise products (taken from *The Development and Growth of the Cruise Industry,* Cartwright & Baird, 1999, with permission).

in Korea, may make a series of identical products which have the brand attached when they arrive in the county of re-sale. Many brown goods (TVs, hi-fis, computers etc.) are made in the same factory and then have a 'brand' attached by the retailer.

Differentiation

To be successful against its competitors an organisation needs a **unique selling point** (USP). It is the USP which will, hopefully, persuade the customer that they should partake of that product or service over any other, i.e. to gain a competitive advantage. Michael Porter considers that there are only a limited number of ways to gain differentiation over the competition (1980, 1985):

- Compete on quality
- Compete on price
- Compete on uniqueness.

The latter, despite patents, is quite difficult to sustain. One method is to make the brand unique. Indeed if you can make the name of your product synonymous with all products of that nature, there is considerable competitive advantage. Hoover is an excellent example. In the UK, people refer to 'hoovering' the floor even when using a competitor product!

Much differentiation is therefore based on price or quality, with the brand name often making a difference as customers often associate certain brands with high-quality standards.

Delighting the customer

It is no longer, as stated earlier, enough just to satisfy the customer. Chapter 4 will show that the loyalty of a just satisfied customer cannot be relied on. In order to retain customers and to ensure that they tell their friends and colleagues about you (as discussed in Chapter 1), it is necessary to delight them. Delight is when a customer receives more than they expected. Much of the remainder of this book is about how you can delight your customers, be they internal or external, individuals or groups.

It was stated earlier there was a time when customer satisfaction was the 'in' phrase. Today mere satisfaction is unlikely to gain lasting customer loyalty. What organisations need to do, as mentioned above, is to delight their customers.

Customers are delighted by a variety of factors. Research in the course of writing this book showed that the main ones are:

- Higher quality than expected for the price
- A feeling that the customer was important
- Supplementary products that really added value
- Quick recovery if things went wrong.

MacDonald and Piggott (1990) wrote that: 'Quality is delighting the customer by continuously meeting and improving upon agreed requirements'. In essence, a customer is delighted if the agreed requirements are not only met each and every time but are exceeded. There is of course the danger that exceeding requirements on a regular basis will lead to an expectation that this will occur again and again. The relationship between a supplier and the customer must start from the premise that they both agree what is an acceptable standard. The customer can expect that standard and nothing more, anything above it being a bonus. Constant communication between supplier and customer is vital if unrealistic expectations are not to be raised.

Whilst low prices are important to customers, there is ample evidence that as disposable incomes rise then so does a requirement for high quality. Clutterbuck *et al.* (1993) make the point that even those organisations that are able to achieve cost savings and thus undercut their competitors may well have to convince customers that quality has not been sacrificed.

Modern technology is enabling zero fault products to be brought to the marketplace. In the 1950s and 1960s, the owner of a new motor car would have expected a series of trips back to the dealer to have minor (and sometimes major) faults rectified. It was all part of the process of buying a new car. The modern customer expects it to be right first time, every time.

Summary

This chapter has concentrated on looking at the wants and needs of the customer and introduced the concepts of internal and external customers.

The relationship of the customer to the market and to the products and services offered by the organisation in a particular marketplace is all-important.

By understanding segmentation, differentiation and branding, organisations are able to offer the right products and services, at the right price and to the appropriate standard for their customers.

Terms introduced

- AIDA
- Client
- Competitive advantage
- Competitiveness
- Core product
- Delighting the customer
- Differentiation
- End user
- Generic products
- Hygiene factor
- Lifetime value of the customer
- Market segmentation
- Motivator

- Needs: Basic
          Primary
          Secondary
          Tertiary
          Facilitory
- Purchaser
- Supplementary product
- Unique Selling Point (USP)
- Wants

QUESTIONS

1. Why is the internal customer just as important as the external one? Explain the relationship between the customer chain and the value chain in terms of the relationships between internal and external customers.
2. In what ways can an organisation seek to differentiate its products and services from its competitors and so gain competitive advantage? What benefits do you believe that this can bring to the purchaser/end user?
3. Explain AIDA in terms of a recent purchasing decision you have made. How did each stage manifest itself?
4. Describe the marketing mix and show how it is important that each factor receives due care and attention.

▼ 3 Value for money

What's it worth? – Value expectation – Porter's forces – Bowman's strategic compass – Excellence and quality – Quality gurus – Deming – Juran – Crosby – Peters & Waterman – Excellence equilibrium – Clutterbuck et al. – Total quality management (TQM) – Service – Branding and quality – Consistency of service – Quality standards – Mystery customers

What's it worth?

This section could be titled 'The Great House Selling Conundrum'. A couple wish to sell their house. Unfortunately it is in an area where prices have been at best fairly static. Three years ago they paid £70,000 for the house and have fitted a new kitchen at a cost of £6000 and added a conservatory which cost them £10,000, a total cost of £86,000. The estate agent values the house for them at £75,000. Their insurance agent advises them that the insurance value for rebuilding should be £95,000. Plenty of potential customers (and not a few time wasters) come to see the house and eventually they are offered £72,000.

Is the house worth the £86,000 they have spent on it, the £75,000 the estate agent has valued it, the £95,000 it would cost to rebuild or the £72,000 they are offered?

Something is only worth what somebody else is willing to pay for it. This is a key concept when considering value for money. It is the customer who decides whether something is value for money. An organisation can make as many statements as it likes regarding its beliefs that its products/services represent value for money but those statements can only be proved if customers are prepared to pay.

Indeed value for money, or VFM as it will be referred to for the rest of this book, may well be a very individual matter as it comprises a series of factors, which may be very personal to the customer:

- Desire for the product/service
- Amount of finance available
- Cost of competing product/service.

A product/service can only be deemed value for money if the targeted customer can actually afford it. A Porsche may well be considered good value by many but nevertheless they cannot afford to buy one.

One of the major theories of motivation is that proposed by Vroom (1964) and commonly known as **expectancy theory**. Vroom's concept was that the perceptions that effort will lead to effective performance, that effective performance will lead to rewards and that such rewards are available produce a motivational effort on the part of an individual, the effort leads to performance and the performance to some form of reward. Achieving the reward starts a feedback loop in that it reinforces the original perceptions. From Vroom's ideas it is possible to develop the concept of **value expectation**.

Value expectation

Based on the above ideas of Vroom, this new concept uses the model shown in Figure 3.1.

The model is based upon four basic perceptions held by the customer. The first is a widely held one that has some, but not a complete basis in experience, namely that there is a direct relationship between price and quality. In many cases the higher the price, the more likelihood there is of higher quality. There are, however, many exceptions and indeed this is what often leads to customer dissatisfaction.

The second perception is based around the strength of the customer's need (or want) for the particular product or service. Highly felt need will tend to enhance the 'value' of the product in the customer's mind.

Thirdly there are the perceptions gained from previous experiences. If they

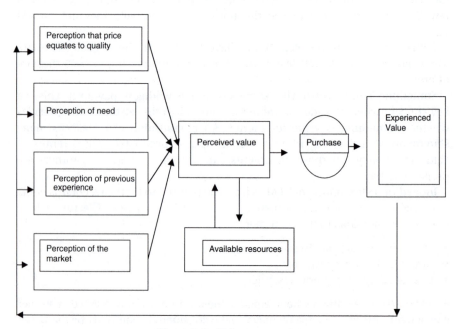

Figure 3.1   Value expectation.

have been bad, then there may be an expectation of dissatisfaction. An excellent previous product or service from the same supplier will lead to an expectation of quality. This is important to the discussion of consistency later in this chapter.

Lastly there is the perception of the customer in regard to the market. How well does the customer know the alternative etc.?

These four perceptions feed into an overall perception of value. If the customer has a good idea of the true relationship between price and value, i.e. they understand that prices are based on costs (see Chapter 2), if they have a high level of need, good previous experiences and know the market and what is on offer then there will be the likelihood of a high perceived value. The opposite could also apply: bad previous experiences, ambivalent need, lack of understanding of both the market and prices can lead to a low perceived value.

If the perceived value is equal to or greater than the available resource to match the price then a buying decision is likely.

After experience of the product or service, the customer is able to make an objective judgement of the actual value to them of their purchase. This can then feedback to inform revised perceptions of price v quality, there are new experiences, a measure of need fulfilment and enhanced knowledge of the marketplace.

The model provides a theoretical underpinning of the concept of a 'free trial'. If the customer is able to experience the product before making an actual purchase then their perception of value will be much more objective and if the product or service is in fact VFM, then the customer will be far more willing to part with cash.

The model also emphasises the importance of individual perceptions. Two people experiencing the same product or service at the same time may have very different perceptions of the value. This is one of the great problems of customer relations – each customer is an individual. Disney emphasises this factor in their training and Cartwright & Green (1997) and Cartwright & Baird (1999) found it was an important factor in customer care in the cruise industry.

A partial answer to the problem lies in ensuring that an organisation listens to and understands where its customers are coming from and what their expectations actually are.

Porter's forces

Michael Porter (1980, 1985) produced what has become known as the '5 Forces' model to explain the competitive situation that organisations find themselves a part of. Cartwright & Green (1997) refined the model with the addition of two additional competitive forces. The revised model is shown in Figure 3.2.

The competition most organisations recognise and are used to is that between existing players within their particular market, i.e. Ford compete with General Motors, British Airways with United Airlines, Tesco with Asda etc. However a true understanding of competition and its connection to customer relations and

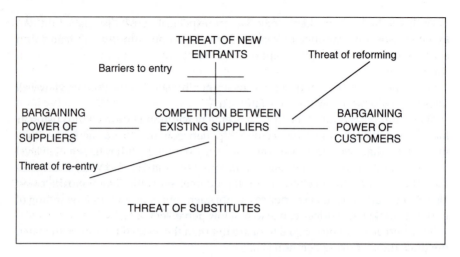

Figure 3.2   Competitive forces (adapted from M E Porter by Cartwright & Green, 1997 and copied, with permission, from Cartwright & Green).

perceptions of value requires a consideration of the question: 'what business is the organisation actually in?'

This is not as trite a question as might seem at first glance. Simplistically one might say that Ford are in the motor car business, British Airways in the airline business and Tesco in the supermarket business. However it is necessary to ask a further question: 'what is it that the customer is actually acquiring and are there alternatives?'

Substitutes

Ford, in respect of their motor cars, are actually in the personal transportation business, as are bus and rail operators. During 1999 the UK government announced that they intended to adopt policies that would encourage people to use public transport instead of motor cars for environmental and anti-congestion reasons. The main methods to achieve this were to be increasing the cost of using a car through fuel prices, road tolling and parking restrictions/costs, coupled with newer and more comfortable buses and trains, the latter becoming substitutes for the privately owned motor car. British Airways are in the business of moving large numbers of people over long distances. For airlines on the London–Paris route, as well as for the cross channel car ferry operators, the Channel Tunnel was a substitute competitor. Shopping from home via the INTERNET could become a substitute threat to supermarkets as indeed has the arrival of amazon.com® (see Chapter 7) to the book selling market, allowing as it does the ordering of books from a computer at home with delivery through the post.

Caledonian Cinemas (see case study in Chapter 10) have realised that they are not in the cinema business, nor indeed the movie business but the family entertainment business, and thus their competitors include not only other cinemas, video outlets and television but also theme parks and leisure centres which may attract families.

Substitutes, because they are often new, may well offer a novelty value to customers, who if they are satisfied may stay with the substitute product. They may often be able to demonstrate considerable customer advantages in the form of supplementary benefits. Whilst the air travel time from London to Paris is only 35 minutes compared to the 2+ hours on the Eurostar train, the air time saving is offset by the time taken to get to Heathrow and then from the French airport into Paris. By offering a city centre to city centre service, Eurostar have been able to make serious inroads into the air market and thus gain considerable market share. It is likely that many of those who used Eurostar in its early days of operation did so for the novelty value of travelling through the Channel Tunnel but decided to stay with the product when they experienced the benefits.

New entrants

Substitutes tend to be totally new ways of satisfying the market but any flourishing market is likely to tempt newcomers into it. The cruise market as profiled by Cartwright & Baird (1999) has been one of the fasting growing industrial sectors (not just within tourism) over recent years. By 1999 the traditional UK operators, including P&O and Fred Olsen, had been joined in the cruise market by, amongst others, two of the largest names in UK packaged holidays, Airtours and Thomson. These two companies had sufficient financial resources to equip themselves with suitable vessels and thus overcome the very high entry cost barriers to market entry. Direct Cruises, who also entered the UK market at that time, then as part of the large Direct Holidays operation, were less successful and failed to make a positive impact, the operation being sold to Airtours.

The higher the barriers to entry, which include cost and customer perception – that is, has the new organisation the skills, knowledge, resources and background to deliver? – the harder it is to become established.

There is also the problem of too many players in a market diluting the possible profits and, whilst intense competition can lead to temporary value for money deals, if the drop in margin leads to organisations withdrawing from the market, the customer may eventually suffer both through a lack of choice and the raising of prices when the market stabilises with fewer players.

Virgin Atlantic run by Richard Branson is an example of a company that succeeded despite the massive cost barriers and the hostility of existing players in the airline industry as profiled by Gregory (1994).

Competition is, from an organisation's viewpoint, less about providing value for the customer and more about driving away other competing players. The natural tendency for any organisation is to seek to achieve as near a monopoly situation as possible so as to maximise income and to control rather than react to the market. Thus many countries have enacted anti-monopoly legislation (see Chapter 6).

Bargaining power

In Chapter 1, the relationship between supply and demand was introduced. In many ways the relationship between the relative bargaining powers of customers and suppliers mirrors the economic supply and demand model. Let us consider a simple relationship between a single supplier and a single customer.

The customer wishes to obtain the highest quality at the lowest price. Conversely the supplier wishes to supply the lowest acceptable quality (note the word acceptable, we are not talking about low quality) at the highest price he or she can obtain. A purchase is likely to be made when the highest quality the supplier can produce matches the lowest acceptable standard the customer requires, and when the lowest price the supplier can sell at matches the highest price the customer will pay.

Customers want highest quality at the lowest price; suppliers want the lowest acceptable quality at the highest price. This is a natural law of supply and demand. Because of the value chain, the supplier may well be a customer of other suppliers and the same rule will apply.

Another factor that can complicate the equation is availability. The more available a product or service is then the more bargaining power a customer has. The customer may find it relatively easy to go elsewhere.

It is sometimes cheaper to fly from London to New York than it is to fly from Aberdeen to Orkney, why? The answer is simple, there are more available seats on more air carriers across the North Atlantic than there are in the North of Scotland. Where supply exceeds demand, prices fall and customers are able to strike better deals. Where demand is high but there is restricted supply then prices rise and the supplier has the bargaining power.

If a car dealer has three vehicles and only two customers then the customer has the upper hand. If the dealer has three vehicles and four customers all desperate to buy then the supplier is in control. This phenomenon has been seen at Christmas over the supply of much wanted (one hesitates to use the word needed) toys. Parents have paid over the odds and have even flown across the Atlantic to avoid disappointing their offspring.

It follows that it is in the supplier's interest to ensure that demand always exceeds supply but not by too much. If demand greatly exceeds supply there may be the threat that other players may enter the market to satisfy the unsatisfied demand or that the customer will seek a substitute.

The dynamics of the process can be interesting. Increased costs from a supplier are normally passed along the chain to the ultimate customer who becomes dissatisfied with the prime supplier through no fault of that supplier. Indeed if margins are not affected too much it may be a good customer relations' exercise to absorb all or part of cost increases for as long as possible. Savings rarely go the whole way along the chain.

When home computers first came on the market, considerable demand was generated by one UK company which they were then unable to satisfy, with the result that other players came into the market, satisfied the demand and went on to dominate the marketplace, forcing the original company out.

The message is simple: if you create a demand, satisfy it or the customers will go elsewhere and may stay there. Being first into a market gives a short-term competitive advantage but this does not last. For many years the philosophy of the Douglas Aircraft Company in the USA was always to be the second to enter a market. Their literature quoted Pope: 'Be not the first by whom the new are tried, Nor yet the last to cast the old aside' (Eddy *et al.*, 1976).

It is an interesting statistic that whilst Boeing, who were second into the commercial jet airliner market behind the UK built Comet, were able to sell no fewer than 917 Boeing 707/720 (Green *et al.*, 1987), only 113 Comets were built (Stewart, 1986). Douglas, coming in later than Boeing, sold 556 DC8 aircraft, a product very similar to the 707. Coming in second paid dividends for Boeing as they were able to learn from the problems of the Comet (which were many) and design a totally different and highly successful aircraft (Stewart, 1986; Irving, 1993).

The first player into a market may gain all the initial business but they also have to iron out all of the bugs etc. in the product and this can lead to a deterioration in customer relations.

Cartwright & Green (1997), as mentioned earlier, added two extra 'threats', **re-entry** and **reforming** to the Porter model, both of which have implications for customer relations.

Re-entry

Organisations may leave a particular marketplace for a variety of reasons, financial, geographic, political etc. At such a time their customers may well go to another organisation. However, should the organisation return to the marketplace with the same name, there is every possibility that they will be able to regain at least part of their customer base. The degree to which this can be achieved will depend on how dissatisfied and inconvenienced customers were when the organisation left and how loyal they feel to their new supplier. Airlines often leave and re-enter routes but they nearly always take care to ensure that there are suitable alternatives for their regular customers.

Reforming

It was shown earlier that there can be considerable barriers to entry into a particular marketplace. One method of overcoming this is through a process known as **reforming**. In 1972, P&O (a UK company) attempted to break into the growing US cruise market with a ship named *Spirit of London*. P&O, whilst well known in the UK, were virtually unknown in the USA. The venture was not a success. However in 1974 P&O were able to purchase Princess Cruises (owners of the original *Love Boat*® from the television series). This gave P&O an immediate entry into the US market which they capitalised on when Princess (now part of the P&O operation) purchased Sitmar Cruises in 1988. The Princess identity, which is very strong in North America, was kept. Similarly Carnival Cruises expanded by purchasing Holland America Line, Costa (an Italian company) and eventually, in 1999, Cunard, owners of the QE2. The availability of corporate finance allowed, in those examples, the purchaser to 'reform' the original company in order to break into a marketplace and, critically, to keep the customer base of the indigenous company.

The importance of the Porter model

The Porter model is important because it stresses the relative powers of the partners to a transaction and provides a framework that considers the alternatives available to the customer. Using the model one can begin to understand that the value of any product or service is not vested within the product or service itself but in the customers' perceptions of what it will do for them. Ownership of a car may change somebody's life completely as it provides new possibilities.

Bowman's strategic compass

Clutterbuck *et al.* (1993) use Bowman's strategic compass as a tool to inform organisational decision-making as to the direction an organisation should take.

The model uses two axes, one relating to price and the other to perceived added value, as shown in Figure 3.3.

Looking at each of the strategies in turn:

Classic

The traditional strategy, an increase in perceived value, leads to the ability to charge more. This has been the classic Western approach since the industrial revolution.

Downmarket

The opposite of the classic strategy. Just as price can be increased if the perceived value increases, so lower value allows for price-cutting. Discounting often follows this strategy. Ward (1994, p. 291) has linked a slippage of standards on some cruise ships to the practice of discounting.

Failure

It perhaps stands to reason that an attempt to charge a high price for low perceived value is a doomed strategy. It can only work in a monopoly situation with a very highly desired product. It is certainly not a medium- to long-term strategy for success.

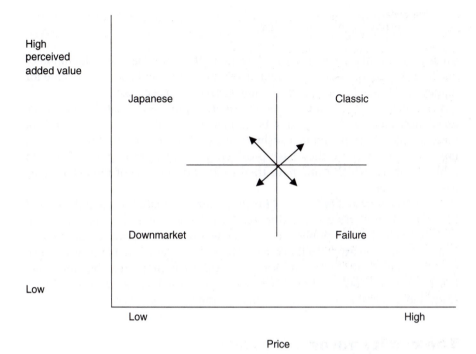

Figure 3.3 Bowman's strategic compass.

Japanese

This is an interesting strategy as it links high value with low price. This is a classic method of gaining market share. Pascale & Athos (1981) have pointed out the many differences between the Japanese and the Western style of management after World War II. The Japanese have traditionally regarded market share as a prime success criterion whereas the West tends to look for Return on Investment (up to 15% per annum in many cases). Japanese electrical goods and cars made massive inroads, especially in the USA, by offering quality products at low prices. They were, at times, accused of dumping goods onto the market and making no profit at all. True or not, they were able to gain a massive market share through this strategy. Interestingly, in the late 1990s, Japanese goods are no longer the cheapest, Taiwan and Korea have also learnt how to play the game!

The important point to note about the strategic compass is that it is perceived value that is important; it is the customer who ascribes value, not the supplier.

Excellence and quality

Excellence and quality are key factors associated with value for money. The *Concise Oxford Dictionary* (1990) defines excellence as:

'. . . surpassing merit or quality'

Quality comes first, excellence goes beyond it. It follows that a consideration of quality is key to any study of customer relations. It could be said that value for money (VFM) is achieved whenever quality exceeds expectation.

A number of authorities have considered precisely what is meant by excellence, collectively they may be termed the 'quality gurus'. The work of these people – Deming, Juran, Crosby, Peters & Waterman, Clutterbuck *et al.* – is important not because they have provided a detailed prescription of how to achieve quality (which some have tried to do) but because of the debate they have stimulated.

Peters & Waterman's *In Search of Excellence* made a major impact in the United Kingdom when it was published in 1982. Its themes were taken up with great gusto, especially by the public sector which was perhaps unusual at that time as it might have been expected that the lead in considering and debating excellence would be taken by the private sector. It was even rumoured that the Chief Executive of one local authority had one copy of the book at work, one in his study and one in the bedroom, so important did he think it was.

The quality gurus

The first of the recognised modern quality gurus was W Edwards Deming. Deming had been invited to Japan after World War II to assist the Japanese in rebuilding their industry because of the reputation he had gained assisting the allied war effort. Deming was probably the first person to articulate the principle that raising quality can actually lower costs. Whilst this might sound paradoxical, high-quality first time saves money on fixing faults.

Deming's philosophy revolves around the belief that 'happy people, delighted by what you have provided become loyal customers' (Deming, 1988). Deming produced 14 Points for Management in respect of quality. Those wishing to pursue Deming's philosophy are advised to consult Neave (1990) who has written a definitive account of the Deming approach.

Neave, as quoted in Wille (1992), makes the point that Deming's 14 Points are not a straightforward, just do this and everything will be OK approach but vehicles for opening up thinking about quality.

Deming's 14 Points are reproduced below:

1. CONSTANCY OF PURPOSE
Quality is a constant process. There are not times when one does quality work and times when just anything will do. Quality, like customer relations, is an attitude, a way of thinking.
2. A NEW PHILOSOPHY
Building on point 1, if quality is an attitude then organisations need a new philosophy that will not tolerate anything less than the best. If an organisation expects the best it tends to get the best and if it expects the worst then that is what will happen – a self-fulfilling prophesy!

3. REMOVING MASS INSPECTION

If quality is built into every stage of a process, the costly need for mass inspection of both tangible artefacts and intangible procedures will be removed. Work with quality circles has shown that those delivering a particular product, component or service are best placed to ensure quality. If somebody else inspects for quality, it becomes that person's concern and quality should and must concern all those employed by an organisation.

4. RELIABILITY OF SUPPLIERS

This book has already referred to the customer and value chains. Quality is the business of everybody in the chain up to the final customer. It is to an organisation's advantage to work closely with suppliers and to insist on a consistent standard of delivery.

5. CONSTANT IMPROVEMENT

Deming makes the point that organisations should be constantly looking to improve. Even if it is not possible to improve (and that is rare), it is still worth analysing the processes and products to see where value can be added.

6. TRAINING

An organisation committed to quality needs to provide constant training to its staff to ensure that their skills are up to date. Money spent on effective training is never wasted, a point made by Peters (1987) where he points out that constant training is the only way to ensure that staff can meet and exceed customer expectations.

7. LEADERSHIP

Deming saw managers as people who were there to help others do their job properly. He saw the leader's primary role as that of ensuring that the systems in place in an organisation aided the workforce to produce to a high standard. This is a far cry from earlier ideas of management, for example Taylor (1911) where the manager has a control/disciplinary role. Deming's ideas see the manager more in terms of the Peters & Waterman (1982) model where the manager in successful US companies was more of a coach and facilitator.

Quality must pervade an organisation and it requires both a top down and a bottom up approach. Senior management needs to create an environment where employees can take responsibility for their own quality issues.

8. REMOVING FEAR

A suitable environment for quality is difficult to sustain in a blame culture. Peters & Waterman (1982) stressed the importance of allowing controlled risks to be taken if organisations are going to develop. Fear is not conducive to producing products and services that will delight the customer. The work of Herzberg (1962), discussed in the previous chapter, showed that achievement and recognition were good motivators. Fear will never encourage staff to go the extra mile or to develop new products and services. That can only be done effectively in an environment where blame is not used as a punishment.

9. PULLING DOWN BARRIERS

Departmental and other organisational barriers can prevent a quality culture pervading the organisation. Multi-functional teams such as the Unipart OCC (Our Contribution Counts) groups profiled by Cartwright & Green (1997) allow quality issues to be discussed along the value chain and not just at nodal points. Involving everybody gives everybody shared ownership of quality issues.

10. ELIMINATE SLOGANISING

Deming, unlike Crosby (1979), believed that exhortations and slogans promoting quality did little. Deming believed that slogans without the necessary resources in the value chain were of little use and could lead to harmful frustration.

11. REMOVING QUOTAS

Externally set targets, especially if not set to C-SMART criteria (see Chapter 1), do not inspire quality. There is a great danger that just asking somebody to produce a set number of items without specifying the quality may lead to considerable later re-working. Deming believed that everybody should work to his or her capacity with quality not quantity being the prime factor. This proved to be one of the most controversial of his 14 Points.

12. PRIDE OF WORKMANSHIP

Engendering pride in a product or service should be the goal of every manager. The case study on the Scottish Prison Service (SPS) in Chapter 10 shows that even under prison conditions, products can be made that reflect pride. If workers feel a part of an organisation they are better able to empathise with its values, and if quality is one of those values then quality will pervade the workplace. Pride in workmanship comes from within; it comes from people who care.

13. SELF-IMPROVEMENT

Deming made the point that not just the product/service should merit continuous improvement, it is also the people making/delivering the product/service. A well-developed workforce understands the environment within which the organisation operates. Such knowledge is vital and forms part of the customer relations' strategy in Chapter 11.

14. TRANSFORMATION IS EVERYBODY'S JOB

Everybody means everybody: senior managers, middle managers, clerks, sales people, operators, cleaners – everybody. All have a role to play in the quality process. A dirty floor may lead to an accident that leads to a bad product; a badly answered telephone can lead to a lost order. Quality is everybody's business and everybody should have their quality and customer care skills enhanced. Even if they never meet an external customer they are all part of the internal customer value chain.

Juran

Joseph Juran began writing about quality issues in the 1950s and made a major impact with his book *Managerial Breakthrough*. Juran has emphasised the systematic approach to quality and developed what has become known (Wille, 1992) as the Juran Trilogy of quality control, quality planning and quality improvement.

Just as Deming produced 14 Principles, so Juran devised 10 Steps that are required to deliver quality products and services:

1. Develop awareness of the need and opportunity for improvement
2. Set goals for improvement
3. Design and set up the organisation to reach those goals
4. Train staff
5. Solve problems using a project approach
6. Report progress on a regular basis
7. Recognise people who produce quality
8. Communicate results
9. Keep scores
10. Maintain the momentum of improvement.

Juran has made the point that quality is not free. However the extra income that quality products and services can provide together with the decrease in expenditure rectifying errors will normally lead to a positive gain.

Crosby

Philip Crosby has been the exponent of a 'zero defect' approach. Whilst it may well be that no defects is an impossibility, Crosby maintains that this should be the aim. Crosby considers that quality is free as the financial penalties of adopting a zero defect approach are far outweighed by the financial benefits, as discussed earlier (Crosby, 1979). Crosby's ideas centre on four basic principles:

- A common definition of quality
- A system to manage quality
- Zero defects as the aim
- Quality is effectively free.

Crosby has, like Deming and Juran, produced a series of steps; interestingly he, (like Deming) uses 14:

1. There must be managerial commitment to quality
2. The use of quality improvement teams
3. Measurement of quality should be displayed for all to see
4. The definition of the cost of quality should be used as a managerial tool
5. Communication of quality awareness throughout an organisation
6. Systematic problem solving
7. Adopt a zero defect approach
8. Train supervisors to run quality improvement programmes
9. Run special zero defect events
10. Set quality goals
11. Develop an effective communication system
12. Appreciation of those who deliver quality
13. Set up quality councils
14. 'Do it over again' – improvements must be continuous.

Crosby has been described as an evangelist for quality and many of his books have that evangelical feel. Nevertheless, in stressing zero defects he makes the very important point that nobody should make do with second best. The more people strive for zero defects then the nearer to that goal they will become.

It must be stressed however that zero defects is an approach most easily suited to manufacturing. However, even if a product is defect free it is important that the service procedures that deliver it to the customer are also defect free. Even when the physical product is perfect, there are still possible improvements that can be made to service. Crosby is not only relevant to manufacturing but to any aspect of customer relations. If the organisation attempts to deliver perfection then they will get closer to that goal by adopting a continuous improvement process.

As MacDonald & Piggott (1990) have written: 'The customer's perception of quality includes more than the satisfaction obtained from the primary product or service. Their view of the company that provides the basic need will include how the original inquiry was handled on the telephone, the method of timing of delivery, the clarity and helpfulness of the operating instructions and the timeliness and accuracy of the invoice. Clearly if we are to delight the customer, quality management must be extended to the administrative areas'.

Quality, as described by Deming, Juran and Crosby, is the concern of all and includes supplementary as well as core products/services. There is considerable common ground between the Principles of Deming and the Steps of Juran and Crosby. Indeed many of their ideas, especially relating to the commitment of management and the need for pride in workmanship (a point considered in the case study on the Scottish Prison Service in Chapter 10), could have been written by one of the first management gurus, Fayol, as early as 1916. Fayol wrote of the importance of unity of direction, centralised policies, and *esprit de corps* and initiative as part of his treatise on management.

Peters & Waterman

In their very important work on excellence (*In Search of Excellence*, 1982), Peters & Waterman looked at a large number of US organisations that had a reputation for excellent products and services. They found that there were a series of attributes that these companies exhibited: they were all dynamic, they were very customer oriented ('Close to the Customer') and they gave their people responsibility and backed them when they took risks. They recognised that all productivity comes through people, and they made sure that all their employees understood the values and mission of the organisation. As organisations they stayed close to what they were good at and didn't try to branch out into unrelated areas, they had simple organisation structures and they kept a close control on values and costs but allowed employees freedom of action within those constraints. They discovered that in excellent organisations, the employees believed that their organisation was the best in its particular business.

The Peters & Waterman attributes are worth examining in some detail as they have provided much of the foundation for studies of excellence and quality from the 1980s onwards. Their studies concluded that there were eight basic attributes of excellent companies backed up by seven basic beliefs. The basic, underlying beliefs of the excellent organisations studied were:

- a belief in being the best
- a belief in the importance of getting the details right
- a belief that the people who worked for the organisation were at the heart of its success
- a belief in superior quality and service
- a belief in encouraging innovation and tolerating failure where this was a genuine effort to move the organisation on
- a belief in the importance of internal communications
- a belief in the need for the organisation to grow economically.

Supported by these beliefs, the organisations demonstrated the following eight attributes:

Bias for action

The organisations were ones that were innovative and were willing to try things. This attitude is demonstrated by the organisations considered in this book. They are PROACTIVE rather then REACTIVE. Proactivity is about anticipation and making things happen rather than reacting to others all of the time.

Closeness to the customer

It is only by talking to the customer that you can find out what they want. Tom Peters has coined the phrase 'Management by Wandering Around' (MBWA) and stresses the importance of talking to your customers, not just for a hard sell but to find out about their wants and needs. It isn't enough to know what the customer requires and feels; systems need to be in place to communicate the information throughout the organisation (see Crosby earlier in this chapter). Communication with the customer needs to be in the language of the customer and not jargon. Jargon and technical 'speak' may sound clever and knowledgeable but if the customer cannot understand or feels patronised, they may well go elsewhere.

Autonomy and entrepreneurship

Excellent organisations encourage people to take responsibility for decisions within corporate guidelines and in accordance with the mission and vision of the organisation.

One key characteristic of an excellent organisation is that it realises the contribution of its entire staff. This means celebrating success throughout the organisation. Excellent organisations ensure that internal customers know what is happening and share in good external customer comments. All quality ultimately depends on the people in the organisation.

Hands on, value driven

In excellent organisations, the core values and beliefs of the organisation are known and understood by all of the staff. It doesn't matter whether it is a huge multinational, like a regional leader, or a small organisation, perhaps an independent retailer with one outlet, everybody who works for the organisation needs to understand its philosophy and communicate that to the customer. Values are not something for the boardroom; they are for the hands on staff as well.

Stick to the knitting

One thing that Peters & Waterman found was that although there may be gaps in unrelated markets, organisations were most successful when they stuck to what they were good at. This does not mean that there should be no diversification but that it does need to be planned.

Single form, lean staff

Organisations work best with simple structures. Customers, too, understand simple structures. A complex organisation often pushes customers from department to department and the more complex an organisation is, the more difficulties are encountered with communications. If you have to set up any structure within your organisation, KIS (Keep It Simple).

Productivity through people

One key characteristic of an excellent organisation is that it realises the contribution of its entire staff. This means celebrating success throughout the organisation. Ensure that internal customers know what is happening and share in good external customer comments. All quality ultimately depends on the people in the organisation. There can be as many quality systems as you like but without well-motivated, well-informed staff, customer service will suffer.

Simultaneous loose–tight properties

Whilst sounding complex, this is a very simple concept. Give the staff at the customer interface as much flexibility as possible but keep a close control on the core values (and the finances) of the organisation.

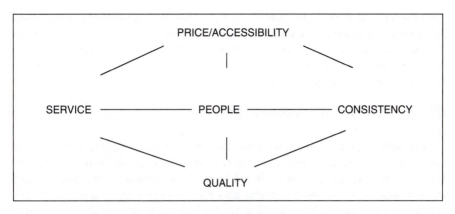

Figure 3.4 The excellence equilibrium (reproduced from Cartwright *et al.*, 1994, with permission).

Cartwright *et al.* (1994) took this concept to develop the 'excellence equilibrium' and their ideas are adapted and reproduced in Figure 3.4, with permission.

A Rolls Royce is possibly the best car in the world and in pure terms it is truly excellent. One of the most highly rated cruise ships in the world in 1999 (according to the *Berlitz Guide to Cruising and Cruise Ships* (1999)) was the *Crystal Symphony* of Crystal Cruises, but how many people can own a Rolls Royce or travel on the *Crystal Symphony*? If the *Crystal Symphony* was full to capacity for 52 weeks of the year and allowing therefore for 52 seven-day cruises, only 52 000 people would be able to enjoy the experience and no ship can be in operation for 365/6 days without needing time out for maintenance. Rolls Royce and Crystal Cruises are undeniably excellent, they are probably amongst the best in the world, but for most of us, excellence is connected with things that we can do or experience.

Marks and Spencer and Tesco in the UK and Macy's in the USA may not be in the same league as very expensive stores but they offer an excellent service to a large number of customers. Ford Motors may not be perceived as in the same class as Rolls Royce but they provide good, reliable transportation for millions of people across the world. British Airways operate the largest route network in the world and at prices a large number of people can afford and they do it to a consistent high level of service. Princess Cruises, operating all of their vessels over a full 52-week period on a mixture of 7–21 day cruises could carry approximately 400 000+ passengers in a year. To do that with a consistently high service and at prices that are described as moderate in the Berlitz guide is, for most of us, a truer example of excellence.

Excellence in the real world is a balance between the best service or product for the price with the highest quality, delivered to a consistently high level. All this is done through people. Excellence is the equilibrium between the various components. If a conscious decision has been made to go for a small 'niche' market, then one cannot compare the products or services so developed with those that are aimed at a wider market. When considering excellence it is important that like is compared with like.

Whilst not all of the companies Peters & Waterman looked at have been successful over the years since the research was carried out, many have and the work of Tom Peters and Bob Waterman has served to inform the debate on quality and excellence world-wide.

Clutterbuck and associates

David Clutterbuck has been one of the UK's most prolific writers on quality and excellence. *The Winning Streak,* written with Walter Goldsmith and published in 1983, and its sequel *The Winning Streak Mark II* , published in 1997, both looked at what made companies successful and have a degree of commonality with Peters & Waterman (1982). Writing with Clark and Armistead, Clutterbuck produced *Inspired Customer Service* in 1993, a book that is commended to all involved in delivering service to customers. Amongst the important points made in the latter is the balance between quality and productivity. Clutterbuck *et al.* make the point that it is easy to achieve high quality if low productivity is accepted and it is a danger that huge gains in productivity may lead to a diminution of quality. The trick is to get them into balance. If a company can make a maximum of 200 products but with a high defect rate, might it not be better to make 150 with a lower defect rate. Defects not only cost money to put right; if a product is delivered unrectified to a customer there will not only be the cost of rectification but also the loss of customer goodwill which may cost much more to regain. Clutterbuck *et al.* have also provided excellent examples of how to benchmark, not only against competitors but also against successful organisations in other fields, a technique that forms part of Chapter 11 of this book.

Total quality management (TQM)

The concept of Total Quality Management (TQM) gained a high profile from the early 1990s onwards. In effect the ideas of the various quality gurus, discussed earlier were combined into a concept that saw quality as the responsibility of everybody in the organisation and placed quality, like customers, at the centre of the organisation's activities.

Going right back to ancient times there is a quotation from King Hammurabi of Babylon in 1700 BC:

> 'If a building falls into pieces and the owner is killed then the builder shall be put to death. If the owner's children are killed then the builder's children shall also be put to death'.

Rather harsh one might think but nevertheless it does show a concern about quality and the concept of the provider being responsible to the customer for the standard of workmanship. The craft guilds of medieval times were formed both to control the market and to impose quality standards so that a customer who purchased products or services from a guild member would have guarantee of quality and would know that shoddy work would be rectified and that culprits could be punished by fines or expulsion from the guild. Organisations such as ABTA (Association of British Travel Agents) and the BMA (British Medical Association) are the modern-day successors to the medieval guilds.

Modern thinking, as promoted by the quality gurus, centres around the concept of continuous improvement often referred to as *kaizen*, this being the term for continuous improvement in Japanese. Continuous improvement leads to a belief in the totality of quality. Total quality is not just a control system based on constant inspection (QC – Quality Control), nor is it purely an assurance mechanism reliant on self checking (QA – Quality Assurance) but a holistic approach that requires an organisational attitude and culture that run through every operation (TQM – Total Quality Management).

TQM is very much a people oriented as opposed to a control centred approach. TQM considers that all employees actually have two work roles, one being their actual job and the second being to find ways of improving the work that they do. Given that the second role involves personal initiative it is obvious that the TQM approach has implications for the senior management of an organisation. Senior management must subscribe and support the TQM approach as it is their commitment that will lead to the TQM culture pervading the whole organisation.

Service as the prime supplementary

As organisations have put the ideas of Deming, Juran etc. into their cultures, so the products they deliver have moved nearer and nearer to zero defects. There are few consumer items in the Western world that can be differentiated by considerable differences in quality. As stated earlier, defects in new cars are now rare, TV sets work first time, computers have very few faults etc. Where companies can differentiate is in the level of service they deliver. Cartwright & Green (1997) found that customers in a free market economy are prepared to pay for good service and are beginning to see service as moving from a supplementary part of the product to its core.

In discussing the importance of customer service, Clutterbuck *et al.* (1993) describe how organisations can be classified in relation to their actual service standards and their commitment to the delivery of outstanding service. Their organisational typology is as follows:

Naturals

In a 'natural' (as regards customer relations) company, excellent service is embedded into the total philosophy and culture of the company. In many instances this can be traced back to the founder(s) of the organisation. Because they are known for their excellent customer relations these companies tend to attract, as employees, those who share the customer first philosophy. If service declines then word will spread rapidly. Such companies do not need to spend vast sums setting up customer service initiatives, they already form part of the operating procedures, but they do need to ensure that the momentum of continuous improvement is maintained.

Aspirants

Aspirant organisations have a keen desire to become naturals and share many of the same characteristics of excellent service and flexibility. Clutterbuck *et al.* believe that the difference between the two is that aspirants talk more about service but perhaps deliver less, whilst naturals don't talk much about service but are renowned for their delivery.

Followers

Clutterbuck *et al.* describe followers as organisations that are being forced to adopt a customer centred approach against their will. Top management may well believe in the concepts but these are rarely communicated downward. Clutterbuck *et al.* note that such organisations frequently embark upon costly customer care campaigns because of insistence by their larger customers.

It may seem strange that any organisation could undertake customer care unwillingly but it is unfortunately the case that there are many product driven organisations still in the marketplace. Anybody who doubts this should consult the consumer advice pages of national newspapers or the television programmes dealing in customer complaints; some of the stories would be farcical if they were not, unfortunately, true.

Laggards

The very worst service, according to Clutterbuck *et al.*, comes from laggards. They really do not care. Survival in a competitive environment is naturally very difficult for such organisations and many of them have been in protected, monopolistic situations. They can improve but they have such a bad reputation that they have to work much harder than aspirants or naturals.

Pre and after sales service

To return to the motor dealership theme, which provides so many useful examples for a study of customer relations. A customer purchasing a vehicle is increasingly interested in the supplementary products that form part of the package. As stated earlier, it can be assumed that the vehicle (if purchased from new) will have very few faults. What distinguishes it from the competition may well be the supplementaries and of those, service is a vital component.

A customer is interested not only in the service at the point of sale or delivery but throughout the life of the product. This is why so many people buy extended warranties; they are concerned that the product will receive the proper maintenance that it requires. More and more organisations are stressing their ability to provide good after sales service, as this is what will lead to repeat business.

Pre sales service is also important because the first contact a person has with an organisation sets the tone for their future dealings; this is when perceptions are developed. Thus the first contact, be it an advertisement, a telephone call or a visit, should be steeped in quality. The importance of first impressions will be examined in Chapter 8 when the concept of Organisational Body Language (OBL) is introduced.

Branding and quality

Branding is an important part of the relationship between an organisation and its customers, as shown in the previous chapter. Brand loyalty can be quite high and the basic concept is to encourage the customer to identify with a particular brand. There are many, many brands of washing powder on the UK market but most are made by just two or three companies. Chocolate bars of different brands fill the shelves but there are only a few major manufacturers. Certain VW, Skoda and Seat cars look very similar; this should be no surprise as the brands are all owned by the same group. British Airways are able to franchise their BA brand to regional airlines in the UK and other parts of Europe. BA has a particular position in the marketplace and it is advantageous to the franchisees to be associated with that particular brand.

Once a brand gains a reputation for quality then its position is strengthened. Quality is not the only reason for brand success; fashion too may play a part. It is difficult to tell whether different 'trainers' for children sold in a shoe shop are actually worth the large differentials some brands are able to gain. In this case the name itself is more important than the product, hence the problem of pirate copies. Branding and the loyalty of a customer to a particular brand is an important weapon in competition and take-over attempts may be purely to acquire a particular brand. Carnival Cruises have already been mentioned in this book. Carnival as a stand-alone brand appeals to a particular customer base and it is interesting that when the Carnival parent company acquired Holland America, Seabourne, Costa and Cunard they did not re-brand the products. All four of the acquisitions had their own loyal customer base and thus it was more effective to leave the brands as they were rather than risk losing those customers (Cartwright & Baird, 1999).

The popularity of particular brands can be culturally and geographically specific. In August 1999, a list comparing the 50 most popular UK wide brands with the 50 most popular Scottish brands was produced. The results of the top ten for each are shown in Figure 3.5.

Consistency of service

Organisations that operate across multiple sites need to ensure that not only is the quality of the product consistent but also that service is delivered to a consistent level. Local conditions may require differing types of service but the

	UK wide	Scotland
1	Coca-Cola	Irn-Bru *
2	Walkers Crisps	Coca-Cola
3	Persil	Pepsi
4	Nescafe	Walkers Crisps
5	Andrex	Nescafe
6	Stella Artois	Golden Wonde
7	Muller Yoghurt	Wiseman's *
8	Pepsi	Mars Bar
9	Pampers	Andrex
10	Ariel	Muller Yoghurt

* Irn-Bru is a very popular soft drink in Scotland and Wiseman's are well known in Scotland for their milk.

Figure 3.5   Top 10 UK and Scottish brands, August 1999.

overall standard should be the same. This is one of the reasons why mystery customers (see later) are employed as they can visit a number of sites to check up on service levels. Even within an organisation it is vital that internal service is consistent, as the value chain is only as good as its weakest link. If a company is operating theme parks in different countries it must ensure that customers receive the same basic standard wherever they are; a chain of shops needs consistency of service, as do the departments of a local authority. Customers will base their overall impression of the organisation on the worst service they receive at one of its sites and not the best.

Quality standards

Many organisations boast about the quality standards they have achieved. ISO 9000 and BS 5750 are two of the better-known quality standards. Clutterbuck *et al.* (1993) make the point that gaining a standard only represents part of a service quality approach. Many organisations are required to gain standards in order to be suppliers to large concerns and especially governmental bodies. Just being able to undertake the paperwork may be no indication that the customer will receive a better standard of care. Standards may be of more practical use when they can be removed as well as awarded. In the summer of 1999 the UK Passport Agency lost the 'Charter Mark' it had been awarded by the government because of the huge delays experienced by its customers. Standards need to be reviewed regularly, it is no use achieving the standard and then allowing things to slip back – customers will soon notice.

Mystery customers

A frequently used method of acquiring hands on information about the standard of service delivered to customers of the organisation or its competitors is to use the services of a 'mystery customer'. Usually employed by an agency, this is a person (also known as a 'mystery guest' or a 'mystery shopper') who undertakes to sample the service offered and then reports back using a set of agreed criteria.

The mystery customer acts, as far as possible, as a normal customer, selecting and paying for goods or partaking of services as any customer would. A report is then sent to the relevant authority in the organisation on the standard of service, usually covering the whole of the experience from entry to exit.

Provided that it is not obvious to staff from the type of questions asked that this is a mystery and not a normal customer, the information can be very helpful. It is important that staff do not feel that they are being spied upon in an underhand method. It is good practice for organisations to make clear that the mystery customer is not basically looking to catch people out but would rather 'catch people in', i.e. doing and saying the right things.

When briefing a mystery customer prior to their observing the organisation, it is unhelpful if they have a huge checklist to complete as this will make their actions rather mechanistic and thus give the game away. The mystery customer needs to behave as normally as possible if the exercise is to be of benefit.

When the report is received it is important that there is an opportunity to provide objective and positive feedback to staff. Managers must deal with those areas of concern indicated by the report but also need to praise staff for the things they have done well.

Many organisations undertake formal or informal mystery customer exercises on their competitors. There may be specialist staff employed to use the competitors as though they were normal customers or the organisation may seek informal information from its staff on the efficiency of competitors that they may have gleaned through their normal shopping, hotel, travel activities etc.

Summary

This chapter has centred on the importance of value for money, quality and excellence. Value is a very personal thing as different customers may have different perceptions of value. The Value Expectation model shows the importance of the perceptions that the customer holds. Porter's 5 Forces model provides a model for competitive forces and has been added to by Cartwright & Green (1997), and can be linked to Bowman's strategic compass.

The role of the quality gurus – Deming, Duran etc. – was explored and these were linked to the ideas of Peters & Waterman and Clutterbuck *et al.* The Excellence Equilibrium provides a model for understanding excellence in a pragmatic way that relates to the real world.

The chapter considered branding, pre and after sales service and the importance of achieving consistency of service across multiple sites and along the value chain. The final section pointed out some of the dangers associated with quality standards and considered the use of mystery customers.

Terms introduced

- Aspirants
- Bargaining power
- Excellence
- Excellence equilibrium
- Followers
- Laggards
- Mystery customer
- Naturals
- New entrants
- Porter's forces
- Pre and after sales service
- Quality
- Quality gurus
- Re-entry
- Reforming
- Standards
- Strategic compass
- Substitutes
- Total Quality Management (TQM)
- Value expectation
- Value for Money (VFM)

QUESTIONS

1. Explain the nature of the competitive forces operating upon an organisation and how these forces can affect the relative power of the customer and the organisation.
2. Show how common themes relating to quality run through the ideas of Deming, Duran, Crosby and Peters & Waterman. How can organisations use these ideas to achieve continuous improvement?
3. Explain how service has become a prime supplementary product and what implications this has for product/service providers.

M 4 Customer loyalty

Belonging – Comfort zones – Types of loyalty – Customer behaviour – Apostles, Loyalists, Hostages, Mercenaries and Terrorists – Measuring loyalty – Loyalty schemes

Mention has already been made in Chapter 1 of the importance of the lifetime value of the customer. With the exception of those few organisations normally in the criminal justice or medical sectors whose aim is to never see the customer again, successful organisations view the initial transaction with a new customer as just the first of many. The point has already been made in this book that it costs far more to gain a new customer than to retain an existing one (Cartwright & Green, 1997). The actual cost difference has been placed as high as a factor of 5. This cost reflects the amount of advertising and the time it will take to build up a working relationship with a new customer. There is also a hard to define but very real benefit in having loyal customers as they often act as a marketing organ for the organisation. Unfortunately as Cartwright & Green (1997) pointed out, satisfied customers seem to have fewer friends than dissatisfied ones and the latter appear to have louder voices. Put simply, people are far more likely to be vocal about things that go wrong as opposed to those that go right. Whilst there have been a number of TV and radio programmes in the UK dealing with consumer problems, there has not been as much mention made of the things that have been done well. Bad news sells better than good news, as a casual glance at any newspaper will show.

It is clearly to the advantage of the vast majority of organisations to have a loyal customer base. It is perhaps also advantageous, psychologically for customers to be loyal to a particular product or organisation. Chapter 2 introduced the motivational theory ascribed to Abraham Maslow (1970). Belonging, according to Maslow, is quite a high-level need for humans. As a species we gain comfort from a feeling of belonging and being with others who share similar ideas and values to ourselves. Organisations that can provide this sense of belonging to their customers are tapping a very important psychological vein within humans.

Much of the fashion industry works on the sense of belonging. It is important to the fashion conscious to be identified with others of a like mind. It matters what name is written on the side of a pair of trainers or on the breast of a pocket. Princess Cruises, who are considered in a case study in Chapter 10, operate, like other cruise companies, a special club for regular customers. After a first Princess cruise, customers are automatically enrolled in the 'Captain's Circle'. Members receive a regular newsletter and when embarked on a Princess cruise are invited to a special party. There is a ranking scheme for members whereby after a certain number of cruises they are 'promoted' from First Officer to Chief Officer to Captain and eventually to Commodore, receiving a badge with the appropriate number of gold stripes. All of this strengthens the sense of belonging and conversations with Captain's Circle members in the course of preparing this book indicated that membership was valued. At the party, the ship's Captain is expected to give details on comings and goings in the company and a real family atmosphere is generated.

Comfort zones

Change of any type, even if for the better, can be very uncomfortable. Kurt Lewin (1951) suggested that people become frozen into a particular situation and whilst it may not be the best situation available, the effort and uncertainty of changing can inhibit even a change for the better.

Tice (1989) has developed the concept of a comfort zone in which people operate. Any movement away from the zone of comfort, be it for better or worse, is resisted. This can explain why people who upgrade into first class on airline flights can feel uncomfortable and for the fact that a huge lottery win may well bring discomfort as the winner is moved completely out of their comfort zone.

In terms of the relationship between customer relations and loyalty, the concept of comfort zones can be used to explain why customers stay loyal to an organisation or product even if another is convenient, thus making the change relatively easy. Customers tend to stick to what they know or as the saying goes: 'better the devil you know. . .'. We could term this form of loyalty, **COMFORT LOYALTY**.

Linked to the effect of comfort zones is the cost to the customer of switching to another supplier or product. In the case of everyday household goods (Fast Moving Consumer Goods, FMCG) there may be no cost. However switching, say, computer operating systems may require the purchase of new software, changing to another make of car may require building up a relationship with a new supplier and dealer, and these costs can be perceived as too high. They may not be monetary at all, often they are time and effort but they are costs to the customer nevertheless.

Product and brand loyalty

Wind (1982) has examined customer loyalty and has postulated that there are six classifications of customers in respect of loyalty:

- current loyal customers who will continue to use the product or service
- current customers who may switch to another brand

- occasional customers who would increase consumption of the brand if the incentive were right
- occasional customers who would decrease consumption of the brand if a competitor offered the right incentive
- non-users who could become customers
- non-users who will never become customers.

It is important to distinguish between loyalty to the generic product, the brand and a particular supplier.

Many people are loyal to coffee as a beverage. There are also those who are only occasional coffee drinkers and those who never drink coffee, often for medical or religious reasons. Those who drink considerable amounts of coffee can be described as having a product loyalty. Within that group there will be some that buy just the cheapest coffee or drink whatever is available. For them a new term is being introduced in this book, they are product loyal but brand **A-LOYAL**. They are not disloyal as that implies that there has been a loyalty, but they have no loyalty at all to a particular brand, Later in this chapter these brand a-loyal customers will be equated to a type of customer known as a mercenary. Within the group of those who are product loyal there will be those who have a particular **BRAND LOYALTY.** They always buy a particular brand or at least a brand from the same producer.

According to Alsop (1989) who studied brand loyalty in the USA, cigarettes, mayonnaise and toothpaste carried a 60% brand loyalty, with plastic bags and tinned vegetables having very little brand loyalty. The situation has become more complicated as suppliers have begun to introduce their own brands, a point picked up later in this chapter.

Supplier loyalty

As was mentioned in the section on comfort zones, many customers are creatures of habit. Not only are they loyal to particular brands, there is also a loyalty to particular suppliers. The work on customer behaviour to be covered later in this chapter introduces a type of customer known as a hostage, i.e. somebody who has no choice but to be a customer of a particular brand or supplier. Such a situation could occur in a small village community where there is only one shop selling perhaps just one brand of baked beans. A customer who is without transport could be forced, if they really want baked beans, to be loyal to that one brand and that one supplier. The term introduced for this is **PSEUDO-LOYALTY**. A statistical analysis of that customer would show considerable loyalty but it is known as pseudo-loyalty because given the opportunity the customer might well choose another brand from another supplier. The introduction of large edge-of-town supermarkets in the UK provided a dramatic illustration of pseudo-loyalty as smaller shops saw customers they had previously thought of as extremely loyal defecting to the supermarkets in large numbers, lured by lower prices and increased choice. In cases such as the above there may well be product and brand loyalty but no supplier loyalty.

Supra-loyalty

Supra-loyalty is a term that can be applied to those who are extremely loyal to an organisation, product or service. In the case of loyalty to an organisation they have normally built up a personal relationship with the organisation over a period of time or in the case of a product/service they identify themselves with it. It is as if they have internalised the relationship and consider themselves almost part of the organisation instead of being a customer. Cartwright & Baird (1999) found examples of such customer behaviour in their study of the cruise industry. Some customers could not conceive of taking a cruise on the ship of a competitor company and were, in fact, very knowledgeable about the history and operations of their preferred company. Such supra-loyalty can be very beneficial to an organisation as its customers actually perform a marketing function for it by telling their friends, relations and colleagues, but if they become disillusioned then they can wreak havoc as will be shown later.

De-loyalty

A customer who makes a deliberate decision to move to another organisation because he or she has been let down by an organisation that they were previously loyal to can be described as being **DE-LOYAL**. This is not the same as disloyalty, which suggests that it is the customer who is doing something wrong. In the case of de-loyalty it is the organisation that has let the customer down. There is evidence that people are willing to forgive one mistake or one case of poor service, that the forgiveness is actually inherent has been suggested by Dawkins (1976), and Cartwright & Green (1997) have pointed out that customer loyalty can be retained even after a mistake provided that rectification (and an apology) is speedily forthcoming. However if a supra-loyal customer becomes disenchanted they may take their business elsewhere, in effect becoming de-loyal. If they are very, very disappointed they may become **ANTI-LOYAL**, seek retribution against the organisation and become what are known as terrorists, a phenomenon that will be covered later in this chapter.

Disloyalty

It is a mute point as to whether a customer can actually be disloyal. Customers owe nothing, in terms of loyalty, to suppliers. Many customers may feel that they are being disloyal if they go elsewhere but feeling disloyal is not the same as being disloyal. The only obligation actually placed on a customer is to render payment for the product or service provided by payment in monetary or other terms.

Organisations, however, carrying as they do a responsibility to their customers, can be disloyal. Disloyalty is not providing a product or service deliberately to a previously loyal customer. An example of this would be an organisation that treated a new customer better, deliberately or not, than an existing customer. In this case the organisation would be being disloyal to the relationship that had been built up. If the existing customer decided to go elsewhere then they would be making a perfectly valid and proper decision. Disloyalty implies an act that is somehow immoral and one can argue that only the organisation and not the customer is capable of such an act. The customer may be a-loyal, de-loyal or even anti-loyal, as discussed earlier, but never disloyal.

Customer behaviour

This chapter has introduced a number of terms that can be used to describe the degree of loyalty a customer has to a particular generic product, brand or supplier: A-Loyal, Supra-Loyal, De-Loyal, Pseudo-Loyal and Anti-Loyal. In effect they describe a variety of customer behaviours. Work by Jones & Strasser in the USA has also considered customer loyalty and in particular why satisfied customers defect. In short, the question can be answered by stating that mere satisfaction is no longer enough. As has been already stressed in this book, the aim of any supplier of goods or services should be to delight the customer. Unless they are A-Loyal, delighted customers do not defect unless they cease to become delighted or are even more delighted by the offering of a competitor. The concept of comfort zones discussed at the beginning of this chapter indicates that a competitor will need to provide considerably more delight in order to woo a customer and that may well not be a cost-effective method of gaining new customers.

Jones & Strasser have made the point that many organisations believe that if their customer feedback mechanisms indicate satisfaction then the organisation is in a good position. Their research however showed a weak link between satisfaction and loyalty. As products and services improve, so satisfaction becomes in effect the minimum acceptable standard. As this book has used the terms supra-loyalty and pseudo-loyalty, Jones & Strasser have referred to long-term loyalty and false loyalty. Many commercial operations have competition curtailed either by government restrictions or by (sometimes illegal) arrangements between the various players. Whilst monopolies are becoming rarer in free market economies, Cartwright & Green (1997) have described situations such as duopolies where there are only two main players in a particular segment of the market, or what they have described as oligopolies where the supply is restricted to a limited number of suppliers. High cost barriers to entry, as discussed in the previous chapter, may restrict membership, as may the illegal setting up of cartels. The oil and airline industries have been accused of restricting membership to the favoured few, situations that benefit the suppliers but not the customer (Sampson, 1984; Gregory, 1994). Jones & Strasser have concluded that in the case of monopolies or oligopolies, as soon as there is increased competition then the level of satisfaction required to retain previously 'loyal customers' increases. They point out that whilst in monopoly/oligopoly situations it is the customer who has restricted choice, as soon as competition opens out it is the supplier who has only one real choice. They must provide their existing customers with higher and higher levels of satisfaction. The easier it becomes to switch, the more likely it is to happen.

UK banks have made a point of targeting students to open accounts with them despite the fact that students have little if any disposable income. The fact is that graduates are likely to earn more over their working lives and thus provide more business and revenue for their bank. There has also been a considerable lack of switching of bank accounts. Part of this may be due to loyalty but it has also been relatively complicated to do so. Banks are now making it much easier for customers to change to them by easing the complexities that the customer could experience. This is, off course, a two-edged sword. If you make it easier for somebody to switch from a competitor to you, your competitors will make it easier for your customers to defect to them. Changing one's email provider may require a new email address and people will have to be informed; perhaps it is easier to remain with the current provider. When the UK government deregulated telephones, gas and electricity in the 1990s, the various suppliers made it relatively simple for customers to switch provision. British Telecom, as the UK market leader for telephone services, also made it easy and cheap for defectors to return.

The importance of total satisfaction (or delight) against mere satisfaction was demonstrated by the example of the reprographics giant, Xerox, as profiled by Jones & Strasser (1995). They found that delighted Xerox customers were a staggering six times more likely to give repeat business to Xerox than merely satisfied customers. As it is unlikely to cost six times more to delight a customer than to merely satisfy him or her, then the financial advantages of delighting the customer seem self-evident.

Jones & Strasser have developed terminology for six types of customer behaviour that can be linked closely to the types of loyalty discussed earlier.

Apostles

Apostles demonstrate supra-loyalty. The apostle is delighted with the service or product and, as stated earlier when considering supra-loyalty, may actually identify with the organisation or the product. This is of course good news for any organisation. Apostles in effect carry out a marketing function for the organisation. They are highly loyal and delighted and they tell their friends and relations.

There are downsides to having too many apostles in the customer base. Their identification with the organisation may be so close that they can come to believe that they are actually part of the organisation. When this happens the distance that should rightly be present in the customer–supplier relationship is destroyed. The apostle can become a nuisance by demanding special treatment and interfering in matters that are really not their concern, such as internal arrangements that have no effect on the customer. There is a delicate balance to be struck by organisations that want the benefits of apostles but must militate against the disadvantages.

The biggest danger associated with the apostle is the tendency to become highly disruptive if dissatisfied. Apostles are paradoxically the most fertile source of the organisation's worst enemy, the terrorist. It is said that 'Hell hath no fury like a woman scorned' but to an organisation 'Hell hath no fury to compare to a highly dissatisfied apostle'. The dissatisfied apostle does not just feel let down, because of their perceived close link to the organisation they can feel betrayed and with betrayal may come a wish for revenge and retribution.

Apostles are unlikely to switch unless they become very dissatisfied, but when they do it will be in such a manner as not to go unnoticed.

Loyalists

Loyalists form the most important component of the customer base. They are akin to the 'Cash Cows' described by the Boston Consulting Group to describe those products that form the basis for organisational success. Loyalists require much less effort on their behalf than apostles do and are very loyal customers, coming back time and again. They tend to be less volatile than apostles are and thus more tolerant of mistakes. They are less voluble in their complaints but that does not mean that the organisation can afford to ignore them. An organisation that loses the support of its loyalists is on the downward spiral to major problems.

Whilst there might be a certain glamour attached to apostles and their effusive praise of an organisation, loyalists are the true firm foundation for any customer base. Loyalists provide the stability and objectivity required for sustained growth. Loyalists form useful members of focus groups as they will not be afraid to tell the truth as they see it, but they will be objective in doing so and that will provide useful data for the organisation.

Jones & Strasser make the point that loyalists are the easiest customers to deal with. That is true but customers only become loyalists as a result of high-quality products and services delivered over a period of time and when there have been complaints, they have been rectified expeditiously.

Mercenary

Mercenaries are the hardest customers to deal with, as they are basically a-loyal. Mercenaries will tend to go for the cheapest or the most convenient option. They are difficult to deal with because they may well be satisfied but they are not loyal. Mercenaries may demonstrate product loyalty but brand a-loyalty; they may be brand loyal but supplier a-loyal. They may well move from brand to brand or supplier to supplier. If asked why they moved, the answer may be in terms of cost or convenience but it may well be just a desire for a change.

The problem for an organisation is whether to expend energy or indeed money on trying to turn a mercenary into a loyalist. The organisation will need to satisfy the mercenary as even they will tell people about bad products and services, but unless they are incredibly pleased it may well be that they will continue to shop around. From the organisation's point of view it is important not to pander too much to the mercenary. Too big a discount on the first transaction may well mean that they will always want such levels if they return, but they are just as likely to go down the road and quote your discount to a competitor in the hope that it will be bettered.

Hostage

In Chapter 10 of this book there is a case study on Caledonian Cinemas. During a training session on customer care with a group of their managers there was an illuminating discussion on loyalists and hostages. It was interesting to see the recognition of the hostage category when it was described.

Hostages appear to be very loyal but that is only because they have no choice. If a town only has one cinema then it will receive the vast majority of the cinema trade. An organisation will not know whether its customers are loyalists or hostages until a competitor or a substitute (see previous chapter) appears on the scene.

Hostages have no choice; there is only one convenient shop, one local supplier, one hospital to go to etc. They have no choice but to demonstrate attributes of loyalty even when dissatisfied, hence the use of the term pseudo-loyalty.

The time for an organisation to assess the loyalty and the satisfaction of its customers is not when a competitor opens up but before then. Hostages will leave as soon as they have an opportunity if they are dissatisfied. Even satisfied hostages may leave for a while in order to assess a new competitor. The original supplier will have to hope that the original product/service was of sufficient quality to tempt them back. It is too late to offer discounts and/or enhancements after competition starts. Hostages will ask, and rightly, 'why are you offering this to me now but not before?'

Defector

Dissatisfy even a loyalist often enough and they may well defect from the organisation. Once a customer has defected and given their custom to another organisation it may well be difficult to recover the situation, as their comfort zone (see earlier in the chapter) will have changed.

Organisations need to ensure that complaints (see the next chapter) are dealt with in an expeditious manner so that any temporary dissatisfaction does not become permanent and thus lead to defection. One organisation's lost customer is a gain for a competitor, with the financial penalties as shown in the Customer Accumulator introduced in Chapter 1.

The defector displays characteristics of de-loyalty, as discussed earlier.

Terrorist

The terrorist in customer relations' terms is the worst nightmare an organisation can have. Just as the political terrorist acknowledges no rules, neither, it appears, does the customer relations' terrorist.

Terrorists were often apostles displaying supra-loyalty until they were let down and the situation was not recovered. They are not so much dissatisfied with the organisation, product or service as at war with it. They have a desire for revenge and retribution. Many of those who appear on consumer affairs television programmes have been previous apostles. On being let down, they have no problem in letting the world know about it.

The longer a situation remains unresolved, the angrier the terrorist becomes and sometimes their actions may be extreme, irrational and even criminal. The threat of a court appearance for harassment or breach of the peace in respect of their relationship with an organisation may well have an unexpected and negative effect. Court means publicity and by the time a customer becomes a terrorist, putting the problem right is no longer enough, they want to see the organisation humiliated.

The best method of dealing with this type of terrorist is to do what should never be done to a political terrorist – give them what they want and more if necessary and hope that they go away. The organisation will not want them as customers in the future. The organisation should concentrate on cutting its losses rather than trying to win back the custom. Terrorists are not de-loyal or even disloyal, they are anti-loyal; to use a metaphor, love has turned to hate!

Jones & Strasser's work is useful in that it provides an easy-to-understand explanation of why mere satisfaction is no longer enough to generate loyalty. Loyalty must be earned and should never be taken for granted. A summary of loyalty and satisfaction is shown in the loyalty matrix in Figure 4.1.

High	HOSTAGE (PSEUDO-LOYAL)	APOSTLE (SUPRA-LOYAL)
		LOYALIST (LOYAL)
LOYALTY		
	DEFECTOR (DE-LOYAL)	MERCENARY (A-LOYAL)
Low	TERRORIST (ANTI-LOYAL)	
	Low SATISFACTION High	

Figure 4.1   The loyalty matrix.

How can loyalty be measured?

This is a question that can only be answered in a situation where there is considerable choice available to the customer. Customers will be truly loyal and not displaying pseudo-loyalty when the quality and value for money that they receive are sufficient for them to ignore the competition even when the competitor can offer either a slight cost saving, enhanced convenience or both.

Even changing one's regular supermarket can affect the comfort zone and it appears that there is a threshold that needs to be reached before many customers will defect.

Loyalty schemes

The 1990s saw a proliferation of loyalty schemes, in part due to the opportunities presented by the introduction of new information technology systems, as will be covered in Chapter 7 of this book.

Loyalty schemes have, however, been around for some considerable time. Since the earliest days of commercial activity, discounts have been offered to repeat customers, thus encouraging them to come back to the same supplier. What new technology has allowed is for loyalty schemes to become highly sophisticated.

However, as Brassington & Pettitt (1997) have pointed out, if every supermarket and every airline and every department store have their own loyalty scheme, much of the competitive advantage may be lost. Cobb (1995) has reported that once the market for loyalty schemes becomes saturated they generate very little extra revenue. Mitchell (1995) has shown that over 25% of scheme members are happy to switch to a scheme offering marginally better benefits and as such display a-loyalty, as discussed earlier. Once saturation is reached it may be that lower prices may well become, once more, the determinant in customer choice. Nevertheless loyalty schemes grew considerably in the 1990s and seem set to be a feature of retail operations for the foreseeable future.

Brassington & Pettitt (1997) provide a useful case study on supermarket loyalty schemes in their book *Principles of Marketing*, pp. 694–5.

A number of the schemes that will discussed in the following sections involve the awarding of points, stamps or vouchers to the loyal customer. Such rewards are known as alternative currencies as they can be traded in for goods and services at an agreed exchange rate, in the same way that actual cash is used to purchase goods and services (Brassington & Pettitt, 1997).

Co-op dividends

The various Co-operative Societies that sprang up in the UK during the industrial revolution, the first being opened in Rochdale in 1844 under the title of 'The Rochdale Pioneers', were based on the concept that they were owned by their members. In effect they were an early example of the share-holding democracy that became a touchstone of the Thatcher government post 1979. The major benefit of membership was the dividend that was paid out either as cash or goods at the end of the year. Each transaction a member made attracted a certain discount that was recorded on a slip and placed in the dividend book. The author can well remember as a child his grandmother using her dividend from the Stockport (Greater Manchester) Co-operative for presents and food at Christmas and her Co-op number, 31292, is still etched in his memory. It was this 'shared' ownership that set the Co-operative movement apart from other retail operations and it is only in recent years that other retail operations have begun to operate similar loyalty schemes. The Co-operative movement was also different in that it had social and political aspects, being closely associated with the working class and the labour party. It should also be noted that in its earliest years there was no provision for the transfer of benefits from one Co-op to another, the operations being very much based on geographical location.

Features of a successful loyalty scheme

The Co-op dividend was successful in attracting customer loyalty in that it displayed most, but not all, of the attributes of a successful loyalty scheme. The most important attribute of a successful scheme is that the customer perceives added value. If they do not, then the scheme is doomed. To add value it must offer benefits that the customer wants as opposed to those that the organisation may wish to give.

Be mutually beneficial

The original Co-op schemes need to be viewed from the sociological perspective at the time. By owning the organisation the members were able to control prices to some degree. Given the smaller amounts of disposable income available to a working class family at the time, this was of considerable benefit when linked to the payment of a dividend. The organisation benefited from a customer base that was locked into it via ownership and culture.

Today the benefits to the organisation of an effective loyalty scheme can be viewed not only in terms of customer loyalty but also in the information they can provide the organisation about the customer. As will be covered in Chapter 7, Electronic Point Of Sale (EPOS) equipment linked to the information held on the cards issued to members of a loyalty scheme can allow an organisation to build up a profile of the customer. Viking Direct, a UK office equipment and supplies company, is able to use customer-ordering information to make targeted special offers based on previous purchases. This is not only beneficial to the customer, who can receive extra discounts on regularly purchased items, but it allows Viking Direct to make the customer feel special – it is 'their' special offer and not just a general one open to all.

As will be shown in Chapter 7, this new technology may be able to bind the customer and the organisation even closer together. By identifying buying patterns it may be possible for organisations to be even more proactive. It should be possible for the cashout operator to be able to ask a customer if they have forgotten an item; it only requires the EPOS computer to compare the current spend with previous ones to produce a very personalised service.

Reward increased spending

A successful loyalty scheme will reward spending differentially. Whether it is a points system such as that operated by many supermarkets, the Tesco 'Clubcard' being a well known example, or a percentage scheme such as the 'POSH' Club operated by P&O Cruises for repeat cruisers who care to join and are then offered, in addition to a newsletter and extra shipboard activities, percentage discounts on items purchased on board, the scheme should provide higher rewards the more that is spent. That the POSH Club really is a loyalty scheme and not just a marketing ploy is shown by the fact that when, in August 1999, P&O decided to offer an increased discount to members who booked on a particular cruise departing in November of that year, the same discount was then made retrospectively and automatically to members who had already booked on that cruise. There was no legal requirement to do this but the company decided to reward all its loyal customers in the same way. By acting in a generous manner it is likely to have generated extra business from those members. The British Airway's 'Executive' Club for frequent travellers, in addition to awarding air miles, has three levels of entry available to most customers depending on the number of flights they undertake in a year. The Blue, Silver and Gold cards offer an increasing range of priviledges both in airports and in the air. Thus the more a customer spends on air tickets, the more privileges they receive. It is interesting that one of the Unique Selling Points (USPs) of the Easy Jet airline operation based at London's Luton airport is that they do not offer any such loyalty bonus, concentrating instead on cheaper seats. Easy Jet make the point to companies that staff may book more expensive seats with airlines offering a loyalty programme in order to benefit personally and that if a booking is made on an Easy Jet flight there will be cost savings to the company.

Communication

One of the most important functions of a loyalty scheme is that it provides the organisation with the name and address of the customer. This then allows the organisation to mail out to the customer. Mailings cost money and anything that can allow those monies to be targeted should be welcomed. General details about the organisation can be sent to the customer, as can special offers (see the comments about Viking Direct, earlier in this section). Receiving a personalised mailing can also strengthen the customer's sense of belonging, thus binding the customer closer to the organisation.

Cost

In the main the costs of a loyalty scheme should be borne by the organisation and not the customer. It may well be that there is an entry barrier requiring a certain level of initial purchase to enter the scheme. Many of the loyalty schemes operated by companies in the cruise industry allow entry automatically after the customer's first cruise with the company. The POSH Club operated by P&O Cruises is unusual in the industry in that there is an annual subscription required in order to continue membership but the scheme does provide for discounts on shipboard purchases. The Captain's Circle loyalty scheme operated by Princess Cruises, P&O's US based operation, is free but does not provide for discounts onboard.

Multi-site

The original Co-operative dividend schemes were very restricted in that there were no transfers between Co-operatives in different parts of the country. It was only when the Co-operatives merged to form a nation-wide organisation in the 1960s that a national stamp based loyalty scheme was introduced. (Generic stamp based schemes will be discussed later in this section.)

The development of card reading computer systems (see Chapter 7) has allowed organisations to offer multi-site loyalty schemes. Thus a Tesco Clubcard can be used in any Tesco branch anywhere and, as will be shown later, at branches of certain other organisations. Modern customers are much more mobile than their predecessors were. Prior to the introduction of cheque guarantee cards by the UK banks, special arrangements to draw out cash had to be made by customers going on holiday; today they can withdraw cash either at the counter or at a cash dispenser at any branch of their own bank or indeed at competitor banks.

Multi-organisational

Not only have successful loyalty schemes developed a multi-site function, many are increasingly offered as a multi-organisational scheme. Hence the Tesco Clubcard can also be used at branches of the Do It Yourself (DIY) retailer B&Q. The loyalty scheme operated by the British Airports Authority (BAA) allows the customer to collect points based on purchases at a wide range of retail and food outlets in the airports controlled by the BAA. As airlines have formed strategic alliances, so their loyalty schemes have expanded to cover the partners in the alliance. The Air Canada 'Aeroplan' scheme allows the customer to collect and spend Aeroplan miles not only with Air Canada but also British Midland, Continental, Austrian Airlines, Finnair, Lufthansa, Cathay Pacific, Swissair and United. In addition, points can be collected when making purchases from certain hotel and car rental operations. Whilst there are certain similarities with the highly successful Air Miles scheme in the UK, the latter is much more a successor to the generic stamp schemes that will be covered later in this section, as Air Miles are gainable and redeemable from and at outlets other than those operated by airlines and associated operations. Air Miles will be covered later in this chapter.

Whilst the logistics of operating a multi-organisation scheme may be more complex, they are eased by the ability of computers to communicate very effectively and thus there is no real problem in operating such a scheme provided that the partners have the equipment in place to read each others' cards. The scheme operated by the Summerfield supermarket chain involves Premier points that are redeemed at the Argos stores group. These points can also be collected at certain petrol stations. Points are added to the card, which has magnetic storage facilities and is thus able to keep a record of the accumulated points. The total can be checked on a simple machine that is located in each Summerfield store.

The Tesco Clubcard has been a very successful loyalty and promotional scheme since its introduction in 1995. At that time UK supermarkets were undergoing a major expansion, especially in the form of 'edge of town' sites offering increased facilities. Whilst Sunday trading had been the norm in Scotland for many years, changes in the law in England in the 1990s allowed the supermarkets to offer a seven day per week service. The provision of ample parking spaces, café facilities, cash dispensers, florists and an increasing product range was allowing a successful supermarket operation to become a 'one stop shop' for customers. The competition for suitable sites that provided both the space needed for customer vehicles and proximity to major roads and motorways was intense and the supermarkets were keen not only to acquire new customers but to retain those customers in order to boost their market share. The Tesco Clubcard scheme recorded the monetary value of a customer's purchases at the cashout point and then sent the customer a series of money off vouchers according to the spend made. The scheme was very successful and by June 1996 there were over eight million members (Brassington & Pettitt, 1997). The expansion of the scheme to allow customers to collect points not only at the B&Q 'Do it Yourself' stores but also at branches of Lunn Poly travel agents provided not only an increased bonus for customers but further added to Tesco's database of its customers and their spending habits and preferences.

Brassington & Pettitt (1997) claim that the Clubcard scheme assisted Tesco in boosting its turnover by 25% and profits by 15% in 1995 alone, despite the fact that over £40 million had be given back to customers as a result of Clubcard discounts.

Whilst the Clubcard scheme in its original form provided for discounts on spending at Tesco, by 1999, members could receive discounts at theme parks, on holidays, air tickets, entertainments, rail travel, ferry crossings and a host of other products and services. To this extent Clubcard has moved nearer to the *Air Miles* concept covered later in this chapter.

To celebrate the fourth anniversary of the Clubcard scheme in 1999, Tesco introduced an enhancement known as Clubcard Deals. For every £25 spent, Clubcard holders received a 'Clubcard key', each key being valid for one year. Holders of 50 keys could receive a series of half price offers including holidays, travel etc. from a special brochure, whilst holding 100 keys gave a 75% discount.

It is not surprising that Tesco's competitors have followed suit. Loyalty schemes in the UK have flourished, mirroring the US experience, and nearly every purse and wallet contains a series of such cards issued by a variety of organisations.

Ease of redemption

As will be shown later, one of the problems with earlier types of loyalty schemes was the effort required by the customer to redeem their reward for goods. Modern technology makes it very easy to store the accumulated rewards on a magnetic strip on the customer's loyalty card and to use this information to ease redemption. The easier it is to redeem a reward, the more likely the customer is to use that particular scheme.

These characteristics of rewarding increased levels of spend, personalised communication, ease of redemption and wide inter and intra organisational use typify the vast majority of contemporary successful loyalty schemes.

Whereas most current loyalty schemes are based around a card that can be read by a computer, there are two earlier types of scheme which have been largely superseded by modern technology but were very popular and built on the Co-op dividend schemes.

Trading stamps

After the merger of the locally based Co-operative stores, the organisation replaced the dividend with a stamp scheme. Stamps were given by each store based on the value of the customer's spend and could then be used to pay for subsequent items exactly as cash. The Co-op scheme was, naturally enough confined to Co-op outlets but a much larger, nation-wide multi-organisation scheme was developed that offered Green Shield Stamps.

Large numbers of outlets across the whole of the retail sector offered these stamps which were collected by customers who then redeemed them for items out of the Green Shield catalogue. As Brassington & Pettitt (1997) have pointed out, the problem with this scheme was that it tended to drive prices up as retailers had to pay to take part. Nevertheless, up to the 1970s, large numbers of consumers collected the stamps and there was pressure on retailers to offer them in order to match their competitors. The introduction of cards that could be read by computer helped hasten the demise of stamp schemes as the cards could be read quickly and easily whereas stamps had to be placed somewhere safe and then stuck into a book, which had to be redeemed against catalogue goods.

Vouchers

The idea of a voucher included with each purchase of a particular product was used by the cigarette companies in the years after World War II with considerable success. The best known UK scheme was that run in conjunction with the Embassy brand of cigarettes. Given the increasing campaigns against smoking, such a scheme that encouraged increased purchases would be much less acceptable today but in the 1950s and 1960s, large numbers of smokers collected Embassy and other vouchers that were, like trading stamps, redeemable against goods in a catalogue. As with trading stamps, the vouchers had to be stored, counted, collated and then sent through the post.

Air Miles

One of the most successful UK loyalty schemes has been that of *Air Miles*. According to Churchill (1999) the scheme was conceived almost informally by Keith Mills, an advertising executive and Alan Deller, an ex British Caledonian Airlines marketing director in the late 1980s. Instead of the more mundane goods offered by the trading stamp and voucher companies, *Air Miles* was designed to offer the glamour of air travel. All airlines have a proportion of empty seats on many flights and the concept was that *Air Miles Promotions* would purchase seats from British Airways that it could then sell on to retailers in the form of vouchers in a series of air mile denominations. British Airways took a 51% stake in the company but eventually in 1994 decided to acquire the operation in its entirety. Various large organisations had begun to offer air miles to both loyal customers and as a staff incentive, and with the arrival of electronic registering of *Air Miles* both the Sainsbury supermarket operation and Vodaphone began to offer air miles. It was also a sensible strategic move to offer other rewards in addition to flights and these now include admission to theme parks and holidays. Only about a third of *Air Miles* is actually used for flights. As Churchill (1999) points out, it is also possible for a customer to increase their reward by using a credit card from a bank that offers *Air Miles* to pay for goods at a retail outlet also offering *Air Miles*. By switching to electronic registering, *Air Miles* has been able to bridge the gap between the earlier voucher and trading stamp schemes and the current loyalty cards as offered by more and more organisations.

Pseudo-loyalty schemes

The major car manufacturers operating in the UK began to offer payment options that had many of the hallmarks of loyalty schemes from the early to middle 1990s. By guaranteeing a residual value for a new vehicle after so many years (normally 2 or 3) and with an allowable annual mileage, a customer would be able to pay only the difference between the purchase price and the residual value. There was also a guarantee that there would be enough money left over in the deal for the deposit on a new vehicle at the end of the scheme period. Thus the customer received lower repayments and the manufacturer, in effect, locked the customer into buying a new vehicle on a regular basis. Provided that the customer is happy with the products of the chosen manufacturer these schemes can be useful but, as with all such arrangements, there are financial penalties if the customer wishes to leave the scheme early.

Forms of credit arrangement as offered by certain retail outlets also lock customers into deals which may sound an attractive method of making an initial purchase but can considerably increase the customer's financial indebtedness to the supplier. Such options are not really loyalty schemes as such but a financial arrangement between customer and supplier.

Summary

In considering customer loyalty this chapter looked at the types of loyalty that can be displayed, namely Product Loyalty, Brand Loyalty, Supplier Loyalty, Supra-Loyalty, A-Loyalty, De-Loyalty, Anti-Loyalty and Disloyalty. These were linked to the work of Jones & Strasser and their concept of Apostles, Loyalists, Mercenaries, Hostages, Defectors and Terrorists, leading to the construction of the loyalty matrix. A variety of loyalty schemes using cards, stamps etc. was then introduced and the benefits and disadvantages discussed.

Terms introduced

- Air miles
- A-Loyal
- Anti-Loyal
- Apostles
- Boston matrix
- Brand loyalty
- Comfort zones
- Co-op dividends
- Defectors
- De-Loyal
- Disloyal
- Fast Moving Consumer Goods (FMCG)
- Hostages
- Loyalty matrix
- Loyalty schemes
- Mercenaries
- Product loyalty
- Pseudo-Loyal
- Supplier loyalty
- Terrorists
- Trading stamps

QUESTIONS

1. Using the descriptions of various types of loyalty given in this chapter and the work of Jones & Strasser, explain why the link between satisfaction and loyalty is not straightforward. In what circumstances may loyal customers actually be dissatisfied and why might satisfied customers defect?
2. Why might a Supra-Loyal customer present such problems to an organisation that they would rather the customer defected to a competitor?
3. Describe, using examples, the attributes of a successful loyalty scheme and explain the mutual benefits to the organisation and the customer.

▼ 5 Complaints and recovery

How and why customers complain – Recovery – Professional complainers – Reluctant complainers – Non-complainers – LICAL – Handling complaints – Complaint fatigue – Conflict resolution – Rectifying the situation – Perishable goods – Complaints and front-line staff – Solving problems/taking decisions

Clutterbuck *et al.* (1993) make the very important point that even in the best run organisations, something will, at some time, go wrong and that much of the emphasis on TQM has been on ensuring everything is right first time, so that the issue of complaints may well have been given a lower emphasis than it should.

There is also no doubt that it is the customer who nearly always makes the first move in a complaint situation. Note the use of the term 'nearly always'; if a company finds out that there is a fault with a product, they can be proactive and announce a recall before there are too many complaints. Companies that know of faults and do not try to inform customers can be heading into dangerous product liability (Chapter 6) waters as the US aircraft manufacturers McDonnell Douglas discovered over the defective rear cargo door on early model DC10 airliners (Eddy *et al.*, 1976).

Newspaper reports and the growth in television programmes dealing with consumer problems suggest that by the late 1990s Britons had become the world's number one complainers (see Figure 5.1). The tendency to complain shows every indication of rising. 1999 saw the regulator of rail operations in the UK warning franchise operators that unless complaints came down, massive fines were likely and that poorly performing companies would be forced to cut prices.

The fact that nearly 1 in 3 of complainants saw fit to inform others bears out the point made by Cartwright & Green (1997) that dissatisfied customers tend to be more voluble than satisfied ones.

The report also made the point that whilst consumer problems, especially with holidays (where complaints to the Association of British Travel Agents were up from 14 931 in 1994 to 18 403 in 1998) predominated, professions including the medical and legal services had also seen a considerable rise in complaints.

No organisation can avoid complaints. Whilst it would be ideal if every customer was delighted with every transaction, common sense says that this is unrealistic. In every organisation there are bound to be times when things don't turn out as expected. In fact things may well go completely wrong. As Cartwright

Method of complaint	% of those surveyed
By telephone/email	46%
By letter/fax	18%
Telling friends and relatives	32%
Informing the media	4%

Figure 5.1   Method of complaining (author's figures).

& Green (1997) have pointed out, it is rarely the fact that something goes wrong that causes customers to be lost but rather the way in which the organisation responds to it.

Customer/service recovery is a crucial issue in managing the relationship between customers and the organisation if things go wrong. The effect that terrorists can have has already been demonstrated in Chapter 4. Apostles often become terrorists not because of the original mistake but because there was not a satisfactory attempt at recovery.

This volume has already stressed the importance of the lifetime value of the customer. There are bound to be some complaints during that lifetime and the customer will judge the organisation as much on how it recovers the situation as on the times when everything is just so.

Customer recovery becomes a very important issue if this 'lifetime value of a customer' approach is taken. The additional costs that might (but not always) be incurred by customer recovery need to be viewed against the 'lifetime cost' of losing him or her.

Not all customers are lost through complaints. Customers may move and eventually die. However they cease to be customers, it is better that they leave saying positive things about the organisation than telling their friends and relatives about poor recovery.

One, almost paradoxical, of Cartwright & Green's (1997) Golden Rules for Customer Care is 'Welcome complaints, they allow for recovery'; in effect complaints can, if properly handled, turn a disaster into a triumph. Indeed organisations may be able to enhance the relationship with the customer by effectively dealing with a complaint.

Complaints often escalate from minor problems into disasters because of a lack of perception from the organisation as to the apparent seriousness of the situation as viewed by the customer. Cartwright & Green (1997) set out a series of scenarios relating to customer complaints:

1. The organisation knows what has gone wrong and it is the organisation's fault.
2. The organisation knows what has gone wrong and does not think it is the organisation's fault but the fault of a supplier.

3. The organisation knows that the fault is beyond the organisation's control.
4. The organisation does not know whose fault it is.
5. The organisation cannot believe the customer expected that particular service.
6. The organisation has no idea that there is a complaint as the customer walks away and never uses the organisation again.

There is also a clearly defined typology of complainers:

- Professional complainers
- Reluctant complainers
- Non-complainers.

Professional complainers

Professional complainers are a sad fact of life for many organisations. These are individuals who have often decided to complain before the product or service has even been delivered in the hope of financial gain or some enhancement to the product or service. Very often the complaint is about a small matter that the complainant seeks to magnify. Once such people are recognised, the organisation may well decide that they are not worth having as customers and may well wish to warn others through professional associations and trade bodies. Whilst all complaints should and must be treated seriously, the professional complainer may be relatively easy to spot if they develop a pattern to their complaining. If there is something genuinely wrong then it should be rectified, but organisations should be careful about the degree of reaction lest they find themselves hostages to one of their customers!

Reluctant complainers

The vast majority of people who make a complaint do so reluctantly. They have no wish to make a fuss and may even feel embarrassed about having to complain; they may well not know how to complain effectively.

One reason why an organisation may well receive few complaints is not because of the quality of the products and services but because it is made difficult either for the customer to actually make a complaint or having made one to receive effective redress.

Complaint procedures need to be simple enough for those with a genuine complaint to be able to make their grievance known, but not so simple as to give the professional complainer a free run at the organisation. It is a tricky balance to achieve and what often happens is that complaint procedures are made unnecessarily complex and succeed in turning reluctant complainers into non-complainers. The number of complaints received may well go down but there is little link between the number of complaints received and the actual number of complaints!

Non-complainers

Non-complainers are not people with no complaints. They have legitimate complaints but for one reason or another do not see fit to make a complaint to the organisation although they may well complain to their friends and relatives.

A classic restaurant scenario is when a customer is asked if they are enjoying their meal and they answer 'yes' even when they are not enjoying the meal and have no intention of patronising the establishment again. If the staff was asked if the customer was happy they would have to answer in the affirmative.

A person with a complaint who does not voice it is of much less use to an organisation than one that does. As stated earlier, to put things right the organisation needs to know what was wrong in the first place. If the customer does not voice a concern then it is difficult for the organisation to recover the situation.

Chapter 8 of this book considers relationships, and those who are able to empathise with the customer may recognise dissatisfaction in the body language displayed and thus be able to intervene. It is important for organisations to have procedures in place to make non-complainers into reluctant complainers because then there will be data available about the customers' perception of the operation.

Hopefully most customers are at best satisfied but when asking, 'is everything alright?', well-trained staff should be able to distinguish between a satisfied 'yes' and one that displays dissatisfaction but it will be too much bother to complain.

It is not unusual to see an organisational objective of reducing the number of complaints received when what should really be stated is reducing the number of actual complaints. As we are told from an early age, we learn from our mistakes; it is better to receive a greater number of actual complaints provided that the number of complaints is declining. Every complaint received should be seen as an opportunity to recover a situation. This does not mean that it is good to make mistakes in order to recover the situation, just as St Paul cautioned against sinning in order to receive forgiveness! However, if it is recognised that mistakes will happen then it is important to ensure that mechanisms are in place to rebuild the situation with the customer and to incorporate learning into the future operations of the organisation.

Why do customers complain?

Unless the customer is a professional complainer whose objective is to receive money or enhancements, customers complain because what they have received falls below their expectations. It was John Wannamaker, a Philadelphia department store owner, who said in 1869: 'The customer is always right'. Experience tells us that the customer is not always right. The customer can be wrong, can be stupid and can be unrealistic, but they are the customer and their money pays the wages of the organisation.

In many cases when the customer appears wrong it is because expectations and perceptions were raised by the organisation that it could not meet.

There are three basic reasons why a customer complains:

- Lower than expected quality
- Lower than expected service
- Higher than expected price.

Chapter 6 considers the legal aspects relating to the contract between a supplier and a customer but whatever the legal remedies, if the quality, the service or the price do not meet the customer's expectations there is a danger that the relationship between the customer and the organisation will break down. If the matter comes to court then the breakdown will be irretrievable.

Earlier in this chapter, six possible scenarios for complaints were introduced. Taking each in turn it can be shown that different strategies are required for each:

1. The organisation knows what has gone wrong and it is the organisation's fault

Cartwright & Green (1997) introduced the acronym LICAL for the five easiest ways to lose a customer, namely:

- LYING
- IGNORANCE
- COMPLACENCY
- ARROGANCE
- LETHARGY.

(LICAL is covered in more detail in Chapter 9 of this book.)

If the organisation knows that it is at fault then it is pointless to try to cover the facts up. Sooner or later the customer will realise what has happened and may well become very angry indeed. Lying to the customer never, ever works in the long term. There is no point in being complacent and there is absolutely no point in treating the customer in an arrogant, 'we would never do that' attitude. Sooner or later the truth will come out and the organisation will be embarrassed.

The organisation can enhance its reputation by admitting its faults and pointing out the steps it is taking to remedy the situation. It can be highly embarrassing, thankfully vicariously, to listen to an organisational spokesperson on national television trying to defend the indefensible. They lose potential customers that way when they might have gained new customers by a policy of honesty. People will forgive mistakes but not a lack of integrity, as countless politicians have discovered to their cost.

It is often the case that customers want just two relatively simple things – the situation rectified and an apology. The latter is often the hardest to obtain perhaps because, by apologising, employees feel that they are somehow betraying the organisation. However an apology is often what an aggrieved customer most requires and the longer it is delayed, the more frustrated and angry the customer may become.

2. The organisation knows what has gone wrong and does not think it is the organisation's fault but the fault of a supplier

The first point to make is that although the organisation does not believe it is at fault, there is still an aggrieved customer and therefore an apology is appropriate. This will be an apology for the inconvenience caused to the customer and should be followed by a promise to work with the supplier to rectify the concern. The organisation should recognise that it has a duty to act on behalf of its customers to rectify problems along the value chain. The contract is between the customer and the immediate vendor (Chapter 6) and thus there is a legal obligation in many instances for the organisation to rectify problems even when caused by suppliers some way down the value chain.

3. The organisation knows that the fault is beyond the organisation's control

As in the previous scenario the organisation should apologise for the inconvenience caused to the customer. There are times when through what is legally termed *force majeure* or an *Act of God* (see Chapter 6) a supplier is unable to fulfil a contract through no fault of their own. Any insurance contract will exclude such unforeseeable events. Holiday companies can hardly be expected to take their customers into a war zone or the aftermath of a natural disaster.

Even when events are completely outwith the organisation's control, they should still do everything they can to provide alternatives if they wish to retain the customer's goodwill.

Organisations need to be careful that they only use *force majeure* etc. as a reason when the events really are outwith the organisation's control. Many events can be foreseen and contingency plans put into place. Staff illness should not be used as an excuse unless the country or region is in the midst of an epidemic.

The vast majority of customers are reasonable people and will recognise and reward an organisation that is trying to assist them in difficult circumstances. Provided the full facts are supplied, organisations are likely to find that their customers show true loyalty and form a partnership with them to assist.

4. The organisation does not know whose fault it is

Put simply, the organisation should find out. Whoever is at fault, the relationship is between the customer and the organisation and the onus is on the latter to find out what is happening and rectify the situation.

An example of the above scenario could occur when a piece of equipment ceases to work. Many organisations will send it back to the manufacturer for the customer who is then inconvenienced by not having the equipment available. A customer centred organisation will provide a replacement (on loan if necessary) whilst an investigation is carried out. By doing that, the organisation is recognising that the customer's problem is not that the equipment is faulty but that they have lost the use of it.

Vehicle dealerships now loan customers vehicles when their vehicle is in for a service or repair. The customer's real problem is not that the clutch does not work properly but that they cannot drive to work etc.!

5. The organisation cannot believe the customer expected that particular service

Wannamaker's statement (see earlier) about the customer always being right did not also say that the customer is also reasonable.

Modern advertising can serve to produce an unreasonable perception in the customer's mind. Toy advertisements in the run up to Christmas may, intentionally or not, produce a false perception of size. Advertisements that offer a particular motor car for what appears to be a very low price will only state in the very smallest print that the details refer to the basic model only. In the UK the Trade Descriptions Act (Chapter 6) covers advertisements that are deliberately misleading but it is still possible for customers to develop unreal expectations.

Chapter 3 introduced the Competitive Forces Model (Porter, 1980, 1985; Cartwright & Green, 1997) and considered the bargaining power of customers. The customer will want the best possible quality and service for the lowest possible price. There will be a price or enhancements below which the supplier cannot go without losing money. If there is the possibility of large-scale repeat business there may be a temptation to take a loss on the first transaction, but the organisation should be aware of the fact that the customer is then likely to want all their transactions at that price.

If a customer is being totally unreasonable in their demands then the organisation needs to stand firm on the bottom line but in such a manner that the customer still feels valued. It is a delicate balance. Most negotiations are carried out in a ritual manner, as illustrated in Figures 5.2 and 5.3.

Provided that the minimum the customer will accept is lower than the maximum the organisation can offer, agreement is possible. If not, then there is no zone of agreement and it is unlikely that there will be a transaction.

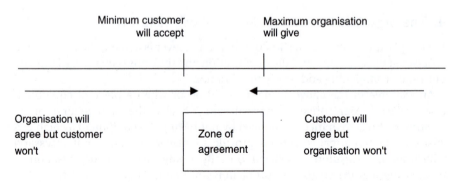

Figure 5.2   Zone of agreement.

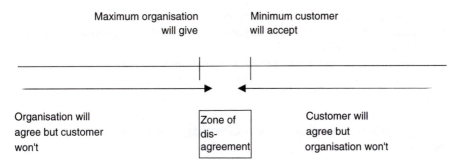

Figure 5.3   Zone of disagreement.

6. The organisation has no idea that there is a complaint as the customer walks away and never uses the organisation again

This is the nightmare scenario for any organisation because it is believed that the customer is satisfied when this is not the case. Unless it is possible to make contact with the customer, not only are they lost but the organisation has no idea why. Chapter 9 of this book uses an example of good public relations from the UK mail order firm of Cotton Traders who use their database to contact customers who have not ordered for some time, inviting them to make contact if the reason for not ordering was any defect in product or service.

Clutterbuck *et al.* (1993) report that 96% of dissatisfied customers do not bother to complain. For an organisation this means that it will only hear from four out of every hundred dissatisfied customers and thus only be able to recover the situation for a tiny minority.

The importance of checking back with customers in an objective manner as to their satisfaction or otherwise cannot be stressed too highly. Just asking: 'Is everything alright?' is not enough as that nearly always elicits a 'yes' response, even if the customer is not satisfied. This chapter will examine means of eliciting useful, objective feedback.

It may seem strange that customers do not complain when they have every right to but the avoidance of conflict can be quite an important part of human behaviour. Any form of conflict leads to an altered body state, driven by the hormone adrenaline. Whilst there are those who seek excitement, so-called 'adrenaline junkies', most people would rather be relaxed than tense. People would rather walk away from a stressful situation than get into an argument.

It has already been shown that far from being a negative point, receiving complaints can be quite positive for the organisation, as such complaints can provide useful feedback and an opportunity to recover the situation.

Cartwright & Green (1997) have identified a number of barriers that inhibit people from complaining:

- It is too much bother to sit down and write a letter
- It might be embarrassing to ring someone up and talk to them
- It is particularly embarrassing to complain face to face

- Taking things back will cost extra money for bus fares etc.
- Sending things back means wrapping them up and going round to the post office or other carrier
- The company probably won't do anything about it anyway.

Customers are more likely to complain:

If the product/service is perceived by them as being expensive

Clearly, people are much more likely to complain if they are dissatisfied with what they consider to be an expensive product, expensive that is in their terms and not the organisation's. Just because a customer buys a product at the bottom of the range, which will thus be perceived as the cheapest product by the organisation, might conceal the fact that, to the customer, this purchase is on the very limit of what they can afford and thus expensive in their terms.

If the product/service is very important to them

If the product is a vital component of the customer's own end product or something they need urgently then they are very likely to complain if there are problems. What an organisation may perceive as a relatively unimportant item may be crucial to the customer. Organisations that make a point of getting to know their customers will be able to assess how important an item is in the customer's eyes. Those who have excellent customer service skills are able to be proactive in suggesting alternatives if the desired product/service is unavailable or fails in use.

If the product/service is not what they expected

If the customer expected that the product would have a better performance or would last longer, they will be dissatisfied and are likely to complain. This can often apply when a company has a range of products aimed at different market segments. A customer may be drawn to the supplier by the reputation or advertising of the top of the range product and assume that certain key features may apply to the lower range product. Organisations should ensure that the customer is kept fully informed about specifications etc.

If the customer's background or culture encourages complaints

Whether people complain may depend upon their nationality or culture. British people, for example, have a reputation for being reluctant to complain while other nationalities have a reputation for complaining. If the cultural barriers to complaining are high then the organisation is more likely to lose customers without a word of complaint. In these cases it is all the more important to receive customer feedback.

If they have not made many complaints recently (absence of complaints fatigue)

Most people, even if they are prepared to complain, don't really enjoy it. If, therefore, they have come across several cases of poor service in a relatively short space of time, it is unlikely that they will take up every issue.

In addition, if the customer has already complained to the same organisation in the past they may be reluctant to complain again, fearing that the company will regard them as a professional complainer. There is a responsibility on the customer not to cry wolf and complain about every tiny thing and then wonder why they are not taken seriously when something major goes wrong. Organisations can suffer from complaints fatigue as well as customers!

If the complaints procedure is easy

If an organisation makes the process very difficult, then they will probably receive fewer complaints and unfortunately even less feedback. There is an onus upon the organisation to make the procedure for complaints (and praise) as simple and as easy as possible for the customer.

The above suggests that there might be a number of psychological and procedural hurdles that the customer must overcome before making a complaint. The person who does complain has overcome all of these obstacles already and for this reason they are probably:

- angry
- resolute
- disappointed.

Each of these factors makes it very easy to turn a bad situation into a worse one. Anger and the feelings associated with it trigger an emotional state driven by the hormonal (endocrine) system in the body. The major hormone in the anger response is the 'fight or flight' hormone, adrenaline secreted from the adrenal glands above the kidneys. It is adrenaline which prepares the body for action by transferring blood from the digestive system to the muscles (hence the red face often associated with anger), which makes the hair stand on end (in many mammals this makes them look bigger and more threatening) and in general tenses up the body and quickens heart rate.

The hormonal system works using chemical levels in the body whilst the nervous system is more akin to an electric current (although it too works on a chemical differential). Imagine a standard incandescent light bulb – it emits both light and heat. Press the light switch and the light is emitted immediately but the heat takes slightly longer to build up. After an hour if the switch is moved to 'off' then the light is immediately extinguished but the heat remains for some time (as anybody who has burnt his or her fingers removing a light bulb that has just been switched off can testify). The light is analogous to the human nervous system, the heat to the hormone system.

Once a hormonal response has been triggered it will take time to subside and thus anger responses may continue even when the cause for the anger has been removed.

To deal effectively with anger requires considerable interpersonal skills. If it is a face-to-face complaint, it is useful to move to a quiet area and sit down. People who are standing are much more likely to invade each others' personal space and thus appear threatening. Even if the customer raises his or her voice, responding in the same way will only make matters worse. If a customer is shouted at then their adrenaline levels will rise even further and they will take much longer to recover. The whole idea should be to calm the person down and this is best achieved by letting them have their say, providing a drink and above all appearing to be as concerned as they are. Initially it is no use making excuses as angry persons will only hear what they want to hear.

The person dealing with the complaint should make written notes of what is said, summarising and clarifying where necessary. It may well be that it is a relatively junior member of staff who receives the first 'blast' from the customer. All staff should be trained so that they can recognise problems they can deal with and those that require a more senior member of staff. An angry customer should deal with a member of staff who is empowered to provide a solution and thus effect recovery. The customer may well still appear angry but it must be remembered that anger takes time to subside, as covered above. There are many cases on record where a customer has received a solution, and has left still appearing angry, but has telephoned later to thank the person who handled the complaint – anger takes time to subside.

If the complaint is in writing, it may well be necessary to separate the substance of the complaint from the anger with which it was written. It is useful to make notes of the key parts of the complaint, as these will not contain any emotion and will allow for a much more effective investigation. Complaints in writing should always be acknowledged by return, with the customer being given an indication of how long an investigation will take. If there is any delay in the investigation, the customer should be informed immediately. Nothing raises the anger levels than a promise of a communication that is not kept.

People who are resolute are unlikely to be easily fobbed off by excuses. Organisations need to investigate complaints thoroughly to find out what, if anything, went wrong. If the organisation is at fault then it should admit it and tell the customer what the organisation intends to do or, better still, ask the customer what they require to rebuild the relationship.

Whilst the customer may be disappointed in the product or service, the whole point about recovery is to ensure that they are not disappointed in the organisation's response to the complaint.

There are four states to any complaint situation (or, indeed to most human transactions), as shown in Figure 5.4.

The ideal state is WIN/WIN where both sides are satisfied. The organisation has recovered the situation and retained the customer and the customer is satisfied that the organisation has done all they can. The organisation may have incurred costs but these will be offset by further business with the customer.

A situation where the organisation WINS but the customer LOSES is to be avoided. A typical case would be where the organisation does not make a refund

RESULT FOR ORGANISATION	RESULT FOR CUSTOMER
WIN	WIN
WIN	LOSE
LOSE	WIN
LOSE	LOSE

Figure 5.4   States of conflict resolution.

and thus saves money. They do, however, lose the customer, probably for good, so it is a very short-lived victory especially if they lose other current and potential customers because of what the 'loser' says about the organisation. There may be some short-term satisfaction to be gained from 'getting one over on a complaining customer', it may be one of those destructive 'games that people play' as described by Berne (1964), but in the end the customer will always WIN!

A situation where the customer WINS but the organisation LOSES may not be as bad as it looks if the customer stays with the organisation. Unfortunately these are often cases where arbitration or court action has been needed and the organisation does not just lose on one occasion but they also lose the customer for good.

LOSE/LOSE is an all too common situation. The customer may defect from the organisation if it fails to recover the situation but be unable to find another supplier offering the same product/service/terms. Pride, however, prevents a return to the original supplier and both parties become losers – a situation that effective recovery could prevent. It is a fact that if the customer is about to LOSE, then realising they cannot WIN, they often prefer that the organisation LOSE as well. Perhaps for many, LOSE/LOSE is the next best option to WIN/WIN. The whole of nuclear defence strategy in the Cold War was based on a concept of MAD – Mutually Assured Destruction. If the other side launched their missiles at us, in the few minutes we had left we would launch ours at them. We might be dead but at least they would be dead to – a classic (and sad) LOSE/LOSE scenario!

Dealing with complaints

Many people become defensive when dealing with complaints because this is a person's natural reaction to someone who is angrily criticising their organisation or department in the case of an internal customer complaint. Organisations seek to instil loyalty into their employees but complaint situations are times when employees need to be honest and objective. Within the bounds of commercial confidentiality it is counterproductive to not be honest with the customer. As the LICAL (see earlier) showed, lying to the customer is nearly always found out and only serves to make recovery more difficult. Dealing with complaints requires three actions that have traditionally been carried out in the order of:

- INVESTIGATE
- ACTION
- LEARN.

Organisations have, traditionally, on receiving a complaint carried out an **investigation** to see whether the complaint is justified. If the customer has been found to be justified in making a complaint, some form of remedy has been applied as an **action** and the organisation has, hopefully, **learnt** from what has happened and taken steps to ensure that there is no repetition.

More modern thinking suggests that the order of the above should be changed to put the action in rectifying the customer's complaint first and the investigation second. Organisations have argued in the past that they need to carry out an investigation in order to prevent spurious and even fraudulent claims. Such claims however are only a tiny minority when compared to the majority of perfectly justified complaints. If the sums of money involved are large then most customers would consider an investigation reasonable, but when only small sums are in question then immediate action is more likely to recover the situation and retain customer goodwill than a long investigation. The investigation and learning are still important even if there has been only one complaint, because whether the complaint was justified or not the product or service has angered one person, so it could anger someone else. The organisation needs to find out what has happened and what lessons can be learnt.

People usually complain and may become difficult for a reason. Whatever the staff of the organisation feel about the complaint, they cannot deny the customer's feelings of anger or disappointment and that is what the organisation needs to deal with.

Customers do make mistakes but organisations need to bear in mind that if one customer can make a mistake when using the product or service, then others can too. There may be instructions on the packaging, for example, that the organisation needs to change in order to prevent further mistakes. Just as employees do not wish to admit a fault of the organisation, customers may be embarrassed by having to admit they have made a mistake. Embarrassed customers can quickly become ex-customers.

If the organisation is in the right, then it is paradoxically at its most vulnerable because that means that the customer is in the wrong and it takes a great deal of tact to tell the customer that they have made a mistake.

Customers who complain should, with the exception of professional complainers, be thanked because they give the organisation an opportunity to put whatever is wrong right, not only for that customer but also for others who are going to be acquiring the product or service in the future. Complaints can also provide the organisation with valuable market research. Many organisations spend huge sums on market research to find out what people like and dislike. The person who has complained is offering the organisation free information. If justification for the cost of customer recovery is needed this might well be it. By acting quickly to put things right the organisation may save considerable sums in the future, or be able to design new products and services in a better way as a result of the customer feedback gained through complaints.

Complaining customers usually want to give the organisation another chance. As Cartwright & Green (1997) have pointed out, those who walk away without complaining are really saying '**Goodbye**'. They are saying: 'You let me down and you won't get another chance'. Those who complain are saying '**Hello**'. They mean: 'You have let me down but I want to give you a chance to make it up to me'.

Most organisations spend a lot of time and money trying to identify customers who want to buy their products. Complaining customers are offering themselves up free!

Rectifying the situation

Customer recovery means doing something for the customer that mitigates against some failure in the product or service. Many organisations appear to forget that the first, simplest and possibly the most important thing the customer wants is:

1. An apology
Any apology must be sincere. Even if the organisation is completely in the right, the customer has still suffered some inconvenience and therefore some frustration. In effect, staff can express the fact that they are sorry that the customer feels the way they do, even when expressing confidence in the product or service. Employees should always endeavour to avoid the customer losing face if they want to retain their custom.

2. A clear customer relations policy
A successful policy adopted by many organisations is to set out a clear policy for dealing with complaints. The UK store chain of Marks and Spencer has been renowned for their policy of replacing goods or refunding money. Provided goods (often clothing) are unused, the company will make a 'no questions asked' replacement or refund (a refund will, of course, require a receipt). Even though the person seeking a replacement or change of item is not the purchaser (with whom the actual contract exists, see Chapter 6), they can still avail themselves of the service. No wonder that Marks and Spencer are a popular choice for birthday and Christmas presents. Even if the item was not suitable or the wrong size, the recipient of the present can still acquire something to their taste.

Signalling what the organisation's policies are in advance and making them simple to access for a customer with a complaint goes a long way to putting the customer's mind at rest. Many organisations now have policies similar to Marks and Spencer and there is no evidence whatsoever that they are abused.

Setting up a specialist customer service department

Many organisations have a specialist department to deal with customer queries and complaints. These can be a two-edged sword. By having such a department, specialist staff are able to deal with queries and complaints quickly but they are somewhat removed from the customer. Those at the customer interface may feel that customer service is less of their concern and should only be dealt with in the customer service department. The customer can suffer if front-line staff are not given the resources to deal with complaints and queries on the spot. Any delay in dealing with complaints is likely to heighten customer frustration and anger.

If there is a customer service department it needs to work very closely with front-line staff to ensure that those staffing the centre have not only excellent product knowledge but understand the needs and wants of the customer. Job shadowing, whereby customer service centre staff spend time working with those in the front line and vice versa, can be a very useful exercise in heightening mutual awareness and raising standards of customer service.

Devolving responsibility for customer service decision-making to the front line

In the 1990s, British Airways ran an interesting programme called 'Winning for Customers'. This customer service programme was delivered to BA staff world-wide, encompassing both front-line and back-office staff as well as including major suppliers. The involvement of the latter indicated the importance the airline gave to the value chain.

One of the major messages of the programme was that customer service is everybody's business and that staff should be empowered to make decisions to resolve customer problems.

Obviously such delegation cannot be given as a blank cheque and there were limits placed on the amount of money or resource an individual could use on their own initiative before calling in a more senior member of staff.

What the programme was attempting, with considerable success, to achieve was a situation whereby all but the most major complaints and problems could be resolved at the check-in desk, at the departure gate, onboard the aircraft, at the baggage reclaim or in the arrivals' hall etc.

By giving staff ownership and responsibility to deal with problems at the first point of contact, organisations are able to stop minor complaints escalating. In effect, staff are able to take ownership of the customer's problem and work with the customer to achieve a solution or recovery without recourse to lengthy organisational procedures. As front-line staff are likely to have the greatest knowledge about their customers, such a policy makes the maximum use of the staff resource.

Whatever the situation existing in an organisation, customer recovery will always be a key issue. Successful organisations manage to balance knowing how far to go in order to retain the customer while at the same time preserving the organisation's return on the deal, by ensuring that the remedies are adequate to satisfy the customer but not so expensive that the organisation is put at risk.

In deciding the level of remedy an organisation needs to consider:

• the original cost of the product or service
• the ability of the customer to influence others

- their lifetime value to the organisation
- the power and value of their friends, colleagues and relations
- the views and opinions of the staff members closest to the problem.

Staff who have built up a relationship with customers (as covered in Chapter 8) can feel very let down if decisions are made without reference to them by a senior manager or the Head Office, especially if such decisions appear to give a lower value to the customer than they would have done. Such decisions may not only lose the customer but may also demotivate the staff concerned.

The more training that can be given to front-line staff, especially if it is accompanied by devolving authority, the more likely organisations are to gain satisfactory outcomes to customer complaints, as they can build upon a firm staff/customer relationship. Recovery is also likely to be made at an early stage before any further damage is done.

Such empowerment requires staff to be thoroughly trained before it can be implemented. Members of staff need to know exactly what they can and cannot do to remedy a complaint. Whilst such training will usually require an input of funds, the benefits are likely to far outweigh the costs. Every customer retained is one less for whom marketing money has to be spent.

In their study of organisations providing excellent customer service, Cartwright & Green (1997) found that there were some very inexpensive methods of assisting the recovery process, methods that required little cash but careful thought. Below are some examples from their findings:

- A simple 'sorry' and the offer of a cup of tea might be sufficient in some cases. Often, if the staff member is seen to put himself or herself out on the customer's behalf, this works wonders and is likely to involve little or no additional cost. Most customers will value this extra effort very highly.
- The organisation could keep a stock of presents that they buy in bulk from a manufacturer at low cost which are kept almost exclusively as give-aways in customer recovery. Bottles of perfume or boxes of chocolates are good examples.
- Another inexpensive means is to offer up spare capacity that would otherwise have been wasted. This applies to railways or airlines that might give free tickets or upgrades when capacity is available.
- Other companies use customer recovery as a further sales opportunity. For example, they may give away a free voucher, hoping that the customer will use it as part payment for a more expensive item.

Whichever method the organisation uses the following needs to be taken into account: you can possibly replace the product and this may satisfy the customer up to a point, but he or she will still have the poor product in mind.

Perishable goods

Some products are described as perishable. This might be thought to apply only to foodstuffs but in customer relations' terms, it applies to any product for which there is only a single opportunity for a sale. An example would be an airline ticket for the 11.00am BA flight from London to New York. Any unsold seats on the aircraft will remain unsold after take off (naturally). Similarly a theatre seat for a particular night is either sold or unsold when the play starts; it cannot be sold part way through. A television set is not perishable because if it is not sold one day it can be sold the next. Because of the all-or-nothing state relating to such perishable goods, customers can often obtain discounts the nearer the point of no return approaches. Late deal holidays are a good example of this.

Such perishable goods often cause problems if there are complaints, as it is very difficult to replace like with like. If a television set ceases to function, the retailer can simply replace it. If a customer has a bad experience on a holiday, then that cannot be replaced in its identical form. The holiday company can offer a refund or vouchers off the next holiday but they cannot replace the customer's time nor wipe out the bad memories.

The importance of front-line staff

It is staff in the front line that normally receive and take the brunt of a customer's complaint and any complaints' procedure should support their key role.

The front-line person may be dealing with the customer face to face, over the telephone or by writing, but they are the first point of contact for the customer and, as will be shown in Chapter 8, set the tone for all the customer's future dealings with the organisation.

Complaints are a form of problem that requires a decision, and thus problem-solving and decision-making models need to be applied.

A simple model for problem-solving and decision-making is shown in Figure 5.5.

Looking at the model in detail:

1. DETERMINE EXACTLY WHAT THE PROBLEM IS – imagine that a customer has returned a faulty watch and unfortunately an exact replacement is not in stock. The problem is simple, isn't it? The watch is faulty. However to the customer it may not be that simple. The problem could be that it is the customer's only watch and they need to tell the time, in which case they could be lent a watch until a replacement could be obtained – simple problem, simple solution. However, many watches, especially those designed for the female market, are also fashion items and anything provided on loan might have to match other items owned by the customer, not perhaps as simple. The defective watch might be intended as a present and possibly an alternative will be satisfactory, a different problem again. The watch scenario will be used to illustrate the development of the model.

2. DETERMINE EXACTLY WHAT THE CUSTOMER WANTS – the simple illustration above shows that what the supplier may deem as the problem and the customer's perception are not always the same. The organisation may wish to suggest alternatives – loan, replacement, another model, a refund etc. – but

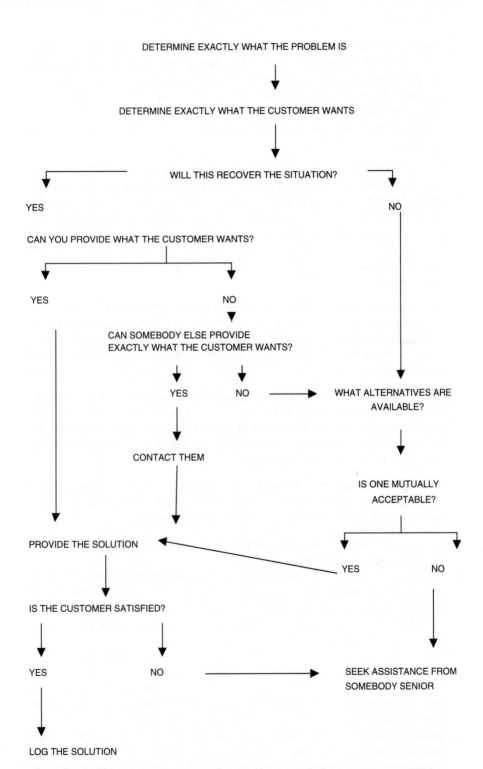

Figure 5.5   A customer service problem-solving/decision-making model.

it should be the customer who determines what will rectify the situation. Customers are rarely unreasonable and asking 'what can we do to remedy this problem?' will often produce a perfectly acceptable response from the customer. If the customer is allowed to say how he or she believes the matter can be resolved, they are then honour bound to accept their own solution and the organisation will have demonstrated that it really does listen to its customers.

3. WILL THIS RECOVER THE SITUATION? – if the answer is YES, then has the member of staff the power and resources to carry out the necessary remedial actions? If YES again, then they should be able to do so without delay and PROVIDE THE SOLUTION. Hopefully the customer will be happy but if not then it is appropriate for higher authority to be involved and the member of staff should SEEK ASSISTANCE FROM SOMEBODY SENIOR. If the front-line member of staff cannot provide a solution, then perhaps somebody else can assist and should be contacted.

4. WILL THIS RECOVER THE SITUATION? – if the answer is NO and nobody else can provide exactly what the customer wants, then it is necessary to explore WHAT ALTERNATIVES ARE AVAILABLE? If one is mutually acceptable then it can be implemented, but if not then, as above, a more senior member of staff should be contacted.

5. IS THE CUSTOMER SATISFIED? – hopefully the answer will be YES, if it is NO then again the matter needs to be referred to higher authority. Even when the result is positive, the complaint and the solution need to be LOGGED so that any unfortunate trends can be identified and/or there is a record of both the complaint and the customer details.

In Chapter 1 the acronym C-SMART was introduced. This acronym can also be applied to the handling of complaints. Whatever procedure an organisation adopts, it should follow C-SMART criteria in that it should be:

C Customer Centred, i.e. it should be primarily designed to give priority to the customer over the organisation.
S Specific in that the customer should feel that they have been treated as an individual. The use of standard letters can be very useful but the organisation must ensure that the customer feels special. When receiving the response to a complaint it will not help the organisation if the customer feels that they are just one of many complainants.
M Measurable, i.e. the customer should feel that the response and remedy measure up to the problem, whether it is in terms of money or not; too low a response and the customer may feel cheated; too high a response and the customer may wonder what else is wrong. Human beings are instinctively good at matching responses to situations. Harris (1970), who coined the phrase 'positive strokes', makes the point that too effusive a response to a situation can be just as bad as one that is not effusive enough. Too high a response to a dissatisfied customer may lead the customer to ask: 'what else is wrong?'.

A Agreed – whatever the solution, it should be agreed between the customer and the organisation. Solutions imposed by one party or the other nearly always lead to resentment, and a resentful customer is nearly always a lost one.

R Realistic – organisations should not promise what they cannot deliver nor should customers ask for what is unreasonable, as that is the fastest method of reaching an impasse.

T Timebound – if the organisation promises a response within 48 hours then that is what it should deliver. Organisations should tell a complainant when to expect a response (not necessarily a final solution) and then stick to it. Broken deadlines lead to customer frustration and that leads to anger.

Complaints will happen but if handled properly and if the situation is recovered to the delight of the customer, triumph can come from disaster.

Summary

Even in the best run organisation with the highest standards of products and services, there will be times when there is a dissatisfied customer. Prompt action by the organisation can recover the situation and produce a situation that is a WIN/WIN scenario. Organisations need to be honest when mistakes have been made and empower staff to rectify the situation in a prompt manner. There are barriers to complaining which mean that only a small percentage of dissatisfied customers actually bother to complain; most walk away and are lost to the organisation. Complaints, if handled correctly, can provide the organisation with both valuable feedback and another method for enhancing their relationship with the customer.

Terms introduced

- Complaints fatigue
- Customer/service recovery
- LICAL
- Non-complainers
- Perishable goods
- Problem-solving/decision-making models
- Professional complainers
- Reluctant complainers
- States of conflict
- Zone of agreement
- Zone of disagreement

QUESTIONS

1. 'My company never receives any complaints', stated the Managing Director. Explain why that might not be the good thing that it appears on the surface. Show

how it could indicate an excellent organisation or one with a poor customer communication record.
2. Describe some of the barriers to complaining that result in only a small portion of dissatisfied customers actually making a complaint.
3. Using the decision-making model, concepts from this chapter and examples from experience, describe how complaints should be handled to achieve a WIN/WIN situation and a delighted customer.

■ ☑ 6 Customer relations and the law

Office of Fair Trading – Law of the UK – Types of law – Contracts – Offers, acceptances and exclusions – Breaches of contract – Consumer Credit Act – Consumer Protection Act – Trade Descriptions Act – Sale and Supply of Goods Act – Health and Safety at Work Act – Product liability – Legal remedies – Codes of Practice – Arbitration – Competition legislation

> 'Ignorance of the law excuses no man: not that all men know the law, but because 'tis an excuse every man will plead, and no man can tell how to refute him' (John Selden, 1584–1654).

Whilst the original quote may be considered sexist in today's climate, the term 'man' should be replaced with 'person', the concept that ignorance of the law is no excuse is still a maxim in UK law.

Previous chapters of this book have concentrated on the development of a positive relationship between the supplier of a good or service and their customer based on mutual benefits. This chapter is somewhat 'harder' in nature as it centres on the legal relationship and the remedies available to either side in the customer relationship if things go wrong. Obviously, nobody ever wishes to go to law, as it is firstly expensive and secondly usually leads to a breakdown in the relationship between the supplier and the customer, but it is sometimes necessary and thus a knowledge of the legal principles that underpin customer relations forms an integral part of this book and leads on from the discussion about complaints covered in the previous chapter.

The material contained in this chapter is not intended to make you a legal expert but to provide a background to the legal complexities that surround relationships with the customer.

In the United Kingdom, the Office of Fair Trading (OFT) has a brief to look after the legal interest of consumers and there are regional consumer councils providing advice and policy suggestions to both the government and the public.

The OFT was set up under a Director General of Fair Trading (DGFT) as a consequence of the Fair Trading Act (1973) which coincided with the introduction of Small Claims Courts (see later). The 1973 Act gave the DGFT powers to identify unfair trading practices and to make recommendations for legislation. The OFT is able to issue notices against organisations that persist in unfair trading, especially where these breach the Trade Descriptions and Sale and Supply of Goods Act (see later). Court action may be taken but of the 400 procedures undertaken by 1986, Montague (1987) reports that few had needed to go to court.

What is worrying in the field of customer relations is the number of employees, often of large organisations and working at a senior level, who have scant knowledge of the legal rights of their customers. Research for this book amongst smaller retailers and suppliers of services to the general public showed a widespread lack of basic knowledge. This lack of knowledge could be very costly in the event of a court case.

To take a simple example: you buy a CD player from a local retailer; it is guaranteed for 12 months. You are offered an extended warranty but decline. After 10 months it breaks down and you go back to the retailer who tells you that it will have to go back to the manufacturer who will repair it and return it to you. You ask for a replacement but the retailer refuses – is the retailer in the right? You will be able to answer this question by the end of this chapter.

Law is a complex subject. Prior to the growth in consumer rights, although there was protection for consumers, indeed the first Sale of Goods Act in the UK dates from 1893, the maxim *caveat emptor* (let the buyer beware) was usually employed.

In 1965 the American Ralph Nader (see Chapter 1) began to champion the rights of the consumer in the USA. Beginning with an attack on the safety features of US-produced automobiles, his work then went on to look at issues concerning the rights of consumers of a wide range of products. This sparked the formation of a Consumers' Association in the UK, whose magazine *Which?* regularly tested and reported on an increasing range of goods and services. Whilst such organisations were able to raise awareness about price and quality issues, they could not act for individual purchasers. Within the UK, in addition to pressure groups there exists a network of Trading Standards offices attached to local government. The work of the Trading Standards Officer will be considered later.

This chapter will concern itself with what is known as 'English Law'. This implies no disrespect to Scotland, where contract law is slightly different, or to the other constituent members of the UK. The reason is that the vast majority of UK contracts (with the exception of house sales and purchases in Scotland) usually have explicit terms relating to jurisdiction and the law to be applied. For instance, included in the booking conditions for the 1999 Direct Holidays Cruise Brochure is the term:

> '21.7 This agreement is governed by English Law and proceedings may only be brought in the English courts'

This is a standard term in UK holiday brochures where products are being sold across the UK and reflects the need to have just one set of conditions binding on the parties. Direct Holidays have a major operation in Scotland and many Scots perceive them to be a Scottish Company (which they are not, in fact) but the booking conditions clearly relate to English law. Indeed in a dispute under English law, the amounts of compensation available through the English Small Claims Courts are higher than those in the Scottish system so the purchaser should not be too disadvantaged! House sales and purchases are conducted very differently in England/Wales and Scotland, and thus building societies etc. have different conditions for mortgages. Basically, in England/Wales a purchaser can withdraw up to the time that written contracts are exchanged; in Scotland, once an offer has been made and accepted, even verbally, it is legally binding and could be enforced.

Law in the UK is derived from three main sources – common law, statute law and European law – and falls into two main categories:

- CIVIL LAW which is concerned with the rights of people
- CRIMINAL LAW, which centres on the types of conduct that society will and will not tolerate.

Most customer relations' legislation falls under CIVIL law but there are cases connected with safety that may have criminal law implications and of course fraud by either a supplier or a customer is a criminal offence.

Common law

Common law provides the foundation for UK law. As Montague (1987) has pointed out, the majority of UK rules of law are based on common law rather than by legislation from Parliament. Common law derives from the succession of decisions made by judges since the conquest of England in 1066. Common law is based on a system of judicial precedent where the decisions made by one judge or by a higher court are used as the precedent for subsequent decisions on future similar occasions. In the UK, the House of Lords is the highest court in the land and thus a decision by the House of Lords will bind all lower courts to its rulings. Key to the application of common law is the concept of 'reasonableness'. In the UK, the European Court of Justice, the House of Lords, the Court of Appeal and the High Court are 'superior' courts whose judgements set precedents. Crown courts, County courts, Sheriff's or Magistrates' courts and tribunals are 'inferior' courts whose rulings do not necessarily set a precedent unless upheld by a 'superior' court.

As common law is not codified in Acts of Parliament, the concept of reasonableness is key to its understanding. Murder has been an offence since time immemorial but it is only recently that it has formed part of an Act of Parliament. A reasonable person would conclude, and so common law has argued, that murder is unacceptable and thus through precedent upon precedent it has always been an offence under common law. In consumer law, reasonableness also plays a part, as will be shown when considering the legal rights of a customer.

Statute law

Statute laws are those enshrined in Acts of Parliament.

Contracts

The key to the legal relationship with a customer as regards transactions is 'does a contract exist?', i.e. has a legal relationship been set up? When one uses the word 'contract', most people think about the contracts that they are most involved in: contracts to buy and sell houses, credit or hire purchase contracts or contracts of employment. In fact, many of the contracts we enter into are not complex legal documents at all – there is no requirement for a contract to be in writing. Every retail transaction that is undertaken involves a contract.

We can define a contract as:

> 'an agreement, enforceable by law between two or more consenting parties (who have the right to make such an agreement) which obliges the parties to undertake certain acts which are not indeterminate, trifling, impossible to perform or illegal'.

For a contract to be valid there must be **agreement** about all the important aspects between the parties. The legal term for this is *consensus in idea*. In addition, the parties must **consent** to the contract. If a party were made to sign a contract under duress, then the contract would be invalid. The parties must also wish to be legally bound by the contract. Business transactions are presumed to create legally binding obligations on the parties whereas domestic situations are not. However there has been a growth in pre-nuptial marriage contracts, and if it is shown that the parties intended that these should be legally binding then they may form valid contracts.

The parties must have the **legal right to make the agreement**. If a person entered into an agreement to sell some goods known to be stolen, then the contract would be invalid as *nemo dat quod non habet*; no one can give that which he does not have and possession is not nine-tenths of the law – only the owner of goods can transfer the ownership of them. Young people under the age of 18 are limited in the contracts they can make, organisations may limit which staff may enter into contractual obligations on behalf of the organisation and those certified as insane are forbidden from entering into contracts. Signing a contract whilst under the influence of alcohol or drugs may also affect the validity of the contract.

It is not possible to enter into a contract to commit an act that is **illegal**. Such an agreement is known as *pacta illicita* (an illicit pact). It would be completely unenforceable by law.

Contracts should relate to important matters and not be **indeterminate** or **trifling**. A court cannot enforce a contract which is too vague and if for any reason the contract becomes impossible to perform, even after it is agreed, then the contract ends. Many holiday contracts include the term *force majeure*, which like Acts of God cannot be covered in a contract. If a hurricane destroys your hotel, you cannot force the holiday company to accommodate you in a hotel that does not exist; careful consideration of the holiday insurance contract is required before purchase to ensure that cover for such events is available.

When does a contract come into force?

There are two major parts to the contracting process, both of which have major implications for customer relations. The two parts are **offer** and **acceptance**. These must match. In simple terms, *A* offers to sell an item to *B* at a certain price. If *B* accepts, then there is a contract between them. If *B* is interested but at a lower price, then *B* can make a counteroffer at the lower price. If *A* accepts the counteroffer then there is a contract. If *B* does not accept *A*'s first price and *A* will not accept *B*'s counteroffer, then there is no contract between them. In retail terms, this is very important. A price on a motor vehicle in a showroom is not an offer to sell at that price; it is an **invitation to treat**, i.e. for a potential customer to begin to discuss a purchase. There is no obligation on the trader to actually sell at that price. The contractual process only commences when the customer begins the negotiation. The classic UK case in this area is Pharmaceutical Society of GB v Boots the Chemist (Southern) Ltd, 1952. Boots had just set up a system where certain proprietary medicines were displayed on shelves and the customer selected items and took them to the counter in order to pay – a common system today but relatively new in 1952. The Pharmaceutical Society argued that under their rules only a registered pharmacist could sell such medicines and that allowing customers to select them broke this rule and also the provisions of the Pharmacy and Poisons Act. Eventually the Court of Appeal ruled that the contract between Boots and the customer only occurred at the moment the customer presented the items for payment and not when they selected them. It was at this point that the customer offered money and the pharmacist accepted. The display on the shelves was just an invitation to treat with the pharmacist, who could refuse to sell the item.

In a similar manner, advertisements are only an invitation to treat, although all such invitations must comply with the Trades Descriptions Act (see later).

Common sense tells us that the number of special-offer items is likely to be limited and thus not every potential customer could be supplied. Responding to an advertisement is neither an offer nor an acceptance but merely responding to an invitation to treat.

It is necessary to be very careful about the wording of advertisements as the famous and much quoted case of Cahill v The Carbolic Smokeball Company in 1893 shows. The company advertised a carbolic smokeball, which would, amongst other things, protect the user from influenza. With much hype (for the 1890s) the company announced that they had deposited £1000 in a bank to show their good faith and that they would pay £100 to anybody who caught influenza after using the smokeball. Mrs Cahill bought a smokeball, used it and during that time caught influenza and claimed her £100. The company refused to pay and Mrs Cahill sued.

The company's defence was:

1. It was not possible under English law to make a contract with the whole world as anybody could buy and use a smokeball.

2. The £100 offer was just an advertising ploy and there was no intention of entering into a legally binding contract.
3. Mrs Cahill had never formally communicated her acceptance of the offer.

The court thought otherwise and in awarding Mrs Cahill her £100 ruled:

1. It was perfectly possible, even if rather foolish, to make a unilateral offer.
2. The deposit of £1000 showed an intention to pay at least 10 claims.
3. By buying the smokeball Mrs Cahill had accepted the offer, no further communication was necessary.

The case is still quoted today and points to the need for care in advertising, the basic message being that if you say you will do X, then you can be held to it.

Withdrawal of an offer

Once an offer has been accepted it leads to a legally binding contract. Time limits can be put onto an acceptance, i.e. the offer is open until such and such a time.

Acceptance of an offer

Acceptance must be a positive step. It is not possible to say that 'the offer will have been deemed to have been accepted if we have not heard from you by such and such a date/time'. It is not acceptable in law that the person who was made the offer should have to go to the trouble of expressly declining an offer. Silence is declining, not acceptance. Where offers and acceptance are made by post, the acceptance is made when it is posted, not when it is received; hence the importance of proof of posting available from the Royal Mail.

Tenders

When you ask for an estimate you are not actually asking for the work to be done but requesting an offer (a tender). You can then decide whether or not to accept. If you do accept, then a contract is formed and you are obliged to pay the tender amount and the other party is legally obliged to deliver to the agreed specification for the accepted price.

Exclusion clauses in contracts

Common law will accept a clause that is inserted into a contract by one party that seeks to limit their liability for the consequences of a breach of contract or negligence. This is because both parties have agreed to the contract and thus it was open to the other party to object to the clause. However it has been realised that one party may have more bargaining power than the other and thus the Unfair Contract Terms Act was passed in 1977 and amended in 1995 to redress the balance, although as early as 1949 courts had been ruling favourably in respect of those who suffered under such unfair clauses.

Many of the cases brought under this aegis have related to tickets with conditions on the back. Airline tickets have a large number of conditions printed on them, often relating to compensation limits in the event of accidents. Eddy *et al.* (1976) have pointed out that US courts have allowed settlements far in excess of the limits because the conditions were not brought to the attention of the purchaser at the point of sale, i.e. when the contract became effective, as discussed earlier. In Thornton v Shoe Lane Parking Ltd (1971), Mr Thornton used a car park controlled by barriers, entry to which was gained using an automatic ticket-issuing machine. At the entrance was a sign stating that all cars were parked at owners' risk. There was no requirement to leave the vehicle in order to collect the ticket and gain entry. Inside the car park was a notice with a list of conditions. When Mr Thornton collected his car he was injured and claimed that this was due to the negligence of the owners. He sued and the owners claimed that they had an exclusion clause on the notice board inside the car park absolving them of responsibility. The court ruled (and were upheld by the Court of Appeal) that because this condition was not made clear to Mr Thornton at the point of sale, it was unfair and that terms notified after contracting are unfair. Mr Thornton won damages.

If Mr Thornton had been required to sign the ticket and if it had the conditions printed on it then he would have been deemed to have accepted them, whether he had read them or not.

You may note that many guarantees for appliances contain a statement that the guarantee in no way affects the purchaser's statutory rights. This is because they have protection under the Sale and Supply of Goods Act (1994) and any clause trying to exclude this protection would be unfair, as was pointed out in the case of L'Estrange v Graucob Ltd in 1934. Mrs L'Estrange, in buying a machine, signed a contract that had the clause 'any express or implied condition, statement, or warranty, statutory or otherwise is hereby excluded'. That removed her rights under the Sale of Goods Act (1893) then in operation and was thus unfair.

Under the Unfair Contract Terms Act (1977), any term in a contract that attempts to restrict liability for death or personal injury is automatically void. In effect you cannot state that you refuse to accept liability for your own actions. Other attempts to circumvent the Act that will also be declared void are those which try to restrict statutory rights, e.g. you cannot say that a person cannot take action under the Sale and Supply of Goods Act (1994), terms which require the customer to indemnify another person plus terms which impose time limits on complaints unless, in all three cases, the party relying on the term can prove that it was a fair and reasonable term under the circumstances.

It should be noted that insurance contracts and the contract relating to the setting up or dissolution of companies etc. are exempt from the Unfair Contract Terms Act (1977). The 1977 Act covers contracts in all the main areas that are related to customer relations.

Standard contracts

Except in the case of large orders, most contracts between suppliers and customers use some form of standard contract. Car sales, holidays and electrical goods are all dealt with using standard forms designed by the supplier. Customers receive protection under the 1977 Act against the supplier who sets up the terms of the contract, in respect of any terms that seek to:

1. exclude or restrict liability for breach of contract
2. enable a party to render a performance substantially different from that which the customer could reasonably expect.

Such terms are void unless the supplier can prove that it was reasonable or fair to include the term.

An example would be that if a coach holiday customer made it known that, for medical reasons, they needed to travel on a coach with a toilet and that the firm's brochure stated that their coaches had toilets, then if a coach was not provided with a toilet, the holidaymaker would have a case. In this example, the fact that the brochure stated that the firm could alter the form of transport used without notice was deemed unfair and the holidaymaker won their case (Elliot v Sunshine Coast International Ltd, 1989).

The terms fair and reasonable are open to interpretation. In general, courts will consider the following factors:

- The relative strength of the bargaining positions of the parties to the contract.
- Were the goods or services freely available elsewhere?
- Was any discount received by the customer for accepting the term?
- Had the customer previously accepted such terms from the supplier?
- Was this a one-off special transaction?

The 1977 Act states quite clearly that the onus of proof that the term was fair and reasonable lies with the party seeking to rely on the term.

Amendments in 1995 brought further protection against terms which sought to allow a trader to vary the price without allowing a vendor to withdraw without penalty, terms which tried to stop a purchaser withholding part payment due to a failure to deliver and terms which sought to absolve traders from the statements of their sales staff.

The ending of contracts

The vast majority of contracts, whether written or not, come to an end because they are fulfilled to the satisfaction of both parties.

Breaches of contract

Many breakdowns in customer relations occur when there is a perceived breach of contract, usually but not always claimed by the customer.

It is important to realise that we are talking about situations where there was an original intention of fulfilling the contract. Where there was no such intention will be covered by fraud or theft legislation. A shoplifter, by not going to the counter, shows an intention not to enter into a contract and to deprive the supplier of goods. This situation is covered by criminal and not civil law, as is an intent to defraud. A shoplifter cannot be described as a customer although, paradoxically, if they tripped over a negligently placed electrical lead in fleeing from the premises they might have a claim under the Health and Safety at Work Act!

Any failure to perform can be considered a breach of contract, as can a failure to perform within a stipulated time limit. Defective performance of one component of a contract can lead to the aggrieved party rescinding the whole contract provided that the breach is serious. It is doubtful whether a customer could refuse to take delivery of a series of items of office equipment because of a very minor defect in one of them. Were it the case that one did not work at all, then there might well be a case for refusing acceptance of the whole order.

Whilst it is hoped that those involved in customer relations are never involved in any form of litigation, it is a fact of life that such litigation is becoming more common. It is important to remember that, even in a simple transaction, once payment has been offered and accepted a legally enforceable contract exists. Courts can and do award damages for breach of contract, especially where it can be shown that a financial loss has been suffered.

Whilst the above has covered general aspects of contract law, the following sections consider important pieces of legislation specifically designed to protect consumers. The *Unfair Contract Terms Act (1977)* has already been mentioned above.

The Consumer Credit Act (1974)

By the 1970s the purchase of goods on credit was becoming more widespread. In a credit sale, ownership is transferred at the point of the transaction as opposed to hire purchase where ownership remains with the vendor until payment in full is made. The Act set out to standardise the forms of contract that could be made and to introduce cooling-off periods. It should be noted that the protection offered is to the domestic consumer more than business users of credit. The Act also provides extra protection for those who pay all or part of a transaction by credit card, in effect making the credit card company a party to the contract and allowing the customer to claim off the credit company for cases of poor performance or defective goods.

The Consumer Protection Act (1997)

This Act defines the standards of safety a purchaser is entitled to expect and thus has some commonality with the Sale and Supply of Goods Act (1994), to be covered later. Importantly, it gives wide rights to those injured by a product to pursue claims for damages against manufacturers, importers, suppliers and even those who put their own brand names on generic products (see Chapter 3).

Trade Descriptions Act (1968)

Often considered a landmark piece of legislation because it attempted to stop growing practices relating to false or inaccurate descriptions of products, the Act regulates the way goods are described to potential customers. The Act deals with three basic aspects of description – claims about the goods themselves, false statements relating to services and incorrect pricing. The Act (section 2) sets out areas that constitute a trade description, namely:

- Physical characteristics
- History
- Quantity
- Size
- Method of manufacture
- Fitness for purpose
- Testing
- Manufacturer
- Use
- Previous ownership.

The Act requires the person selling the product or service (the vendor) to be truthful about these areas. If a box of matches has an approximate number of contents labelled at 100 then, provided that on average there are 100 matches to a box, the Act will have been satisfied. If tests showed that the average was 95 then an offence would have been committed. It would be interesting to postulate on what would happen, or indeed if a case would be brought, if the average were 105!

Interestingly, availability is not covered by the Act and thus items advertised in order to 'lure' customers in but which are not available are not covered and nor are the contents of books or CDs where there is clearly a subjective view as to their quality etc. However if a CD were advertised as being by a band and that band only appeared on one out of twenty tracks, there could well be a case under the Act. It should also be borne in mind that the offence needs to be committed in the course of business and thus purely private transactions are excluded.

The Trade Descriptions Act carries strict liability in that an offence can be committed even if it was not intended to do so. There is a defence for organisations however if a member of staff who should know better carries out an act that renders the organisation liable under the Act. In Tesco v Nattrass (1972), a supermarket manager made a false description of a product unbeknown to his employer. He had received proper training etc. and the Court ruled that Tesco were not liable. This case has been used as a precedent to say that, if an employee makes a false description, there needs to be proof before the company can be held liable for false advertising claims.

The Trade Descriptions Act not only applies to goods but also to services. It is an offence (although strict liability does not apply) to make false statements about specified aspects of service. As strict liability does not apply, it is necessary to prove that the statement was known to be false or was reckless, i.e. not sufficient attention being paid to the truth or falseness of the statement.

The Trade Descriptions Act also covers pricing of products and services and again is related to the truthfulness of statements. Prior to the Act it was not unknown for companies to make blatantly untrue statements about prices: 'was £50, now £20', when in fact the item had never ever been sold at £50.

Under the Act, where a recommended price is quoted and then undercut, that price must have been in operation. Where a sale price is quoted then the original price should be shown together with details of where it pertained. There must be evidence that the non-sale price had been applied somewhere within the organisation for at least 28 days over the previous 6 months. If you look carefully at the sale prices in many large retail outlets you will see statements like: '. . . . as offered in our Manchester store for 28 days between January and June'. It is permissible to make a disclaimer for specially acquired products and this does limit the applicability of this part of the Act.

Pricing, as regards the Trade Descriptions Act, only applies to goods and not services. Thus an untrue statement claiming that the outlet is closing and this is the last chance to buy would not commit an offence.

Many actions under the Trade Descriptions Act are brought by the Trading Standards Department of local authorities. They have been especially vigilant in the area of counterfeit goods. As designer labels have become more and more popular, so there has been a flood of fakes, often sold in markets. Offering such an item for sale is clearly a breach of the Act, as it is clearly not what it purports to be.

Sale and Supply of Goods Act (1994)

The original Sale of Goods Act was enacted in 1893 in an attempt to codify certain parts of common law. The main aim of the Act was to clarify the rights and responsibilities of the parties involved in the sale and purchase of goods in respect of those areas not explicitly covered by the terms of the contract. The Act was amended in 1979 and again in 1994 when it was retitled the Sale and Supply of Goods Act. As shown earlier in the section on contracts, there are explicit and implicit terms to a contract. The Act does not forbid any explicit terms. For instance, if a non-working motor car were to be sold, perhaps as a static display, then the fact that it was non-working causes no problem provided that this is stated clearly in the contract. This is of especial importance when dealing with items that are regarded as 'seconds', i.e. usable but with blemishes. If this is not stated then, as will be shown, there is a breach of the Act.

The 1994 Act provides considerable protection for the consumer by stating that: GOODS SHOULD BE OF SATISFACTORY QUALITY. Prior to 1994 the term used was 'merchantable quality'. The concept of reasonableness has to be applied, as does the vendor's description of the goods. If they were described as seconds, then it would be unreasonable to expect them to be perfect. If there is a defect, then, provided that the vendor makes the defect clear to the purchaser, no breach of the Act occurs as the purchaser is deemed to have accepted a contract.

The Act specifies five aspects of satisfactory quality:

- FITNESS FOR ALL THE PURPOSES FOR WHICH GOODS OF THAT KIND ARE COMMONLY SUPPLIED
- APPEARANCE AND FINISH
- FREEDOM FROM MINOR DEFECTS
- SAFETY
- DURABILITY.

Durability is a key aspect that again raises the question of reasonableness. If goods break down after normal use but within an unreasonable time scale, then the Sale and Supply of Goods Act can be invoked. The definition of a reasonable amount of time will vary from product to product. In the white and brown goods markets (see Chapter 3) there has been much selling of extended warranties over recent years. Manufacturers' guarantees are normally for 12 months. Many extended warranties are sold on the grounds that the purchaser will not be covered for repairs or replacement after 12 months unless they purchase an extended warranty. A washing machine that broke down after 18 months of normal use might well not be covered by the manufacturer's guarantee but the aggrieved purchaser would most certainly have a case under the Sale and Supply of Goods Act.

The Act makes it clear that the purchaser is entitled to a product that is as near to perfect as possible. Obviously, 100% quality, whilst desirable, cannot be achieved every time and thus there are remedies available to the purchaser should the goods be imperfect in any way.

A key point that relates back to contract law as covered earlier is that **the contract is between the vendor and the purchaser and thus the onus for providing redress lies with the vendor and not the manufacturer**. Thus a vendor who claimed that they had to send a faulty item to the manufacturer, or worse, insisted that the purchaser returned the item to the manufacturer, is committing a breach of the Act.

It is not permissible for a vendor to insist that they will provide NO REFUNDS, NO EXCHANGES or CREDIT NOTES ONLY, indeed signs stating this may constitute an offence under the Act. It is for the purchaser to decide the remedy they require. Provided that the time since purchase is reasonable and that the item has not been altered or had abnormal use then, if the purchaser wishes for the item to be repaired, this should be done free of charge, and if they wish for a refund, this should be provided, or the item exchanged if that is the purchaser's wish.

The addition of the word 'supply' to the title of the Act reflects the fact that it applies not only to the sale of goods but also to hire and barter arrangements. The law is very clearly on the side of the purchaser. As Wotherspoon (1995) has pointed out in an article, all those involved in selling or supplying goods should be mindful of '. . . . the buyer should receive goods that are of a satisfactory quality'. If buyers do not, then they can, and increasingly do, sue the vendor.

Many vendors seem unaware of the fact that it is they and they alone who have a contract with the purchaser. If the item is faulty then the vendor may have a case against their supplier, who in turn may have a case against the manufacturer. However the legal relationship is between adjacent links in the customer value chain (Chapter 2). Combining the legal and the economic imperatives for excellent customer relations, it is your organisation that has the relationship with the customer, it is your organisation that they may take to court and it is your organisation that will be criticised for any breach in the relationship.

Should a person receive an item as a present then, according to law, they are not the purchaser and thus any claim has to be made by the person who actually made the purchase. Notwithstanding the above, many retailers will exchange presents but they are under no obligation to deal with anybody except the original purchaser.

It should also be noted that the cost of the return of faulty goods lies with the vendor and not the purchaser.

Services, as opposed to goods, have been covered in law by the Supply of Goods and Service Act (1982). In receiving a service, a customer is entitled to:

- reasonable care and skill in carrying out the service
- have the service performed within a reasonable time
- have the service performed at a reasonable charge if a price was not fixed in advance.

Any materials used in carrying out a service are covered by the same statutory rights as if the customer purchased them personally.

Health and Safety at Work Act (1974)

The Consumer Protection Act (1997) and the safety terms of the Sale and Supply of Goods Act (1994) have already been mentioned. Organisations have, however, an obligation under the Health and Safety at Work Act (1974) to look after the health and safety of all on their premises. This gives them an obligation to customers. Anything which puts a customer in danger or causes them injury can be dealt with under the Act and it should be noted that breaches of the Act can lead to criminal charges. Trailing electrical leads, unsafe buildings and slippery floors can all cause injury, and it is an obligation placed on both the organisation and its employees to ensure that no one (including customers) is put at risk.

Product liability

Product liability is a term imported from the USA where there have been a number of high-profile financial settlements to customers injured as a result of defective products. In July 1995, General Motors was ordered by a Californian court to pay the sum of $3.2 billion to a family of six badly burned when a fuel tank on one of its vehicles exploded. The contention was that the company knew that there was a fault and did not issue a recall notice. General Motors immediately appealed and gained a reduction of damages to £750 million but the case shows how careful companies need to be.

Safety is a key aspect of the Sale and Supply of Goods Act and, since 1988, a European Union Product Liability Directive has been in force which allows for action by anybody injured by a defective product *regardless of whether they were the actual purchaser.* A causal link showing that it was a defective product that caused the injury will need to be demonstrated but the Directive shows the importance that is now placed on consumer safety.

Remedies

Recourse to law has always been expensive and cost has often been a deterrent to the ordinary consumer taking action. The introduction in 1973 of the first Small Claims Courts in the UK made it much easier for actions relating to relatively small amounts to be brought. In the 1990s these Courts became part of the new Civil Court in England and the Sheriff Court in Scotland. The amounts that can be claimed are different in England and Scotland and have been increased upwards a number of times since the original £500 English limit in 1973. Without the formality of a normal court and requiring little or no outlay on legal costs by the plaintiff, these Courts have made it much easier to gain redress. In 1999, the total cost to a claimant in England was £150 for a claim of up to £1000 and £180 if the claim was between £1000 and £5000 (the maximum that could be claimed). Where the plaintiff wins the case, these fees are paid by the defendant.

Larger amounts need to be claimed through the County Court system but with an ever-increasing number of solicitors willing to undertake 'no win–no fee' cases, derived from the contingent approach allowable in the USA, it seems likely that more and more dissatisfied customers may bring legal actions.

It behoves organisations to ensure that they comply fully with the legislation to meet the rights of their customers and to build up relationships such that disputes can be settled amicably without the cost of legal action and the subsequent bad publicity that it can bring.

In 1999 the UK government announced their intention to strengthen the powers of Trading Standards Officers in a white paper entitled 'Modern Markets, Confident Consumers'. Amongst the proposals made were:

- a clampdown on rogue traders using powers to force them out of business
- additional codes of practice
- legislation on INTERNET shopping
- increased consumer protection.

Codes of practice and industry arbitration

Many industries have now set up arbitration schemes to resolve disputes without recourse to the courts. The decisions of such arbitration services may be legally binding but customers cannot be forced to use them if they would rather go to court. The arbitration scheme of the Association of British Travel Agents (ABTA) is typical. Their arbitration fee in 1999 was £65 for claims up to £1500 and £112 for claims up to the maximum claim under the scheme of £75,000. In 1998 ABTA handled 18 000 claims of which 10% went to actual arbitration, with the customer winning 85% of these (*Daily Mail*, 14 July 1999). There is a Chartered Institute of Arbitrators which sets the professional standards for those involved in this work. There are normally time limits on applying for arbitration. As the arbitration service is often linked to a trade association, it is in the suppliers' interest to ensure that they have met their obligations as they may face the wrath of their industry colleagues if they bring bad publicity on the whole industry. Whole sectors have adopted the ombudsman principle first applied from Scandinavia to the public sector. Banking, insurance and financial services are examples of sectors that have appointed an independent ombudsman (or woman) to rule on disputes.

Following the privatisation of many UK public sector industries in the 1980s and 1990s, regulators were appointed to ensure that consumers received a fair deal. OFTEL (telecommunications), OFWAT (water) and OFGAS (Gas) are examples, as are the regulators for the National Lottery, electricity and the rail industry. Appointed through the government, the regulators have the power to penalise unfair practices and monitor standards to see that these are in accordance with the franchise agreements. If they are not, then penalties can be applied and ultimately a franchise could be removed.

Competition legislation

As mentioned in Chapter 1, monopolies do not always serve the interest of the consumer. Since the industrial revolution it has been recognised that monopolies may pose a threat to trade. Anti-trust legislation in the USA was used as early as 1933 when the US Government forced the breakup of the Boeing Corporation, which then included Boeing Aircraft, United Airlines, Hamilton Propellers and Pratt and Whitney Engines, on the grounds that such a concentration was anti-competitive. In the UK, the DGFT (see earlier) has the power to order an investigation by the Monopolies and Mergers Commission into any organisation that controls over 25% of a particular marketplace. In 1980, the Competition Act was passed, which allows for investigations into anti-competitive practices even when monopolies or near monopolies are not involved.

In July 1999, British Airways (BA) were fined £4 million by the European Commission for making what were deemed unfair bonus payments to travel agents. The ruling stated that BA had abused its dominant position in the marketplace contrary to Article 86 of the Treaty of Rome. This was yet another twist to the long saga of BA's bitter rivalry with Richard Branson's Virgin Atlantic as covered in *Dirty Tricks* by Martyn Gregory (1994).

Restrictive pricing

The term 'manufacturer's recommended price' used to be found on many, many price tags. With the ending of the Net Book Agreement in 1996, an agreement that fixed the price of books, only pharmaceuticals remained subject to such price fixing. UK and European price legislation bans manufacturers from setting fixed prices. The contract is between the vendor and the purchaser and it is the vendor who should set the price according to the market. The motor vehicle industry and the suppliers of domestic electrical goods have come under investigation in recent years because of concerns that prices might be being fixed at an artificially high level in the UK as opposed to the rest of Europe and the USA.

Governments consider that competition (in moderation) is a good thing and are thus liable to legislate for any practices that restrict fair competition on the grounds that this disadvantages the consumer.

Summary

Hopefully most organisations will avoid becoming embroiled in a legal wrangle with their customers. It is not only the financial cost of such wrangles that is disadvantageous to the supplier but also the cost of a breakdown in relationships with the customer and the possible bad publicity.

There is a considerable body of law relating to their relationships with their customers that organisations need to be aware of, including:

- Consumer Credit Act (1974)
- Consumer Protection Act (1997)
- Fair Trading Act (1973)
- Health and Safety at Work Act (1974)
- Sale and Supply of Gods Act (1994)
- Supply of Goods and Service Act (1982).

It is said that a little knowledge can be a dangerous thing! This chapter has been designed to raise your awareness of the complexity of the law relating to customer relations and not as a treatise on that law. If in any doubt, always seek professional legal opinion. Customers have increasing rights and the courts can and will uphold those rights.

Terms introduced

- *Caveat emptor*
- Civil law

- Common law
- Consumer legislation
- Contracts
- Criminal law
- Exclusion clauses
- Health and Safety at Work
- Legal remedies
- Offer and acceptance
- Office of Fair Trading
- Product liability
- Sale and Supply of Goods
- Small Claims Courts
- Standard contracts
- Statute law
- Trading Standards
- Unfair contract terms

QUESTIONS

1. Explain, in simple terms, the implications of consumer legislation to the owner of a small retail outlet. What are the implications of a customer purchasing a faulty item from the outlet and what remedies are available to that customer?

2. A car park requires drivers to collect a ticket from a machine before entry. The conditions of use are printed on the back of the ticket and displayed on a notice inside the car park. They clearly state that vehicles are parked at the owner's own risk and that no liability can be entertained for any injuries suffered from whatever cause. Is this legal? Explain your reasoning.

3. What are the implications of the phrase 'this guarantee in no way affects your statutory rights', often found on guarantees, and why might those rights make the purchase of an extended warranty unnecessary?

■ ⌄ **7** Customer care and new technologies

Speed of technological change – PIN numbers – Telephones – 'Plastic' – Credit cards – Debit cards – ATM cards – Store cards – Telephone cards – Loyalty cards – Identification cards – Facsimile machines – email – ecommerce – On-line banking – On-line shopping – Customer relations at a distance – Call centres – EPOS and bar codes

It could be said of any computer that you buy that the only certainty is that it is obsolete before you take it out of the box. The pace of technological change has been increasing that rapidly.

Technological advances are often not linear but synergical. Synergy is the phenomenon that occurs when two or more things come together with the result that the sum of the parts is actually greater than the whole. The linking of telephone technology to computer technology and to copying has produced advantages beyond those which could have been predicted at the time. Computers have been linked using relatively unsophisticated telephone technology to increase their power many fold. The INTERNET is a result of synergy more than anything else: two technologies combining to form a third that is far more powerful than the originals.

To give examples of just how rapid change has been: up to 1830 the fastest that a normal person could send a message to somebody else was about 15 mph – the speed of a horse. By 1829, the locomotives of the Liverpool and Manchester Railway could achieve double this speed and by 1904 the Great Western Railway locomotive 'City of Truro' had achieved 100 mph (Casserley, 1980). The development of railways produced a need to communicate for signalling purposes and this led to the development of firstly the electric telegraph, then the telephone and later wireless (radio) communications. These operated at the speed of light, so thus, in a few short years, communication speeds increased from a few miles per hour to many thousands of miles per second.

Incidentally, the increase in speed brought about by the development of railways led to the introduction of a standard time throughout the UK. When people only moved at the speed of a horse, the time differences caused by using local time, i.e. setting noon as the time when the Sun was directly overhead at each individual location, caused no problems. As the speed of transport increased, it became necessary to keep the same time at both ends of a railway line for obvious reason and so 'Railway Time' was adopted, where noon was defined as the time the Sun was overhead at the Greenwich meridian, this soon becoming known as Greenwich Mean Time – GMT.

The railway revolution really was a revolution not only in transport terms but also in sociological ones. Railways brought towns and cities closer together in time and the tramways that sprang up in nearly every UK city and town in the late 19th Century aided the geographical expansion of those towns. No longer did workers need to live within walking distance of their employment and, in cities and towns across the UK, new housing sprang up along the railways and the tramways in a manner that became known as 'ribbon development'.

The ability to travel brought with it an increase in consumer choice. If it couldn't be found in Stockport, then Manchester was just a short train or tram ride away, and if the branch had not got the item in stock then the ever-increasing rail network meant that it could be delivered from a warehouse within a very short period of time. Advertising changed as well; newspapers could be distributed on a national basis, as could letters – W H Auden's evocative poem *The Night Mail* conveying something of the excitement and importance of a national, cheap mail service. If there was not yet a global consumer economy as we know it today, there was a rapidly developing national one. Soon the high street chains began to develop and a new era in consumerism had dawned, one in which customers were no longer dependent on a local supplier but could cast their nets much wider afield.

The most that can be accomplished in a review of the implications of new technologies for customer relations is to examine how past developments have improved service for the customer and to consider how future developments may proceed. There needs to be a health warning attached to the latter – new developments may come into common use extremely quickly.

The development of the facsimile (fax) machine is a case in point. Up to the middle of the 1980s very few people had actually sent or received a fax. Even large organisations possessed only a limited number of machines (sometimes only one). By the middle of the 1990s, the fax machine was in everyday commercial use and the product was also being marketed for domestic use. Indeed more and more people were finding that a combined telephone and fax machine was useful at home. By the end of 1999, the growth in email both at work and through home computers equipped with modems and scanners was beginning to supersede the fax machine to some extent. Whilst there is always likely to be a market for the fax machine in the foreseeable future, the product life cycle may not be all that long.

This chapter is not designed to consider the technology of new products unless that technology has an implication on the supplier/customer relationship. We may marvel at the proliferation of high tech products but many are bought and sold in traditional ways. This chapter is about how technology can have implications on the relationships between customers and their suppliers.

It is also worth remembering that yesterday's amazing technological advance is today's normality and may be tomorrow's obsolescence. The first flight of the Wright Brothers in 1906 confounded the many sceptics who had declared that manned flight was an impossibility. It should be noted that their first flight was actually less than the length of a Boeing 747 'Jumbo Jet'. By 1969, manned flight had advanced to the stage where not only was it commonplace for people to fly to their holiday destination and think nothing of the experience, but certainly there was a reduced sense of awe and wonder when the first humans had walked on the moon.

In respect of customer relations, technology can be divided into a number of types, although there is considerable overlap between them:

- technology that makes the operation safer for both the organisation and the customer
- technology that provides the customer with something completely new
- technology that provides the customer with a more convenient service
- technology that provides the customer with a quicker service
- technology that provides the supplier with more information about the customer.

Even a cursory glance at the above will demonstrate the overlap.

As was stated in the previous chapter, the Health and Safety at Work Act (1974) lays down a duty on organisations to provide a safe environment on all who have a reason to be on their premises. One problem that began to become apparent with the growth of large retail organisations, aided by the transport revolution mentioned above, was the accumulation of large amounts of cash on retail premises. Very early in the development of the department store concept, methods were put in place to avoid having cash in easily accessible places where the organisation might be vulnerable to either fraud or, even worse, armed robbery. The Stockport Co-operative Store mentioned in Chapter 4 had a centralised cash handling system using what was, for its time, an ingenious piece of technology which went out of fashion for a while but returned in the 1990s. The ceilings of the store were criss-crossed by a large number of pipes that were used by a pneumatic system to take customers' cash in a container to a central facility where the transaction could be recorded, and any change plus a receipt and the loyalty slip sent back to the counter. The author remembers that, as a small boy, he was fascinated by this system and the 'whoosh' made by the container after it was inserted into the vertical pipe and fired off into the system. In the 1990s a number of banks and building societies introduced an updated version of the system to avoid cash being stored at the counters, with the consequent temptation to the criminal fraternity.

The system is a little slower than having cash readily available but the trade-off is in the safety provided for the customer and the staff. The use of credit and debit cards, to be covered below, can also have a safety aspect. Many retailers in the USA, especially at petrol stations, are reluctant to accept cash, preferring the use of a cashless form of payment as this relieves them of the responsibility of having large quantities of money on their premises.

PIN numbers

Much of the technology that will be discussed in this chapter has at its heart some form of computerised operation. In order for any computerised system to be effective it has to recognise the customer who is making the query, transaction, complaint etc. Surname and forename are not enough as there is every likelihood that these may be held by somebody else. How many John Smiths or Alan McDonalds are there in the UK – very many. Name, address and post (zip in the USA) code are more unique but there could well be two people with the same name at an address. The only completely unique method of identifying a customer so that they are not confused with somebody else is to give them a Personal Identification Number (PIN). With ten digits (0–9) to choose from and the ability to repeat numbers, there are literally millions of possible combinations, thus allowing each customer to have their own unique number which can be encoded onto the magnetic strip on the card. The ability of computers to recognise PIN numbers and read information off cards has been one of the truly remarkable technological discoveries of the modern age.

It should go without saying that PIN numbers should not be kept next to items to which they relate nor given to anybody else at all. If the PIN number is revealed then the security of any system will be compromised. It will not be long before other identifiers are brought into common use. The idea of reading palm prints or eyeball patterns may seem far-fetched and from the world of science fiction, but the former is precisely how the INPASS card, covered later, identifies the user.

Telephones

Any review of the implications of technology on customer relations needs to start with a consideration of the telephone, invented by Alexander Graham Bell at the end of the 19th Century and today a standard feature in nearly every home in the developed world and every business world-wide: a piece of equipment often taken for granted and yet at the heart of the communications and computer revolution.

Even in the 1950s most telephone calls in the UK were made either from business premises or from a public call box. The domestic telephone, although gaining in popularity, was not installed in the majority of homes. By the year 2000 the telephone had become a fixture in nearly every house in the developed world, with many people owning two or three landline telephones plus a mobile telephone. The telephone is possibly one of the great icons of the later 20th Century and when, from the 1980s onwards, it became possible to link computers using telephone lines, whole new possibilities of communication and business were opened up. The ATM machines covered later rely on a telephone link to a central computer to carry out the transaction with the customer; without the telephone this would be impossible.

The basic workings of a telephone system are relatively simple. A number of instruments that can both transmit and receive the human voice are connected either by wires or radio to a central switching point where the message is routed to the desired other receiver/transmitter. Originally the switching of calls was a manual task with switchboard operators plugging wires into the relevant sockets.

The author can remember that in the 1950s, until the introduction in the UK of STD (Subscriber Trunk Dialling), any calls other than local ones (that could be handled at a semi-automatic telephone exchange), required the intervention of the operator who would connect the call. International calls needed to be booked in advance. As electronics improved, so it became possible to dial anywhere directly from home. In the UK, until the 1980s, telephony was a government monopoly, subscribers not buying but having to rent a telephone. (Like Henry Ford's famous Model T, you could have your telephone in any colour you liked as long as it was black!)

Without wishing to delve into the technology, an average UK domestic telephone set (or sets, as there are likely to be at least two in most homes) enables the customer to:

- Choose a telephone provider of his or her choice, not necessarily British Telecom
- Have separate lines – most new properties are constructed with at least two telephone line connections
- Place extension sets throughout the house
- See who is calling
- Receive answerphone messages
- Redial the last number automatically
- See who was the last person to call
- Set up call waiting
- Divert calls
- Set up three-way calls
- Send and receive faxes
- Access the INTERNET and email using a modem.

The number of services increases almost monthly.

The first telegraphic connection between Europe and North America was laid by the giant (for the time) steamship *Great Eastern* in the late 1960s and the development of telephone services was limited by wires until well after World War II. The 'space race', which led to the first moon landing in 1969, produced as a by-product the telecommunications satellite and freed the telephone from a total dependency on wires and thus made it possible to use many more channels.

The introduction of ISDN (Integrated Services Digital Network) in the 1990s has led to an explosion of telephone related services. Digital messages, unlike those sent by analogue means, allow the signal to be broken up into discrete packages. Thus a single wire can carry more than one 'conversation'. This allows computers (which use digital codes) to communicate very quickly as well as permitting much more complicated signals to be carried. Digital communications have made video conferencing much more accessible as well as improving the quality of the vision and sound. ISDN is rapidly gaining ground not only for business communications, where vast amounts of data need to be transmitted, but also in the home, where a modem linked to an ISDN line can handle data much more quickly than a traditional analogue telephone system.

As the number of home computers has grown, so has the requirement to access the INTERNET and email from home as well as at work, leading to the development of faster and faster modems and ISDN, as covered above.

'Plastic'

There can be few places in the world that do not recognise and in the vast majority of cases accept plastic cards with the words *MASTERCARD* or *VISA* on them. These are the two major credit card organisations in the world and many millions of people own and use their product.

Credit cards are not the only form of 'plastic' in common use but they are possibly the most important from the standpoint of customer relations. The technological developments that will be covered in this chapter would be of little use unless complemented by an internationally recognised method of payment by customers to suppliers that is secure, quick and easy.

There are a number of types of 'plastic' in current use, which include:

- Credit cards
- Debit cards
- ATM cards
- Store cards
- Telephone cards
- Loyalty cards
- Identification cards.

Credit cards

Credit cards are usually issued by banks, building societies or similar financial institutions. Many charge an annual fee but interest is only charged if the account is not paid off in full each month. There are useful legal reasons for possessing a credit card in the UK, not least is the card issuer's liability if the supplier of goods and services purchased using the card fails to deliver or goes into liquidation. Many of the issuing banks etc. also provide accidental damage insurance for a limited period in respect of items purchased using a credit card.

Hotels and cruise ships provide facilities for customers to register their credit card details at the start of their holiday, the customer then signing for any purchases with the account being settled automatically. This is obviously of considerable benefit to the organisation as it makes non-payment for services much less likely and the customer benefits from not having to carry large amounts of cash.

Credit cards can be very useful when undertaking foreign travel as they obviate the need to change currencies with the losses that always occur during currency conversions.

As with the debit cards covered in the next section, suppliers are able to seek authorisation from the issuer for any amounts over the supplier's own 'floor limit', i.e. the amount over which a member of staff must seek authority before accepting payment other than in cash. Thus if a customer is over their credit limit or the card has been reported stolen, action can be taken.

Credit cards can also be used in many cash dispensers (see later) all over the world.

Debit cards

Similar in appearance to credit cards are the cards known as debit cards, again issued by banks etc. Whereas only a proportion of the balance on a credit card needs to be paid off, a debit card acts like a cheque, with the amount of money being debited from the customer's account and transferred to the supplier. Such cards are nearly always a dual-purpose combined debit and cheque guarantee card.

Debit cards avoid the customer getting into debt as they are in effect paperless cheques with strict limits as to the amounts they can be used for.

ATM cards

Automatic Teller Machines, ATMs as they are known in the USA, or Cash Dispensers using UK nomenclature, have become a common sight firstly at banks and building societies and latterly in airports, shopping centres and ferry ports. Using a special card (often combined as a joint use function with a debit card) or even a credit card and a PIN number, a customer is able to draw out cash from a 'hole in the wall' dispenser. The dispensers normally offer fixed amounts of £10, £20, £50, £100 etc. and work by comparing the PIN number (usually 4 digits) entered by the customer onto the machine with the information coded onto the magnetic strip. Provided the information matches and there is sufficient money in the customer's account, the required cash is dispensed. Banks take considerable care to protect the systems from fraud. There is little they can do about criminals who remove the whole of the apparatus and drive off with it but they can ensure that the machines are set up in locations that are well lit, as those using an ATM are somewhat vulnerable to muggers. It is a fair assumption that anybody walking away from an ATM will have cash on his or her person.

Current security developments to prevent fraud include fixing cameras in the machines to compare the features of the cardholder with digital data encoded on the card. Digital camera technology makes this a technologically possible procedure.

Initially, each bank and building society had ATMs that only accepted their card as issued to their customers but nowadays the LINK network and other similar schemes allow customers to use the machines of other participating institutions.

Store cards

Many large stores and similar retail operations offer a form of credit card applicable to their own operation. The customer is allocated a credit limit and can buy goods up to the limit of their credit, repaying the company (or its agent, normally a financial institution) on a monthly basis. These cards are not like the loyalty cards discussed in Chapter 4, as loyalty cards are used for the customer to accumulate some form of loyalty bonus. Store cards are akin to a form of elastic hire purchase. For the customer there is the advantage that they do not have to pay the full amount for goods at the outset, whilst the company can be fairly confident that the customer will use the card to buy further items when their credit balance allows. The disadvantage to the customer is the ease with which debts can be incurred, especially if he or she holds a number of such cards. As the company has full details of the cardholder, store cards, like loyalty cards, can provide details of buying patterns and allows the company to target the cardholder for special offers etc.

Telephone cards

The growth in the number of telephones world-wide, discussed earlier, plus an increase in travel have led the telephone companies to institute cashless means of using the equipment. There are two methods of achieving this:

Prepaid cards

With prepaid cards the customer makes a purchase at any of the authorised retail outlets for a card containing a set number of telephone units, the number depending on the price paid. The card is then inserted into a slot in a public telephone, a call is made and the number of units used deducted from the information held on the card. When all the units have been used, the card is useless although telephone cards have become collectibles in the same way as stamps and cigarette cards etc., and rare examples can change hands for considerable sums.

Nearly every private and nationalised telephone system has its own cards, some of which are interchangeable between telephone companies. Most of the Eastern Caribbean islands accept each others' telephone cards, easy in this instance as they have a common currency.

The second form of prepayment card is the mobile telephone prepayment cards that were introduced in the UK during the late 1990s. The packages which these supported were designed to free customers from having to enter into contract with mobile telephone operators. The concept is very simple. The customer buys a box from any number of retailers. The box contains a mobile telephone and a starter voucher. The customer follows the instructions to activate the telephone, is advised of the number and provided with their initial credits. Thereafter they are charged for each call made, according to the tariff they have agreed. Credits can be 'topped' up by buying new vouchers from retailers and undertaking a simple activation procedure or by paying directly by credit card. The telephone remains activated provided that the required credits are purchased. The initial problem was that demand exceeded the ability of a number of the mobile telephone companies to handle the requests for top-up credits, leaving customers without the use of their telephone.

Whilst the system obviates the need for a monthly contract, the call can be slightly more expensive than using the traditional contract route.

Telephone charge cards

Most telephone operators offer customers a service whereby they can use public or private telephones world-wide and charge the call to their home telephone account. This removes the need to purchase telephone cards and requires only an account number and a PIN (see earlier) for a customer to, in effect, extend their home telephone to wherever they are. These cards can only be used for making calls; up to the1990s it was only possible to receive calls when not at home if the person calling knew where you were. As will be shown later, call diversion and individualised telephone numbers have overcome this obstacle.

Loyalty cards

Loyalty schemes were covered in Chapter 4. Many people now carry loyalty cards and their use has, as discussed in Chapter 4, developed so that many can be used in a number of linked organisations.

Identification cards

It is a curious aspect of the British character that a driving licence (without photograph) and an envelope with a person's address on it are often all that is required to establish identity. Other countries are stricter about the carrying of identification. There are arguments regarding civil liberties but these are inappropriate for this book. In respect of customer relations, any form of official identification, especially if it carries a photograph, may be useful when applying for credit or settling a bill with a large cheque.

In the USA, a system known as INPASS is in place for frequent travellers. Operating at selected airports, the system allows non-US nationals to use the US national's immigration section; by using a SMART card that contains details of the traveller and a copy of their palm print, the frequent visitor need not queue and answer the normal immigration questions. Using an INPASS card and hand baggage only, it is actually possible to get from the door of an aircraft to the kerbside of the British Airways terminal building at the John F Kennedy Airport in New York in under 4 minutes.

Applicants for the INPASS scheme are screened by the US Immigration and Naturalisation Service and if they have no criminal record and a valid reason for frequent entry to the USA, their palm print is recorded and the details placed together with their passport information, home address, US work address etc. on the card, which is then ready for use.

Facsimile machines

Introduced as a result of developments in World War II, the facsimile machine matches telephone and photocopier technologies to allow documents to be sent over telephone lines. Whilst it may well be superseded by a scanner + PC + email, many businesses rely on 'fax' to send messages quickly and conveniently. It is especially useful when complex instructions or diagrams need to be seen by somebody many, many miles away. As the following case shows, it may be mundane technology today but the 'fax' can still help build useful relationships with customers.

Fiona Farquharson and her husband own and operate the Park View Guest House in Perth overlooking a large expanse of public park known as the South Inch. Although the guest house has only five letting rooms it receives customers from all over the world because the Farquharson's have used modern technology to overcome some of the basic time and language problems potential customers may have. Fiona realised that whilst many foreigners may be hesitant with spoken English, they often had access to somebody who could write in English. By advertising on the INTERNET and because previously satisfied customers had written in to publishers of tourist guidebooks covering Scotland in their own country, Fiona has access to a large potential customer base requiring bed and breakfast accommodation in Scotland's original capital. As Perth is an ideal centre for touring, there are a large number of hotel and bed and breakfast operations in the town, with fierce competition.

By the simple use of a facsimile machine, Fiona's potential customers in Italy, France and even Japan are able to compose a booking request in English and fax it to Fiona without having to worry about time differences or having a difficult telephone conversation in a foreign language. Fiona can then fax a simple acknowledgement and an all-important map back to them, again with no worries about time differences. This may be a very simple use of technology but, by thinking about the needs of the customer, Fiona has been able to expand her potential customer base across the world.

Email

Email (short for electronic mail) is one of the major manifestations of the synergy gained by linking computer and telephone technology. Virtually unknown in the UK before the 1980s, email has become a normal method of business communications and has spread rapidly into the domestic market. With its ability to send document files, pictures and greetings cards to anybody in the world with an INTERNET connection, email has meant that time and distance have been truly overcome. A message typed in London can be in the inbox of somebody in New York in seconds and at the cost of a local telephone call.

Colleagues, family and friends who are on-line can be readily contacted and, as there is no telephone bell to ring and disturb people, the problem of time zones is eliminated. Email, despite its protocols, lacks the personal touch but for instant messages and indeed communications it is hard to beat.

As a simple example of how email and associated technology can aid customer relations, the author renewed a subscription to a US magazine over the telephone using a credit card. For some reason no magazines were received. The home office of the publisher is in Kansas, causing a time zone problem when wishing to get in touch. However, one short email explaining the problem produced not only a very quick reply but also expedited delivery of the missing copies – no fuss and the matter was settled using local telephone charges.

Just examining an email address can provide a number of clues, for example, **.ac** near the end of an address indicates that the address is at an academic institution, **.gov** indicates a government body, **.co** is used for companies etc. and **.com** is used by communication providers with other organisations using **.org**. US addresses have nothing at the end but **.uk** represents Britain (the United Kingdom), **.ca** being Canada etc. Thus **amazon.co.uk**, the UK part of the bookseller Amazon, to be considered later in this chapter, becomes self-explanatory.

INTERNET

Whole books have been written about the development and use of the INTERNET. The combination of telephone and computer technology through a gateway provided by one of the many ISPs (Internet Service Providers) allows people owning a computer with a modem to gain access to millions of web pages covering every possible subject.

There are two major implications of the INTERNET for customer relations, namely:

- Information for customers
- Ecommerce.

Information for customers

Nearly every major organisation, from retailers to governments and charities, and an increasing number of smaller concerns have set up easily accessible web pages where customers and potential customers can find information about the organisation. Whether the customer is searching for a new motor car, wishes to know about a piece of legislation, train times in the Netherlands or wants details of a book, the chances are it can be accessed through a simple INTERNET search. Some searches require the use of passwords but most commercial and public services are open to anybody wherever they are in the world. All that is required is either the URL (Unique Reference Location) of the organisation in question or the use of the search engines provided by the INTERNET SERVICE PROVIDERS. Most addresses begin as **http:///www** etc. Like email addresses, to which they are related, they may appear complex but follow a logical pattern. The growth in the use of the WWW (World Wide Web) has been nothing short of explosive and many individuals as well as organisations now have their own personal web pages where they provide details about themselves.

As more and more people have become 'connected', there has been a massive growth in an area of business known as electronic commerce, or ecommerce for short.

Ecommerce

In September 1999, UK television news services reported that the UK Prime Minister, Tony Blair, was to appoint an 'E-envoy' to promote the effective use of commercial activities carried out using the INTERNET. The reports quoted the fact that in 1999 there were 500 000 companies actually conducting business on the INTERNET, a figure that was expected to grow to a staggering 8 million by 2002 with revenue exceeding £5 billion by 2003. In the UK alone it was predicted that by the end of 2000 no fewer than 9 million Britons would have access to an INTERNET connection (source: ITV Teletext service, 12 September 1999).

Companies using the INTERNET for business in 1999 ranged from the major holiday companies, airlines, travel agents, book suppliers and antique houses down to a small bakery in Whitby in the North East of England.

Home shopping

There is nothing new about the concept of home shopping. As the settlers poured across Middle America in the 19th Century, companies such as Sears realised that the massive distances involved in reaching the nearest department store created a market for mail order shopping. Such companies produced mammoth catalogues containing items as diverse as clothes and farm implements. Even today many people still use a home-shopping catalogue for mail order and this is a thriving sector of the retail industry. No longer do orders have to be placed by mail and an agent used to collect payment. Modern mail order uses the telephone and facsimile technology coupled to credit card payments for those who wish a quicker and more convenient service.

US television stations pioneered the introduction of shopping channels devoted entirely to promoting products and taking orders over the telephone, a development that is now gaining ground in the UK with the introduction of cable, satellite and digital television, which allow more channels to be accessed from home.

Ecommerce is a natural extension of home shopping, recent developments allowing those without a computer but with a digital television to become part of the marketplace.

Given such diversity it would be impossible to mention every type of business operating on the INTERNET as new companies and sectors are being added continually. In 1999, one of the latest applications of ecommerce was the conducting of antique auctions by the major antique houses. No longer did a buyer need to fly from New York to London to bid for a piece or employ an agent. They could see the piece on their personal computer at home, examine its provenance and then bid electronically and, if successful, pay using a credit card.

This section will examine three ecommerce operations, on-line banking, book sales and airline ticket purchases as examples of what ecommerce can do for both the organisation and the customer.

On-line banking

An individual's relationship with their bank used to be a very personal one, with the bank manger knowing the vast majority of the branches' customers by name. For many years after World War II, banks were open six days per week, offering a Saturday morning service, although they tended to open later and shut earlier than the vast majority of retailers and other businesses.

When the banks decided to stop Saturday opening, business was lost to the building societies that were open on Saturdays, a time when many people wished to withdraw cash for shopping. The introduction of ATMs (see earlier) allowed customers to withdraw cash at any time and now virtually every bank and building society offers this facility. However there are other transactions people need from their banks and, for those in work or in remote locations, contact with the bank during normal business hours can be difficult.

One method the banks and building societies have used to solve this problem is the introduction of call centres (see later) where information and certain transactions can be undertaken. Many such centres have extended access hours and indeed the trend is towards a 24-hour service. This provides the customer with greater time to contact their bank but at a further distance and with a less personal service.

The other method that is growing rapidly is the development of on-line banking, linking the customer's personal computer with the bank.

The first UK bank to introduce such a service was the Bank of Scotland, which offered its HOBS (Home and Office Banking Service) to selected customers from 1993 (Winder, 1999). This system required a special modem which, whilst quite revolutionary for the time, would seem very slow today. Working through the DOS system, HOBS basically allowed customers to check their balances, a facility not available on the ATMs of the time, but commonplace today.

Modern on-line banking (Winder, above, lists eight UK on-line banking providers in 1999, together with reviews of their services) allows, in most cases, for customers not only to check their balance but to print out statements, pay bills, transfer monies between accounts and to download data with other types of software, such as accounts packages. In 1999, only the Bank of Scotland and First Direct allowed the customer to apply for an overdraft on-line but the other providers are likely to follow suit. Charges in 1999 were zero or minimal and competitive forces are likely to ensure that any fees remain relatively low given the convenience that such a system offers.

The advantages to the banks are self-evident. Branches cost money both in terms of staff and premises; on-line banking costs far less. The customer is able to conduct the vast majority of day-to-day transactions at his or her convenience. The personal touch is, of course, lost and it remains problematic as to whether the branch network will completely disappear. The trend throughout the 1990s has been for mergers between banks, building societies to convert to banks and for branch networks to be cut. Provided that there is a human being available for those transactions that are not day to day but require discussion and negotiation, then the future of on-line banking seems set to grow.

The challenge for the banks and building societies is to find a method of making the customer feel personally valued. Many of the banks and building societies, recognising this need, have introduced the concept of a 'personal banker' whom the customer can contact in the event of problems. Most transactions can be carried out quickly and conveniently on-line or on the telephone to any member of the bank's staff, but the 'personal banker' is available to discuss and rectify any problems.

Book sales

One of the earliest ecommerce success stories was that of **amazon.com** and its UK operation **amazon.c.uk**. The first INTERNET bookshop, **amazon.com**, was founded in the USA by Jeff Bezos in 1995 (de Jonge, 1999). de Jonge had spotted a crucial niche in the book selling market. Traditional methods of buying books had required a visit to a bookshop or using one of the many book clubs that offered cut price editions via their membership magazines. Unfortunately the titles on offer from the latter tend to be restricted and, whilst browsing through a bookshop is pleasurable, there are many people who know exactly which book they require and just want to acquire that volume with the minimum of fuss.

The concept of an INTERNET bookshop was an idea whose time had come. Book buyers could browse using the amazon web site; this may not be as satisfying as actually holding the volume and browsing the shelves, but many of the books people require are not stocked even by the largest bookshop and thus must be ordered unseen anyway. The concept of an on-line bookshop has certainly proved successful, with imitators entering the market, the expansion of amazon to the UK and, by 1999, no fewer than 6.2 million customers and a 1999 Wall Street valuation of $30 billion (de Jonge, 1999).

Using the amazon service is simplicity itself. Just type in their URL (see earlier) and follow the instructions on the web pages. Enter name, address, preferred password and credit card details over a secure link and the customer can start shopping. Browsing from title to synopsis is done using an HTML (Hyper Text Machine Language) link and required items can be placed in a shopping basket; amazon confirms the order by email and it is delivered by the mail service within the time stipulated by the company. Items in stock are usually received within 2 to 3 days; those that have to be ordered take slightly longer.

For those who live some distance from a major bookshop, like this author, companies like amazon provide a very convenient service.

The company have been expanding, CDs and videos etc. being a similar market and well suited to ecommerce, and Bezos has recently started 'Shop the Web' which offers on-line links to other retailers.

There is no doubt that this is the true successor to the Sear's type catalogues mentioned earlier and provides a convenient method of purchasing those items for which there is little need to browse. Supermarkets etc. are already experimenting with similar services, which will be a boon to the housebound etc.

Travel

If you need to book a plane ticket between Denver and Los Angeles and you live in Manchester (UK), you can do it over the INTERNET. Many specialist flight-booking companies have facilities for searching for the best deals and then making a booking over the INTERNET. Hotels and even guest houses can be booked directly from your own computer.

The UK budget airline, Easy Jet, commenced operations by only accepting telephone bookings paid for by credit card, and in the late 1990s began an INTERNET booking service with one in three bookings being made over the INTERNET by May 1999. INTERNET bookings even receive a discount. In May 1999 there were over 1 million visits to the company's website which provides flight details etc. as well as a booking facility.

Not only are flight details readily available on the INTERNET but so are virtual tours of cruise ship facilities and railway timetables for many parts of the world.

The INTERNET has made the acquisition of travel information far more convenient for potential customers who can make their plans in the comfort of their own home or office.

There is a downside in that facilitating such tasks by computer can lead to job losses amongst high street travel agents etc., in effect the INTERNET brings the same facilities into the home as have been enjoyed by the travel trade for some time. It is too early to see how this will affect traditional trade.

Customer relations at a distance

There is always a danger that technology can remove the personal element from any transaction. There needs to be a trade-off. If a customer cannot have a more personal service, then they need a more convenient one. The books, tickets etc. covered in the previous sections can be purchased at any time, they do not depend on shop opening hours. It has already been shown how banks are introducing 'personal bankers' to redress the balance of convenience v personal service.

The 1990s saw considerable UK growth in call centres.

Call centres

It makes economic sense, as customers become more and more distant geographically, to provide them with a central point of telephone contact. Given the benefits of the technology, this does not have to be in the same country, although the cost of telephone calls needs to be kept in mind, as more remote customers should not be disadvantaged. Fortunately it is possible to set up either freephone telephone calls or local rate calls to ease the burden on customers.

Airlines, especially British Airways, have used their telecommunications network to obviate time differences. A call for information on the London to Glasgow shuttle made at 2000 (GMT) may well be answered in New York, where it is the middle of the day and thus the maximum number of staff are on duty.

Many of the financial and large retail institutions have set up centralised call centres where customer enquiries can be dealt with, often on a 24-hour basis. The computer systems have access to the customer's details and routine matters can normally be dealt with efficiently and effectively, with supervisors on hand to deal with the more difficult queries.

In the UK, a fair number of such centres are located in the central belt of Scotland, as it is believed that the Scottish accent is particularly appreciated over the telephone. Banks that only operate in England and Wales have been known to set up their call centres in the Glasgow area, despite having no (or only a few) branches in Scotland.

Ticketing for flights etc. can be performed in India just as easily as in London, as data travels at the speed of light and so distance is no problem.

Call centres provide a point of contact with a human being and that is still of vital importance to the majority of customers, no matter how good the technology is.

Teleconferencing

It may well not be long before there are also teleconference links to call centres. Domestic videoconferencing software and cameras are now freely available at relatively low cost and their use may make service that little bit more personal, although body language clues (see the next chapter) are hard to spot on a small screen which may not have the best picture resolution possible. One cannot say how this will develop, save that it will become better and cheaper!

EPOS and bar codes

Finally in this chapter there is a consideration of another link between computers and telephones, this time in relation to bar codes and EPOS (Electronic Point Of Sale).

In Chapter 4 it was mentioned that loyalty schemes for supermarkets etc. provide the organisation with a means of assessing the customer's lifestyle. Virtually every product we buy has a computerised bar code. By reading this code at the till point, not only can customer preferences be assessed but data messages sent back to warehouses etc. to ensure that the customer has what they want when they want it, i.e. there is no excuse for accidentally running out of stock. Managers can see the stock situation in more or less real time and ensure that shelves are restocked and new items ordered in a very efficient manner.

Summary

Like the computer mentioned at the start of this chapter, the chapter itself was probably obsolete as soon as it was written, such is the progress of technological advances.

What cannot be denied is that it is important to ensure that technology, however it is used, must benefit the customer and not make he or she feel depersonalised.

The synergy between the computer and the telephone has led to the development of the INTERNET and whilst that promises much for customer convenience, it offers a massive challenge to maintaining and strengthening the relationship with the customer.

Terms introduced

- ATM
- Bar codes
- Call centres
- Credit cards
- Debit cards
- Ecommerce
- Electronic Point Of Sale (EPOS)
- Email
- Hyper Text Machine Language (HTML)
- INTERNET
- On-line shopping
- PIN numbers
- Railway time
- Store cards
- World Wide Web (WWW)

QUESTIONS

1. How can organisations balance the remoteness brought about by technology and the need for the customer to feel a valued individual?

2. Explain how the synergy between telephone, computer and other technologies has benefited the customer by providing greater choices and access.
3. How do you see the future of on-line services and on-line shopping developing in the next ten years? Give examples of what might be possible, based on what is being developed now.

◪ 8 Relationships

Communications and communication model – Noise – Language registers – Means of communication – Umbilicals and mooring ropes – Binding of supplier and customer – CARE (Competence, Attitude, Resources and Empathy) – Types of resources – Power – Assertiveness – The relationship continuum – Relationships and the value chain – Image – Personal body language – OBL (Organisational Body Language)

In Chapter 6 it was shown that there is a legal contractual relationship between the supplier of a good or service and the purchaser. Notwithstanding the legal relationship there are also other relationships, moral, ethical and plain good business sense, between any organisation and its internal and external customers.

Whilst the legal relationship cannot be forgotten, it is the less formal relationships that determine the success or otherwise of the vast majority of transactions between an organisation and its customers, and it is these informal relationships that form the basis of this chapter.

Communications

One of the distinguishing factors between human beings and the rest of the animal kingdom is the complexity of our communications. Human beings have five senses:

- Vision
- Hearing
- Touch
- Smell
- Taste.

Of these five, the one we use most often to communicate is vision – we are a very visual animal. After vision, in order of importance comes hearing, these two accounting for over 90% of our communication. Anybody who has owned a dog will know that dogs communicate in different ways from ourselves. Dogs have a much more highly developed sense of smell than humans do. Indeed when it comes to smell, we are very low down on the list for the effective use of this sense. Many animals use chemicals known as pheromones, which are produced by the body, and use the sense of smell to communicate (Zdarek, 1988). The best we can usually manage is to use perfumes and aftershave, although there is the expression in the English language 'to smell the fear'. It is quite probable that we produce pheromones, it is just that our noses are not sensitive enough to detect them.

Whilst sight is the predominant human sense, accounting for perhaps as much as 80% of communication using writing, signs and body language, it is apparent that the body is able to compensate for deficiencies in a sense. Visually impaired people often have a more highly developed sense of touch, a fact that means they can read using Braille, which requires considerable sensitivity in the fingers. Nevertheless, for the vast majority of people, their communication with each other will firstly be visual and secondly through sound. As primates we have a highly developed visual system that allows us to see colours and is stereoscopic, which serves to aid the judgement of distance. Even our colour vision is restricted to the visible spectrum (so called because it is defined as the range of colours humans can see) and does not include infra-red or ultra-violet radiation. It has long been known that our hearing covers a much more restrictive wavelength of sound compared to that of a dog or a whale, animals that can hear sounds that we cannot.

Communication model

It is possible to build up a simple but highly explanatory model of the communication process. For the sake of simplicity it is assumed that there are two people in a shop and that person A (the customer) requires person B (the salesperson) to communicate the price of an article. A and B possess a multi-function transmitter – a mouth and a hand – and a multi-function receiver – eyes and ears.

The process is as follows. A (the customer) sees an article they are interested in but the price tag is not visible. A's brain, through a series of neural signals, decides to ask a question. At this moment in time the signal is in the form of a neural signal so it needs to be coded into something that B can understand. (If humans ever develop telepathy, this coding stage will become redundant.) A's brain codes the signal into *words* – see Figure 8.1.

An important thing about any code is that the transmitter and the receiver need copies of it in order for the latter to be able to decode the message properly. In this example, A and B are using English. Were A using English and B spoke only French, then extra coding and decoding steps, perhaps using a phrasebook, would be required.

All messages need a medium of conduction. Speech uses sound waves that create a disturbance in the molecules of the air (this is why there is no sound in the vacuum of outer space).

A's request for a price is conducted through the air to B who can also see A and thus gain extra clues as A also points to the object. The message reaches B's receivers, the ears for the sound and the eyes for the visual image – see Figure 8.2.

The sound waves that hit B's ears and the light that enters B's eyes are decoded from speech and vision into a set of neural impulses and are sent to B's brain – see Figure 8.3.

Figure 8.1   Communications step 1.

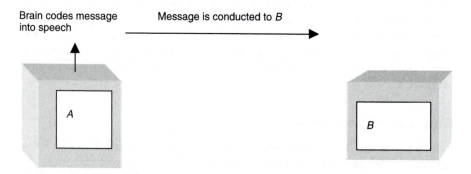

Figure 8.2   Communications step 2.

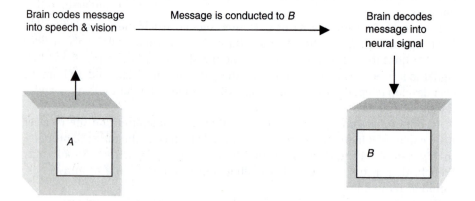

Figure 8.3   Communications step 3.

Complex things will happen in *B*'s brain, as it questions:

- Do I understand the code?
- What am I being asked?
- Have I ever been asked this kind of thing before?
- Where is *A* in terms of space?

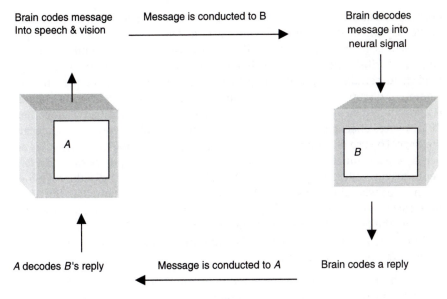

Brain codes message
Into speech & vision

Message is conducted to B

Brain decodes
message into
neural signal

A

B

A decodes B's reply

Message is conducted to A

Brain codes a reply

Figure 8.4   Communications step 4.

The latter may sound a trite question but sound waves etc. are quite directional and need to be accurately 'pointed' in the right direction. Assuming that *B* understands the message from *A*, the process can be repeated, this time with *B* giving the required answer, perhaps by saying '£4.99' and turning the price label around and pointing to it, an aural and a visual message – see Figure 8.4.

B's reply to *A* should provide an indication that *B* has correctly understood the message that *A* sent. History is full of examples where one person *thought* that they understood a message when in fact they hadn't. The 'Charge of the Light Brigade' during the Crimean War is a classic example of somebody acting on what they thought they had been told, when in fact they had been told something completely different.

The way to ensure that a message has been understood is to request feedback. Just asking 'do you understand?' is a very closed question and often receives a 'yes' response because the recipient believes that they have in fact understood. It is often illuminating to ask 'in your own words, what have you been asked to do?' It is often possible to gauge a customer's understanding by analysing the subsequent conversation to see if both the supplier and the customer are actually on the same wavelength.

Noise

The reason messages are often misunderstood is that something interferes with the process. Anything that interferes with communications is called noise. It may be actual physical noise that distorts the message or it may be bad handwriting or conflicting meanings: for example, the old chestnut about the two builders, 'I'll hold the nail and when I nod my head hit it with the hammer!'; hit what? – the nail or the person's head? Noise can be the use of dialect that only one of the people understands or it could be the differences between an apparently common language; British English ascribes different words and meanings than American English to certain things. Anything that distorts the message or prevents reception or disrupts decoding is noise. In any communication with a customer it is important to ensure that noise is kept to a minimum or eliminated altogether. This involves checking that the customer can actually follow and understand the message. The use of acronyms and jargons are typical examples of noise – it is no use saying to somebody who has little experience of computers that 'this is a Pentium chip with 32 megabytes of RAM and a special soundcard' if the customer has no idea what the terms mean. Professions and high tech suppliers can often be accused of using 'in' terms that they understand but the customer doesn't. To illustrate the point, what does EMU mean to you?

On asking a group of managers this question during research for this book a variety of responses were given:

- A big bird made famous by the entertainer Rod Hull who sadly died in 1999
- European Monetary Union (an economic acronym)
- Electro-Magnetic Unit (a scientific acronym)
- Electrical Multiple Unit (a railway term).

Fortunately people can often gain a sense of the meaning of unfamiliar terms and phrases by using the preceding and following phrases to set the term in some form of context. Human nature being what it is, people are often very reluctant to show their ignorance and ask what the term means, and thus misunderstandings can and do occur. Anything that makes the customer look foolish is to be avoided, as a foolish looking customer soon becomes an ex-customer. Plain English with jargon-free terms is the best way to build up a relationship with the customer. Educate the customer by all means, but only in a manner that does not make the customer look or feel foolish.

Governments, both local and national, have gained a reputation for writing documents in a manner that makes them indecipherable to the average person, and organisations such as the Campaign for Plain English have waged battle on behalf of the man and woman in the street in order to have official documents in a more readable and understandable style and format.

As Trudgill (1975) has pointed out when referring to the work of Bernstein, we all speak a number of languages, even if we claim not to speak a foreign language. We have a language type (or register) that we use at home, one for work, one when with our friends etc. It is important that a supplier can use the language register of the customer rather than relying on the customer to learn and understand the language register of the supplier.

Means of communication

As the previous chapter showed, modern technology has greatly increased the speed and methods by which communication between supplier and customer can be accomplished. The advent of email has meant that distance is no barrier to communication and, thanks to the computer and the facsimile machine, time zone differences have been made of little account. Whatever means of communication are used, the points that need to be emphasised are: firstly the medium must suit the customer, not all of whom may be familiar with the technology, and secondly relationships are developed between people and between a person and a machine. In the field of customer relations, social skills are actually more important than technological ones.

Umbilicals and mooring ropes

The above may seem a strange heading for a section in a book devoted to customer relations but is used as an analogy to illustrate the means by which the bonds between customer and supplier develop.

The umbilical represents the core need of the customer and the channels through which it is delivered. It is the need for a product or service that forms the start of the supplier/customer relationship (Figure 8.5). If that need is not supplied or if the customer perceives that the need no longer exists or can be supplied more effectively or efficiently or economically by another supplier, then the relationship is in all probability at an end, albeit temporarily if some form of recovery can be initiated.

Each time there is a successful transaction between the supplier and the customer then a mooring rope is set up between them. As any sailor knows, the greater the number of mooring lines between a ship and the shore there are, the more tightly the ship is held fast and the harder it is to cast off.

When the supplier does something to the customer's satisfaction, the rope goes from the supplier to the customer. When the customer praises the supplier or recommends them to somebody else, they in fact bind themselves closer to the supplier. The mooring ropes of customer relations go both ways and thus bind the supplier and the customer into an ever-closer relationship (Figure 8.6).

The greater the number of mooring ropes between the supplier and the customer, the greater the dissatisfaction that will be needed to force the customer to break free. The early days of a supplier/customer relationship are thus the

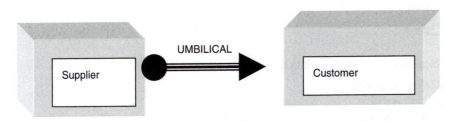

Figure 8.5   The umbilical connection.

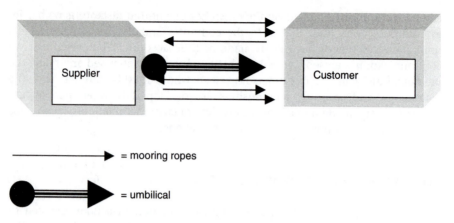

Figure 8.6 The binding of supplier and customer.

most fragile. Because there are few moorings between them, only a small amount of dissatisfaction may be enough to persuade the customer to cast off and look for a new supplier.

In Chapter 4, the concept of 'hostages' was introduced and in their case there are few mooring ropes binding the hostage to the supplier, so casting off is relatively easy when the monopoly is broken and a new supplier is available.

How are these mooring ropes put into place, i.e. how does the relationship develop? In many cases it may be something that grows gradually over a period of time, each satisfactory transaction adding to the customer's perception of the organisation. In other cases there are the 'Moments of Truth', an idea expounded by Jan Carlson of Scandinavian Airlines System (SAS). Carlson believed that his customers experienced over 50 000 Moments of Truth per day when dealing with his airline (Clutterbuck *et al.*, 1993). Moments of Truth occur when the customer instinctively knows that the organisation he or she is dealing with is OK and that a relationship is developing. It may be a single act of one employee or the ambience and atmosphere that the organisation puts out (see Organisational Body Language later in this chapter) but the customer feels it and feels comfortable with the organisation.

What is certain is that unless the staff of the organisation practise CARE (an acronym that will be explained below), a relationship is unlikely to develop.

Care

Care is an acronym standing for:

- COMPETENCE
- ATTITUDE
- RESOURCES
- EMPATHY

the four components for building an effective and long-lasting customer/ supplier relationship.

Competence

A customer has to have faith in the competence both of the organisation and its employees. Cartwright & Green (1997) have pointed out the dangers of lack of product knowledge, and many of the larger UK electrical goods retailers are now shedding their image of employing staff with very little product knowledge and embarking on large training programmes. Customers like to feel that they are in a safe pair of hands and any suspicion that those they are dealing with lack competence is a fast way of losing a customer. One of the barriers to entry discussed in Chapter 3 of this book is a lack of competence in the area of operations in question. Competence and reputation are built up over time and as a result of previous successful transactions. Everybody working for an organisation needs a minimum level of product knowledge. It looks very strange when an employee cannot explain the basic functions of their organisation to an outsider; it does not engender confidence!

Attitude

At the very start of this book the importance of taking a customer-centred approach was stated. Customer relations' policies can only be effective if the staff in the organisation have the right attitude towards the customer. The right attitude is one that recognises the importance of the customer to the well-being of everybody in the value chain. Training and understanding the relationship between the organisation and the customer (in effect, the essence of this book) cannot be overstated.

Resources

There is little point in having trained staff with the right attitude to customer relations if they are not provided with the necessary resources. Any issues relating to the customer should be dealt with as near to the customer interface as possible and that requires the staff at the interface to have the physical resources and the power to act.

The type of resources staff require to carry out an effective customer relations' role include:

Physical resources

If a customer wishes to have a replacement or substitute item then the sooner it is supplied the more likely it is that any problem situation can be recovered.

If staff do not have the authority to take such actions then it is possible that the time taken to supply the item may lead to frustration. There will, of course, be many occasions when it is not possible to take action straight away but the organisational procedures should be such as to minimise any waiting time for the customer.

Nothing is more frustrating to a current or potential customer than to try to make a purchase only to find the item is out of stock. As was shown in the previous chapter, modern information technology systems are able to simplify the task of stock control by providing very accurate instantaneous data and thus there are becoming fewer and fewer genuine reasons for not having stock either available or available at extremely short notice.

Financial resources

Refunding the customer's money (which may be a legal requirement, see Chapter 6) or making a small *ex-gratia* payment is something that can, within strict guidelines, be delegated to the staff dealing with the customer. Unit managers should have the discretion to make refunds and payments for inconvenience without going through long-winded procedures. Provided that the sums do not exceed agreed limits, there are few reasons why the customer should be made to wait if the issue is a genuine one.

Staff should certainly have a delegated budget that allows them to provide basic hospitality for customers.

Information resources

Information is now recognised as a key resource. The current century leads on from the 20th as being the 'Age of Information'. Modern technology (as demonstrated in the previous chapter) allows information about the customer to be widely and immediately available. Staff need to be able to access information that will allow them to deliver a better standard of customer care. Training in the use and applicability of technology is vital if the vast amounts of data are to be used effectively.

Time

Time is a precious resource. Customers can become very angry if they feel that a member of staff has not got the time to deal with them properly. A member of staff may have had to answer the same query time and again during the day and may be frustrated, but *for the individual customer it will be the first time they have asked* and the feelings of the staff member will be of little consequence to such a customer. Management needs to allow staff the necessary time to deal with the customer as an individual.

Power can sometimes be used in an emotive, even negative way. Power itself is neutral and just another resource; it is what is done with power that may be positive or negative. In Chapter 3 it was shown that both suppliers and customers possess bargaining power. However, the staff dealing with the customers also possess power. Two of the most recognisable manifestations of power in the field of customer relations are expert power and authority power. Customers expect a considerable degree of expertise from suppliers and it can be all to easy for members of staff to misuse the power of expertise, either by pretending that they know more than they actually do or by using their knowledge to show off and gain some sort of advantage over the customer. As has already been shown, making the customer look foolish in any way is a guaranteed method of making that customer an ex-customer. Knowledge should be used sensitively so that the customer is reassured by the competence of the employee but not made to feel inferior.

Authority power is the power conferred by the employee's position within the organisation. In the customer's eyes a supervisor may carry more 'clout' when it comes to getting things done than an assistant, and a manager may be perceived as being superior to a supervisor. 'May I speak to your manager?' is a phrase often used by customers who feel that their problems are not being addressed. It should infer no lack of respect for the person they are talking to but rather a wish to talk to somebody with more organisational power.

Empathy

The fourth component of CARE is empathy. Whilst it may sound similar to sympathy, empathy is the ability to understand the situation from the other person's point of view. Sympathy indicates agreement, empathy is about understanding. A good relationship is one where the staff member can put themselves 'in the shoes' of the customer and understand how they feel. To develop empathy requires more than product knowledge, it requires a knowledge of the needs, wants and aspirations of the customer.

The relationship continuum

Under normal circumstances it stands to reason that the closer the proximity of the supplier and customer geographically, the closer their relationship is likely to be. Equally, the smaller the organisation, the more likely it is that the more intimate the customer/supplier relationships are likely to be. Large, diffuse organisations can build closer relationships with customers by adopting a devolved structure and allowing each branch or business unit to develop close links to its customers. Large organisations may appoint client managers whose role it is to look after a small, discrete group of customers on a personal basis.

The relationship between what may be termed the degree of diffusion or degree of concentration of an organisation and the remoteness or intimacy of the customer/organisation relationship can be shown on the relationship continuum (Figure 8.7).

Many large organisations can be described as being diffuse, whilst a local shop is an example of a concentrated organisation that is able to develop a

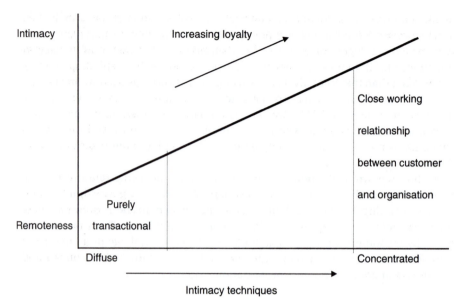

Figure 8.7   The relationship continuum.

considerable degree of intimacy with its customers. The strength of loyalty increases with intimacy and thus it is useful for diffuse, remote organisations to use techniques that make them appear more concentrated and intimate.

Peters & Waterman (1982) coined the term 'close to the customer' as one of their attributes of excellent organisations (see Chapter 3). The larger and more diffuse an organisation is, the harder it is to achieve this closeness without special effort. There are a number of techniques that such organisations can adopt to make them appear more concentrated and intimate in the eyes of their customers. These techniques include:

- Setting up branches with devolved authority to solve customer problems
- Assigning client managers to work with a small number of customers
- Dividing the operation up into discrete brands
- Using technology to appear close to the customer.

Setting up branches with devolved authority to solve customer problems

This is the traditional method of solving the problem of a large, remote organisation. Whilst there are, as discussed above, disadvantages to large organisations, there is the major advantage that they can use their buying power to offer bargains that smaller organisations cannot match. These economies of scale can then be passed on to the customer. By setting up a branch network, the organisation can have the best of both worlds as, indeed, can the customer. Provided that the staff remain at the branch for long enough to become properly acquainted with the customer and have the authority to respond to local needs, a large organisation can behave in many ways like a more concentrated, intimate one. It is unlikely that the manager of the branch of a large organisation will ever have the freedom that an owner manager has, but they can still respond in a personal manner to the customer. As many organisations become larger and more global in nature, it has become increasingly important to respond to the differing cultural norms of the organisation. These norms can differ considerably from region to region and especially from country to country. As Trompenaars (1993) has shown, these differences can be considerable and organisations that ignore them do so at their peril.

Many of the household names in the UK, especially in the retail sector, are large organisations. Some are controlled directly from a single head office and arranged as branches, for example Tesco or Marks and Spencer; others operate on the basis of owner managers banding together in order to boost their buying power, for example SPAR; whilst a third approach is for a large organisation to franchise to owner managers but retaining the corporate image, control and brand, an example being McDonalds – known the world over.

Assigning client managers to work with a small number of customers

Dividing a country or region into specific areas has long been a successful sales technique that allows closeness to the customer by permitting the area representative to build up a close relationship with the customer. If the customer always deals with the same person or small team, the relationship between them can become very close. It is important for the area representative to remember that they are an employee of the organisation and to adhere to corporate-wide objectives and codes of behaviour. Chapter 3 stressed the importance of consistency and it is important for any devolved or regionalised organisation to maintain consistency across the operation.

Dividing the operation up into discrete brands

The example of Carnival Cruises was provided earlier in this book as an instance of an organisation that operates a series of different brands of a similar product. Washing powder manufacturers and the producers of chocolate bars also have whole series of branded products appealing to different segments of a particular market. Customers, as has been shown in Chapter 4, can become very loyal to a particular brand and organisations can capitalise on this by portraying an enhanced relationship with loyal customers. This is part of the attraction of loyalty schemes. The more a customer identifies with a product, the closer their relationship with the supplying or manufacturing organisation.

The problems related to hostages were also covered in Chapter 4, and one means of mitigating against these is for the organisation to recognise that its customers are in fact hostages and then build up a positive relationship with them in the hope that they will not defect when and if more choice becomes available.

Using technology to appear close to the customer

The technologies examined in the previous chapter can aid the building up of a relationship between the customer and the organisation. Whilst 24-hour telephone and INTERNET banking may lack the personal touch of one's own branch, it does allow the bank to offer an enhanced service tailored to meet the customer's lifestyle and requirements, for example their work patterns. In this way it can be portrayed as more personal, even if more remote.

Computer systems that can recognise the customer from their telephone number or which can flash up a personalised greeting when a web page is accessed also provide a very personal touch at a remote distance and compensate for the lack of face-to-face contact by their convenience.

Systems which cause the customer frustration, an example being a long list of options and telephone buttons to press, have been shown to be counter productive, giving neither a personal service nor convenience.

Careful and sensitive use of technology can provide the illusion of personal service and allows organisations to operate from a distance but appear to be much more localised.

Relationships and the value chain

That it is possible to build up a close relationship with the customer at the customer/organisation interface is quite clear. However the success of any transaction depends on successful transactions all the way down the value chain. Unless great care is taken, the close relationship with the final external customer decays very quickly with each step back along the value chain.

Imagine a flashlight beam and the relationship between the distance from the bulb and the intensity of the light. This relationship follows an inverse square rule. Simplifying the mathematics, doubling the distance from the bulb results in the intensity decreasing by a factor of 4, tripling the distance by a factor of 9 etc. The intensity is inversely related to the square of the distance.

The same principle can be applied to the value chain in that unless the organisation takes steps to enhance the relationship, the intensity of the customer/supplier relationship will be inversely proportional to (at least) the square of the number of steps along the value chain. Thus, at best, a supplier three steps removed from the final customer will have a relationship one-ninth that of the immediate supplier to the customer.

Many organisations recognise that, even with the best will in the world, this diminution of the relationship along the value chain can lead to less concern for the final customer from those who are some distance down the chain. Highland Distillers (the makers of Famous Grouse and other fine whiskies) are among a growing number of organisations that send staff from down the value chain out with the salesforce, so that they not only understand the issues facing the sales force but can also meet and gain an understanding of the customer. In this way they 'advance' their position along the value chain and behave as though they were in fact much nearer the interface with the external customer.

Assertiveness

In Chapter 5 dealing with complaints, the concept of WIN/WIN was introduced. WIN/WIN situations can only occur when those involved adopt a position of assertiveness instead of submission or aggression.

In any human relationship, the moment there is any potential or actual conflict, the people involved can adopt one of three states:

- Submissiveness
- Aggressiveness
- Assertiveness.

Unfortunately human beings tend to adopt one of the first two. Submission avoids the conflict for the time being but can breed resentment, whilst aggression may make somebody feel good for a short time but it can lead to violence. Both submission, because it can breed festering resentment, and aggression, because adrenaline is released stimulating heart rate and increasing blood pressure, are actually physically bad for the body. Submissiveness involves giving in and aggression involves forcing somebody else to give in.

All too often a complaining customer receives an increasingly aggressive response to what may well be his or her own aggression. What starts as a minor complaint degenerates into a slanging match and things become personal whereby statements are made that both parties will probably wish to forget. It is certainly probable that if customer aggression is met with aggression, the customer will be lost. There is less likelihood of the customer being lost if their aggression is met with submission and instant apology. Indeed, if the organisation is in the wrong, they need to apologise and recover the situation.

In many cases, however, the customer is partially right, or even completely right, but makes the complaint in an insulting manner. Under the Health and Safety at Work Act (1974), employers have a duty to protect the physical and psychological well-being of their employees, and that includes verbal and certainly physical attacks by irate customers. Whatever happens, however aggressive a customer becomes, they should not be countered by aggression. The answer is to be assertive.

Assertive behaviour is when a person stands up for their rights without violating the rights of the other person.

Aggressive behaviour is when somebody violates the rights of the other person whilst standing up for their own rights, and submissive behaviour is when a person allows somebody to violate their rights.

Assertive behaviour:

- Stands up for one's own views but demonstrates that the views of the other party are understood
- Seeks solutions, not blame
- Enhances the assertive party but does not diminish the other
- Ensures the assertive party wins and at worst the other party doesn't lose
- Is succinct and to the point

- Asks open questions
- Is calm and reasoned.

Aggressive behaviour is far from calm and tends to make quite rigid statements on what the other party *must* do etc.

Even when the customer is right and the organisational representative needs to apologise, assertive behaviour by that party will accept the blame on behalf of the organisation but will defend their right to respect.

Many organisation/customer relationships break down because the aggrieved customer has not thought through what will solve the problem. They are angry and have become aggressive and need to work out that aggression. Working with such a customer, calming them down and showing that a solution that will be acceptable to both parties is being sought, will go a long way to re-establishing the relationship.

Submission normally only produces an apology, assertiveness will produce an apology and then a working with the customer to find an acceptable solution.

If physical or extreme psychological pressure develops or threatens to develop, then every member of staff has the right to refuse to continue and to seek assistance from a superior. No matter how angry the customer is, they have no right whatsoever to abuse anybody verbally or physically.

Body language
(*Illustrations by June A Cartwright*)

Whatever people may say or write, there is one easy method of telling what they are really feeling in a face-to-face situation and that is through an observation of their body language. A customer with a red face, gesticulating wildly, is obviously annoyed; but there are more subtle clues that a knowledge of body language allows those dealing with customers to ascertain the true feelings being expressed. Equally, if a member of staff can work out the mood of a customer via body language, then the customer can work out whether the member of staff dealing with them is interested or bored with the conversation etc.

Konrad Lorenz (1963) was one of the first to study the posture and mannerisms of animals and link these to behaviour. In his work on aggression he was able to show how dogs signalled their aggressive intent through the facial gestures they made and since then many others have studied this area.

Figures 8.8A to 8.8I illustrate a number of body postures that signal the mood and behaviour of an individual. That person may be saying one thing but their likely behaviour is signalled by their body language. These automatic body responses, which are hard to control unless a person is aware of body language, can be called intrinsic body language clues as they involve the body itself. Extrinsic body language clues involving clothing etc. are considered later in this section.

Human beings are unusual for primates in that we are 100% bipeds, i.e. we always walk in an upright position. This confers major advantages on us as a species as we can use our very complex arm, hand and finger joints to manipulate

Figure 8.8A   Honest and open.

tool whilst still being able to move about. The major disadvantage is that the soft, vulnerable parts of our bodies are exposed to attack. The human skeleton is designed to protect the back and deep in evolutionary history it is thought that we moved on all fours with our fronts close to the ground. Thus, when threatened, humans tend to use their arms as a defensive shield across the front of the body and this can be very noticeable in body language terms.

The person shown in Figure 8.8A is being frank, honest and open. As discussed above, they are not adopting any defensive postures and are displaying an attitude that says 'I have nothing to fear from you, so you need fear nothing from me'. Eye contact will be good.

An open posture with open hands as opposed to closed fists (Figure 8.8B) indicates a willingness to listen. The person is not in a threatening posture but neither are they being defensive – they are encouraging dialogue and will probably maintain good eye contact.

In the case of Figure 8.8C the arms are folded and in extreme cases the hands may grip the opposite arm. This person is on the defensive and by closing themselves down physically they are showing both anxiety and disapproval. There may well be eye contact but, because the person is on the defensive, it may be more of a staring rather than an interested nature.

Figure 8.8D shows the classic disinterested or even bored posture. Resting the head on a hand is a clear signal that the person has lost interest and this posture helps conceal any yawns. It is likely that eye contact is being lost.

Figure 8.8E shows another defensive posture that indicates not fear but rather a lacking in confidence. Note that only one arm is in the purely defensive position. Moving a finger across the face is usually a sign of uncertainty. Eye contact may well be lost as this posture frequently results in the eyes being focused on the ground.

Almost the opposite of Figure 8.8E, the very relaxed posture with open non-defensive arms shown in Figure 8.8F indicates that the person is very

Figure 8.8B   Interested and keen to listen.

Figure 8.8C   Defensive.

Figure 8.8D   Bored.

Figure 8.8E   Lacking confidence.

Figure 8.8F   Confident.

self-assured: 'let the world throw what it will at me, I can cope'; plenty of eye contact.

Figure 8.8G is at first glance not very different from Figure 8.8B until the position of the arms and hands and the facial gestures are considered. This is a case when two drawings may look alike but anybody confronted by these two postures would immediately see the difference, indeed they may be able to feel the tension. The arms in this case seem poised, ready to adopt a defensive position. It is likely that there would be little eye contact and a degree of fidgeting.

Figure 8.8H shows a classic interviewer posture. The person is interested, confident and friendly but exudes an air of authority; excellent eye contact and just a hint of defensiveness that seems to say 'I have nothing to fear but I would like to maintain some distance between us'.

In Figure 8.8I the arm will very likely be moving, and there will be good eye contact and a slight smile – this person is making a decision.

Figure 8.8G   Nervousness.

Figure 8.8H   Friendly authority.

Figure 8.81   Decision making.

Those are just a few examples of personal body language. It is difficult to indicate the subtle facial movements etc. in a drawing but if you observe those around you and, of course, your own posture, it soon becomes easy to recognise the clues and thus act accordingly. If a customer is aggressive, adopt a defensive posture; if the customer adopts a defensive posture, then maybe you are being too aggressive. A knowledge of body language is innate. Bullies become more aggressive on seeing a defensive posture; those who value relationships act in the opposite way and try to build up confidence.

Objects can sometimes form part of body language. At least one ex-Prime Minister of the UK was believed to use lighting a pipe to gain time when asked a difficult question. Keys, pens, almost anything people hold, can be played with and, if this happens, the person is displaying nervousness. Beware of such mannerisms.

Hands can be useful tools for illustrating points but it is considered rude and even threatening in most cultures to point directly at a person. It is worth remembering that innocuous gestures in one culture, an example being the thumbs-up sign used in Britain to mean 'OK', can be deeply offensive to some cultures. Personal space should always be maintained. Never get too near to a customer that they feel their space is being invaded – you will soon be able to tell because they will adopt very defensive body language – and also never let a customer come so near to you that you feel uncomfortable.

In Chapter 10, the Princess Cruises Service Credo is analysed and one part of that speaks of answering the telephone with a smile. It is known that the human voice sounds different depending on whether the speaker is smiling or not. 'Smile as you dial' is not just a vague, motivational concept; it is rooted in physiology. People can tell whether the person on the other end of the telephone is smiling or frowning and that can make the difference between a satisfied or a dissatisfied customer.

Extrinsic body language

The clothes people wear, their jewellery even their perfume/after-shave may provide useful clues. A person in business attire will expect to be treated in a business like manner – they may have 'power dressed' for the occasion. It is worth remembering that even the very wealthy may dress casually and that clothes give little indication of a customer's potential value to the organisation.

Staff should always be smart, wear the organisation dress/logo where this is supplied and need to look the part. Customers look at the image a person generates and match that to their perception of the organisation.

In order to study body language, take the time to 'people watch', a great deal about human behaviour can be learnt in this manner.

Organisational body language

As part of the work for their book *In Charge of Customer Satisfaction* (1997), Cartwright & Green introduced the term Organisational Body Language (OBL). They had discovered that it was not only individuals who signalled their true feelings through body language and the resulting dissonance covered earlier in the chapter with the spoken or written message. Organisations also exhibited a form of body language that showed their true feelings about the customer.

OBL relates to the whole atmosphere that an organisation creates. There are organisations that clearly welcome the customer with open arms and there are those that may claim to, although the message the customer actually receives seems to state that the customer is actually rather a nuisance who has to be tolerated!

It might seem strange that there would be any organisation that does not positively welcome its customers but they abound. A typical example is the organisation that has arranged its car park in such a manner that customers park at the end furthest from reception. The parking spaces next to the reception area are 'reserved for company vehicle'. A company mission statement claiming that customers come first will be of little consequence to a customer who has just walked from their car to reception in the pouring rain and passes the company parking spaces right next to the reception area.

An organisation that has thought about OBL will have put the customer first; customer parking should be for the convenience of the customer and not the organisation. Reception will be easy to find and provide somewhere for the customer to sit with newspapers and magazines; there may even be a pot of coffee!

When Cartwright & Green were developing the OBL concept they found many, many examples of the following – all messages that send out negative OBL signals to the customer and give the impression that the organisation thinks about itself first and the customer second:

- There is no car parking space reserved for a customer who is expected
- The customer arrives to find a locked door and no explanation (the door may

need to be locked for security reasons but the means of entry should be made clear to the customer)
- There is nobody in reception
- There are people there but they have their backs to the customer
- There is somebody there but they walk off as the customer approaches
- There are people there but they are interested in each other, not the customer
- There is a large queue and only one person is serving, while others are walking about doing other things
- There is loud music blaring
- There is someone at reception but nowhere to sit and wait
- Reception have never heard of the customer, even though he or she has an appointment
- No one answers the telephone
- The customer leaves a message on an answering machine and no one calls back
- No one answers the customer's letters
- The customer arrives in reception and no one has ever heard of the person that the customer has arranged to see!

The last point may seem far-fetched but often happens when a new member of staff joins the company and nobody remembers to tell reception and the switchboard. OBL proactive organisations ensure that staff changes are notified to reception and the switchboard in advance, with a note of the date and time they take effect.

Outstanding organisations will usually pay close attention to this organisational body language and ensure that the customer is not only told that they are important but that the customer's experience will bear this out. It is a known fact that a good initial feeling leads to a 'halo' effect, whereby subsequent events are judged from a positive point of view. A bad start to a customer/supplier relationship can lead to a 'horns' dilemma. For example, if the first few transactions between an organisation and a customer are good and there is then a less than satisfactory transaction, the customer is most likely to put the bad experience down to a temporary aberration – they have put a 'halo' around the organisation. If the first couple of transactions are less than satisfactory then, provided that the customer has not gone elsewhere, a subsequent good transaction may be thought of in terms of 'well they managed to get it right that time but will it last?' The customer is on the horns of the dilemma as to which transactions really represent the organisation and should they defect anyway in case subsequent transactions follow the initial pattern. Organisations have a perennial problem that one bad event can wipe out many good ones in an instant!

In OBL, as with all interactions between an organisation and its customers, the halo/horns effect will apply. If the organisation is open and welcoming, customers will assume that this reflects the rest of the organisation (halo). If it is the opposite (horns), then they will assume the worst.

Organisations need to be aware that there is a sound version of the halo/horns effect. If customers or potential customers overhear someone talking about an organisation, this is likely to influence them. If what they hear is good it will raise a positive image of the organisation, whilst bad comments are likely to have the opposite effect. Staff need to be aware that if they are wearing company identification, any comments that they make about their organisation may have a halo/horns effect on any listeners.

Another very important aspect of organisational body language is communicating very negatively. This is often manifested in the extremely negative notices that organisations display, for example:

- Don't lean on the counter
- No credit; No cheques; No refunds
- Broken counts as sold
- Do not touch
- No push chairs
- No food to be consumed on these premises
- No children
- No dogs
- No cameras
- Keep off
- No change telephones
- No bags beyond this point.

There may be very valid reasons for the above strictures but it is the manner in which they are communicated that sets the tone for the customer. Every one of the above would send a more positive message if the word 'please' was included. The message would appear much more positive if some form of explanation was given, for example:

- For security reasons, please leave your bags with the attendant
- Newly sown grass, please keep off
- Dangerous area, please keep children away etc.

As Cartwright & Green have pointed out, customers who meet a barrage of prohibition notices are likely to interpret this as 'Go away, you're too much trouble' and this is a very foolish message for any organisation to send to customers and potential customers.

Organisational Body Language can even include the sense of smell. It is possible to purchase essences to place in air-conditioning systems so that the smell of roasting coffee or baking bread can waft through a supermarket and trigger an autonomic reaction in the customers. Having a pot of coffee sending its aroma through a property is a well-known ploy of those trying to sell their house!

Organisational Body Language determines what an organisation actually thinks about its customers as opposed to what it says its policy is. There is no point in an organisation claiming to be family friendly if there are no facilities to change or feed babies and if the seats and counters are too high for children. The British Airports Authority (BAA) is amongst a growing number of organisations that provide baby facilities in the male as well as the female toilets. Many organisations that claim to be family friendly do not provide lowered urinals and toilets for children, a small point perhaps but one that goes a long way to showing how much the organisation has thought about its customer base.

The major aspects to organisational body language

In considering the impact of OBL on customers, organisations need to consider a series of factors, namely:

- Location/buildings
- Security
- Convenience
- Communications
- Ambience.

Each of these aspects has its own OBL implications which the organisation needs to consider, not just in respect of the external customer but also of its own internal customers and suppliers who form part of the value chain.

Chapter 11 of this book, which considers the development of a customer relations' strategy, provides a complete Organisational Body Language audit containing the questions that need to be asked when looking at this important aspect of an organisation's relationship with its customers.

Location/buildings

If an organisation is relocating, management and staff may be able to have a major say in the actual location and the design of buildings etc. In most cases there is little that can be done in the short term to change the location and the basic structure of the organisation's premises. There are however actions that can be taken relatively easily and cheaply to improve the 'look' of the location and buildings.

The actual visual image of an organisation is one of the things that sets the all-important first impressions. Basic items a customer may consider are:

- Do the organisation's premises appear in good repair?
- Are the premises internally and externally clean?
- Has the organisation considered the surrounding environment, for example are there flower beds, trees etc. and are they well tended?

Given that, as stated earlier human beings are highly visual in nature, the visual image of premises is very important. Buildings that incorporate curves may be more pleasing to the eye than purely rectangular ones. Modern architects are well aware of the need not only to consider the functional aspects of buildings but also the aesthetic ones.

Security

Customers need to feel safe. Many a business has lost trade not because its own premises were unattractive but because they were located in an environment that made the customer feel nervous.

There may be little that the organisation can do about its immediate environment, other than lobby the authorities for improved street lighting etc., but the organisation needs to bear in mind the importance of security as a motivator, as discussed in Chapter 2 where the work of Maslow was considered.

Whether it is an office block or a shopping centre, customers need to feel that their security has been considered. Proper lighting, security staff where appropriate, CCTV (Closed Circuit Television) cameras and secure car parking, all send out a message that the organisation cares about the security of its customers.

Convenience

How much has the organisation thought about the convenience of its facilities to the customer? Earlier in this section the example of an organisation that gave precedent to staff parking over the needs of customers was provided. Many of the convenience factors that are put in place for customers will also benefit staff; the important point is that they should have been put in with the customer as the priority.

Is there proper access for the disabled? Proper access does not force wheelchair users to use a back entrance or ramps that have never been checked for ease of operation by wheelchair users. It may seem strange that nobody would actually check that ramps are suitable but during research for this book, two such examples were found. Are the doors arranged in such a manner that a wheelchair user can open them? There are now regulations relating to new buildings that ensure adequate access for the disabled.

Do lifts (elevators) have controls that can be reached by a wheelchair user? There is nothing that shows a lack of OBL knowledge (and customer care) than seeing a wheelchair user have to use a stick to operate the lift buttons because they are situated too high. Modern lifts should also have Braille indicators and possibly voice systems that tell the visually impaired which floor has been reached.

Are the door arrangements easily operated by people carrying shopping or briefcases? Again, a little thought can show the customer that the organisation really does care. Organisations that neglect these simple ideas are actually telling many potential customers that they don't want them. Just because a person has a disability does not mean that they are not a potential customer, and there are very few potential customers who any organisation would want to deliberately disadvantage.

The public sector has been at the forefront of providing access and in recent years many commercial operations, especially in the retail and leisure sectors, have made themselves much more accessible.

Convenience also includes toilet facilities. Are these easy to find and, as mentioned above, are they suitable for children? How well are toilet facilities equipped and how 'comfortable' does the customer feel in using them? Whilst their has been a great improvement in such facilities in the UK in recent years, one really has to consider the 'restrooms' of the USA to see the standard to which such facilities can be provided.

Another important comfort feature is the provision of seating areas for customers. A recent trend in large stores (the Marks and Spencer store at Handforth Dean, near Manchester Airport, being an excellent example) is the provision of a waiting area near changing rooms. No longer should a person have to stand whilst his or her partner tries on clothes. Many motor vehicle franchises now provide a relaxing area with coffee and magazines where owners can wait whilst their vehicle is serviced, and there have been major improvements in doctors', dentists' and hospital waiting areas.

Airports have incorporated increasing numbers of food and retail outlets in a mutually beneficial manner; the customer has something to occupy them whilst awaiting their flight and valuable income can be earned. These developments now extend to many mainline railway stations, again providing a distraction for the customer and income for the retailers and the station operator.

The final feature of convenience is a consideration of opening and closing times. There is no doubt that the decision of UK building societies to remain open on Saturday mornings after the high street banks discontinued the practice led to an increase in custom. There is no point in being open at times when customers cannot avail themselves of a product or service and it is foolish to be closed when they can. The opening of 7–11 stores in the UK following the successful US model has led many other retail outlets to change their hours of opening. As shown in the previous chapter, 24-hour shopping is an electronic reality and may become an actual face-to-face activity in major cities. The introduction of Sunday trading in England (it has long been legal in Scotland) in the 1990s has led to supermarkets being open from early to late up to seven days per week. Experiments are underway to look at differential pricing where those who shop at the quieter times pay different prices from those who shop at peak times. Transport systems have long used such differentials, peak hour travel costing more in an attempt to spread out the customer load.

Organisations need to respond to their customers as to when they operate, rather than the other way around – modern customers are no longer prepared to accept restricted opening hours.

Communications

'If in doubt – ask' is no doubt a good maxim but one which many customers do not follow. Asking may make the customer appear foolish and thus it is not unusual to see customers wandering about and trying to find what they want without having to ask staff. It is therefore very important that signs are customer friendly.

As international travel increased after World War II it became necessary to devise symbols that could replace written signs. On the roads, the huge increase in Britons taking their cars to Continental Europe and other European drivers visiting the UK led to the introduction of standardised road signs. The old UK road sign for a school was a torch and flame, similar to that used for the opening of the Olympic Games – how many German or Danish drivers would have recognised that it was in fact the sign for a school?

It should now be possible to find any of the facilities in a foreign airport, ferry port or railway station without speaking the language. Everything from toilets, to food outlets, to car hire to ATMs (Automatic Teller Machines – cash dispensers) has an international symbol and is thus easier to find.

Nevertheless, customers do get lost and one reason is that those who know their way around usually erect signs. At one site visited during research for this book, a sign was found that was in fact wrong but nobody had noticed. Staff walked past it every day but, because they knew where they were going, nobody apparently noticed the error.

Signs need to be erected bearing in mind that those using them may have no idea of the layout of the facility, and thus simplicity and clarity need to be at the forefront of signage erection. It is also important to ensure that outside signs are erected in such a manner as not to be obscured by growing vegetation. One company erected a number of well-thought-out signs during the autumn, only to find that they became obscured in spring and summer by the beautifully placed plants!

Whenever signs are erected, somebody needs to 'walk the talk' to ensure that a customer with no previous knowledge can find their way around. There is an airport in Northern Germany where there are prominent signs throughout the one-way system that point to car hire return, prominent that is until the very last sign which indicates the entrance. That sign is quite small and is not on an overhead gantry but is affixed to a wall. If a driver misses the entry they have to drive all the way around the airport. That sign was affixed, the author is sure, by somebody who was intimately acquainted with the layout of the airport and never had to actually follow his or her own signs!

The layout of reception or help desk areas is important. They should be welcoming, not threatening. Ideally they should be immediately visible upon entry and manned all the time. There is nothing more off-putting than a vacant reception or help desk. Ideally reception desks should be separate from switchboards. This is not always practical but where they are together the receptionist (if there is only one, as is often the case) has to decide between dealing with the visitor or answering the telephone. Whatever he or she does, one person is going to feel either unwelcome or that their call is not being answered.

One of the roles of a receptionist is to welcome people and the role of the help desk staff is to help customers. This should start with a smile and a polite greeting. Excellent organisations will ensure that reception knows about those visitors who are expected and that name badges etc. are made up and readily to hand. Some organisations display a welcome notice for those who are expected – 'ACME plc welcome Mr Jones', others believe that this may be counterproductive as it lets others (possibly competitors) know who is visiting the organisation. If a customer's name is used, it must be spelt correctly.

Reception areas should always have somewhere for a customer to sit and, if possible, a collection of up-to-date magazines and the day's newspapers. Many organisations use the reception area as a shop window for their products and services; tastefully displayed these provide useful advertising.

If customers are likely to have children with them, are toys etc. provided? Many doctors', dentists' and hospital waiting areas now provide activities for children, and large stores and even car ferries have invested in children's play areas where children can be left in safety whilst their parents (as customers) can carry out their business unhindered.

Non-face-to-face communications

Another aspect of OBL is the way an organisation manages its verbal and written non-face-to-face communications. Is there a policy of answering the telephone within a certain number of rings? There is only a finite amount of time a customer will wait for the telephone to be answered. If answerphones and voicemail are used, how quickly does the company promise a reply? How are out-of-hours calls handled and responded to? As shown in the previous chapter, modern communications can greatly enhance the relationship between supplier and customer but only if used sensibly.

How quickly are letters answered and does the use of standard replies make the customer feel less of an individual? The written communications of an organisation help set the all-important image of that organisation. Much money is spent designing logos but it is important that the written word below the letter heading meets the customer's needs and answers his or her queries.

Ambience

Ambience is a word that relates to the overall impression gained by the customer. The ambience of an organisation is built up from all the above OBL factors. If the customer feels that he or she is important and that their comfort has been thought about in the way the organisation designs its operations, then they will be better disposed to the organisation. If they feel that they are of lower priority than the staff of the organisation, then they are likely to take their custom elsewhere. Organisational Body Language is a very important aspect of customer relations and more and more organisations are carrying out OBL audits to discover exactly how a customer is likely to perceive the organisation – a view that is sometimes at dissonance with the view of senior management.

Summary

This chapter has considered the relationship between organisations and their customers. The importance of effective communications was stressed, together with the importance of maintaining a relationship using umbilicals and mooring ropes. The concept of the relationship continuum and the way that the strength of the relationship can diminish down the value chain unless active steps are taken was discussed. Finally the importance of an understanding and working knowledge of both personal and organisational body language (OBL) was considered.

Terms introduced

- Aggression
- Assertiveness
- Body language

- CARE
- Communications
- Empathy
- Feedback
- Inverse square
- Language register
- Moments of Truth
- Mooring ropes
- Noise
- Organisational Body Language (OBL)
- Personal space
- Pheromones
- Power
- Relationship continuum
- Umbilicals

QUESTIONS

1. Describe a simple model of communication between an organisation and its customers, demonstrating how 'noise' can interfere with the message that either party may wish to put across.
2. Show how to distinguish between aggression and assertiveness, and describe how the latter can lead to a WIN/WIN situation and thus enhance supplier/customer relations.
3. Explain why body language may be a better descriptor of how a customer actually feels than the words etc. that they may use. Why is a knowledge of body language so important to those involved with customers?
4. Use the concept of Organisational Body Language (OBL) to show how the message an organisation sends out may actually be different from the one it believes it has communicated to its customers.

⊻ 9 Public relations

Public relations, publicity and advertising – Public relations and customer relations – The publics served by an organisation and their differing needs – Product recalls – Media relations – LICAL – Advertising – Corporate identity

Three terms that are often confused are Public Relations, Publicity and Advertising. This chapter considers public relations in some detail and advertising in somewhat less detail as it is not really part of customer relations *per se.*

Publicity is the result of actions by or to the organisation and is managed through the public relations' process. Publicity can be active, where there is a deliberate attempt to put over a message or image about products, services or the organisation, or passive, where something happens that is outwith the control of the organisation but an organisational response is required.

Advertising could be classed as a type of active publicity although it is usually considered as a separate subject.

The Institute of Public Relations quoted in Brassington & Pettitt (1997) define public relations as:

'The deliberate, planned and sustained effort to institute and maintain mutual understanding between an organisation and its publics'

The use of the plural form for publics is important. Marston (1979) states that:

'a public is any group, with some common characteristic, with which an organisation needs to communicate'

There are, therefore, a number of publics with whom any organisation needs to communicate, including:

- customers
- suppliers
- shareholders in the private sector
- the electorate for the public sector
- local and national government
- competitors (where there are matters of mutual concern)
- the media
- its own employees
- pressure groups
- professional and trade bodies.

Each of these groups will require different information to be used for different purposes. The Institute of Public Relations definition is rather wide and could be deemed to include advertising and related activities. It is proposed therefore to use the following definition of public relations as it relates to this book:

> **Whereas advertising is related to the raising of interest in products or services, public relations is concerned with presenting a positive image of the organisation to its various publics in response to the needs of those publics**

Thus this chapter will only be concerned with the advertising function of organisations where that function supports an overall message relating to the image of the company. As Jefkins (1980) has pointed out, public relations embraces everyone and everything, whereas advertising is limited to special buying and selling tasks. Public relations may use advertising to achieve its aim but is itself neither a form of nor a part of advertising.

Public relations is also not publicity (Jefkins, 1980). Publicity is the result of something that has happened, public relations is the response to that publicity which may in turn generate more publicity. Let us take a practical example: a holiday company has a number of clients on a Caribbean holiday. Unfortunately their hotel is badly damaged by fire. This will generate PUBLICITY, which may be negative, and the company will be asked by the media to comment. Good PUBLIC RELATIONS (perhaps showing how the company has relocated their customers) will generate positive PUBLICITY and this may be used in future ADVERTISING ('We will look after you whatever happens etc.'). Poor PUBLIC RELATIONS ('Customers should note that their contract with us excludes problems relating to Acts of God etc.') will produce further negative PUBLICITY.

As was shown in Chapter 5, complaints can be used positively and negative publicity can be transformed into positive publicity by good public relations. Much has been said about so called 'spin doctors' in recent years, normally referring to those in the political arena. One of the case studies in Chapter 10 relates to a politician, who provides a product/service just like any other organisation. 'Spinning' in this regard is the putting forward of a positive message about something that may be viewed in a negative manner in the first instance.

Public relations and customer relations

This whole book is concerned with customer relations. In order to remove any possible confusion, in the context of this chapter, public relations is the process used when communicating to whole sections of the customer base rather than an individual customer. The relationship with an individual customer will differ from customer to customer according to their various needs and wants. The public relations' process will be addressed to groups of customers.

In a problem situation, for example a batch of faulty products, a two-pronged process will be required from the organisation. Firstly there will need to be individual contact with dissatisfied customers to solve their individual problems, but there will also need to be a public relations' initiative to reassure not only existing customers but also potential ones that the organisation is able to cope with and rectify such problems.

The needs of the various publics

Each group that has a relationship with the organisation will have different needs, as discussed below. A key component of an effective public relations' strategy is to cover as many of the groups as possible and to avoid providing conflicting messages to different groups.

Customers

The individual nature of dealing with customers has been mentioned above. There will be times, as in the example given above, when the organisation needs to 'speak' to its whole customer base. One such occasion is when there needs to be a product recall.

Product recall

It is especially important to make urgent contact with customers when a fault has been found in a product and which requires immediate rectification. If the organisation has a list of purchasers then they can be contacted directly, but it must be remembered that the purchaser is not always the end user of a product so that additional steps also need to be taken. Notices can be placed in the various outlets that stock the product and notices can be placed in the appropriate media, such as newspapers, magazines and trade journals. Such notices need to do two things. They must provide clear and concise details of how the fault is to be rectified and they must give information about the nature of the fault. If the item must not be used, then this must be clearly stated. It is also possible to use such a notice to reassure the customer. Statements such as 'in a small number of instances' etc. will help achieve reassurance. As product liability has become very important (see Chapter 6), organisations are tending to veer to the side of caution in issuing recalls. Obviously any recall is likely to generate bad publicity but, as discussed earlier, dealing with the problem quickly and effectively can generate good publicity. It is important that the need for a recall should, ideally, come from the organisation and not the media. There have been a number of cases where faults have been highlighted by consumer organisations and television programmes, forcing the manufacturer to issue a recall. Good public relations should be proactive rather than in this case reactive.

Customer newsletter

One of the advantages of loyalty schemes, as described in Chapter 4, is the information they provide about both the customer base and individual customers. This can allow an organisation to write to its customers on a regular basis. British Telecom sends out a regular newsletter to customers, as do many of the supermarkets and utility companies. The organisation can keep its customers informed about products and services and make the customer feel part of the enterprise. When P&O Cruises announced the building of their ship *Aurora*, all members of the POSH Club (the club for repeat cruisers) received regular details of the new ship in the POSH Club newsletter together with an advanced opportunity to register for the maiden voyage.

The UK firm of Cotton Traders specialising in leisure wear and named after the Rugby star, Fran Cotton, use their database not only to send out a regular catalogue but also to write to individuals who have not made a purchase for some time, asking them if there has been a problem with their previous purchases.

Customer events

The launch of a new product or service can be an ideal method of gaining extra personal contact with customers. This is a technique that has been used successfully by a number of vehicle dealerships. Examples of a new model are put on show and past (and any identified potential) customers are invited for a drink and a buffet. Sales staff can then circulate and talk to customers on a more informal basis than normal. Even if there are no immediate sales, the exercise provides a good public relations' exercise and shows that the organisation is trying to get close to its customers.

Customer comments

Comments from customers, especially those that are unsolicited, can provide a useful public relations' opportunity. Such comments, which often appear in brochures etc., should always be available for inspection and the permission of the comment maker must be sought before their name is used.

Suppliers

The importance of the value chain has been discussed in a number of parts of this book. The relationship between suppliers and an organisation is both delicate and dynamic. Suppliers will operate to their own values and culture but if the organisation they are supplying is a large one, then that organisation may be able to insist on its values being applied within the supplier. There may well be issues, especially those of product liability, that concern a number of members of the value chain. Eddy *et al.* (1976) have shown how, in the case of the 1972 Paris DC10 air disaster, the public relations' exercise involved not only Douglas as the main builder of the aircraft but also Convair, who built the fuselage and the defectively designed rear door (to the specification, it must be said, laid down by Douglas), and Turkish Airlines, the operator of the aircraft. Indeed had the engines been considered to be a contributory factor in the crash, then General Electric would also have been involved. In this case the public relations' exercise was not conducted well, with members of the value chain actually suing other members. The case does serve to illustrate the dependency on mutually supporting public relations for the various members of the value chain. In Chapter 6 the point was made that the contractual relation is between the customer and the vendor.

Imagine a case where the failure of a product could be referred back to the manufacturer of an individual component.

Shareholders in the private sector/the electorate for the public sector

The UK Labour government, elected in 1997, brought the word 'stakeholders' into common use. Stakeholders are those who have an interest in the function and performance of an organisation. As such the term encompasses customers, suppliers, employees and crucially those who have a financial stake in the organisation. In the private sector these are the shareholders, in the public sector the whole of the electorate have a financial interest in the organisation.

In the 1980s and 1990s the UK Conservative government began a series of privatisation exercises, taking a large number of publicly owned enterprises into the private sector. The aim was to produce a shareholding democracy with those sections of the public who had never previously owned shares buying into these enterprises. British Airways, British Gas, the electricity generators and British Telecom were amongst the larger enterprises privatised.

These new private sector organisations had very large numbers of shareholders indeed, ranging from financial institutions down to individuals holding just a hundred shares.

Private sector organisations need to communicate to their shareholders. They are compelled to produce an annual balance sheet showing the financial position of the enterprise and it has proved a good public relations' exercise to provide easy-to-read summaries of the yearly accounts for those who had never previously had to read a balance sheet. The early annual general meetings of such organisations occasionally erupted in uproar as small shareholders attempted to make points. As time has gone on, the senior management of these companies have demonstrated a growing awareness that small shareholders have different needs from those who have traditionally held large numbers of shares. In the case of many of the privatised enterprises, shareholders are also customers and this can provide an interesting view of the Porter model discussed in Chapter 3 with regard to bargaining power. As a customer, one wants the lowest price possible; as a shareholder, higher prices may well mean higher dividends!

In addition to the annual report and general meeting there are two other methods used by private sector companies to communicate with their shareholders.

Firstly, large companies make considerable use of the media and often employ their own public relations' consultants. Any stories about the company are likely to be seen by their shareholders and they will always want to present the company in the best light. The stock market can be very volatile and any story that diminishes confidence in a company may lead to shareholders selling stock, and it is normally the largest shareholders who do so first. It is interesting to note that the share price of a company has little to do with its performance and more to do with how the stock market values it. When one reads that a vast sum has been wiped off the share price of a company it does not mean that the company is any worse off than it was the day before. Stock markets can collapse for reasons that have nothing to do with the performance of an individual company. They operate in the manner discussed when looking at value in Chapter 3. The share price is an indication of how investors value the company. Shareholders of course wish the share price to remain high, as they will want to obtain maximum income if they sell.

Secondly, many companies also offer shareholders discounts on products and services. This is a deliberate bid to make the shareholder into a customer. This approach has a certain degree of commonality with the loyalty schemes covered in Chapter 4.

In the public sector there has been a greater emphasis on public relations in recent years. State schools have been compelled to produce an annual report and hold an annual meeting for parents since 1986, hospitals are required to produce reports on their work, and local councils have become much more adept at providing information to council tax payers. Demands for council tax now come with an explanation of how the money is allocated and many councils hold public meetings on planning and budgetary issues to ensure that the electorate can gain information if they so wish.

As regards the payment of council tax, the electorate are in a hostage (see Chapter 4) situation, but whilst they cannot legally withhold money, they can 'spend' their vote.

The UK Labour government elected in 1997 decided to issue a public booklet on how well it was fulfilling its promises, although it came in for considerable criticism for the employment of so-called 'spin doctors' who were employed to put a positive spin on policies and actions.

A phenomenon that has been seen regularly since World War II has been the public relations' aspect to armed conflicts. In 1939 the British Prime Minister, Neville Chamberlain, actually wanted to close down BBC Radio for the duration of the conflict. Today, news is broadcast directly from the front line and governments employ spokespersons to brief the press and through them the general public. Even as late as 1992 the UK government was criticised for the handling of the Falkland's conflict with Argentina in respect of the way it handled the public relations' aspects of the conflict, especially when dealing with operational matters and the tragic loss of personnel, ships and aircraft, the manner in which the sinking of the destroyer *HMS Sheffield* was reported being considered particularly inept (Hastings & Jenkins, 1983).

As more and more democracies enact Freedom of Information legislation, the role of the public relations' staff in those organisations will become increasingly important and challenging. It might, of course, be argued that every election campaign is in fact a major exercise in public relations although, given the low turnout in some recent UK elections, it may well be that the parties have not really succeeded in putting their message across.

Local and national government

The previous section considered the need for local and national government to undertake public relations for themselves. However, a whole range of organisations consider that one of their publics (as defined earlier) is the local, regional, national or even supra-national (e.g. the European Union) government. Individual organisations, trade bodies and professional associations lobby politicians and employ specialist public relations' consultants (known as lobbyists) to put forward their views. Many sponsor politicians and in the UK it is a requirement for politicians to register any such interests. Smaller organisations that cannot afford to employ lobbyists may be able to lobby through trade bodies, and such bodies are often invited to provide the trade or sector viewpoint to legislative procedures.

Competitors

Whilst it might sound strange that a competitor can be regarded as a stakeholder, within any sector of business there will be matters of mutual concern. For instance, if the government is bringing forward legislation on a matter that has implications for all the players in a particular market there may be an advantage in a common approach. In these cases a trade body may handle the public relations' aspects in order that there is a co-ordinated response. Whilst many organisations may be fiercely competitive, they may also work collaboratively on matters of safety. This is only common sense as a lack of confidence in one player in a market may cause a lack of confidence in that sector of the marketplace in general.

Employees

Employees have a vital, if often informal, role in public relations. Chapter 8 introduced the concept of Organisational Body Language (OBL) and covered the important function employees carry out in promoting the image of an organisation. It is often forgotten that, for many retail and public utility companies, employees are also customers, often receiving discounts. The image and the message that an employee sends about his or her company can be very important. Nothing is more likely to dent confidence in a product, service or organisation than an employee talking about it in a derogatory manner. One of Cartwright & Green's (1997) Golden Rules of Customer Care is 'if you don't believe, how can you expect others to?', i.e. if the employee has lost confidence, do not be surprised if the customers also lose confidence. It is vital, therefore, that the organisation makes sure that employees know what is happening and to that extent they become the recipients of internal public relations. Brassington & Pettitt (1997) stress the importance of such internal PR.

Pressure groups

The final half of the 20th Century saw a growth in the number of what became known as Single Issue Pressure Groups. This was not a new phenomenon, the anti-slavery movement of the 19th Century and the suffragettes of the first two decades of the 20th Century are good examples. Such pressure groups can be very focused and may be local, national or even international. They normally campaign on a single issue which allows them to put over a very simple message:

NO BYPASS, BAN HUNTING WITH HOUNDS are examples, as are those that seek redress or justice for a particular individual, the yellow ribbon campaign for the UK au pair Louise Woodward in 1997–98 after she was convicted of manslaughter in the USA being an example of a single issue campaign that was international in nature.

Such groups are often very effective in their own public relations but are sometimes reluctant to listen to the message put out by other organisations. Any issue always has at least two sides and there is very often a public relations' 'war' going on alongside the real issue as each party attempts to rally public support to its point of view. In Chapter 5 the acronym LICAL was introduced. The L stands for lying and whilst organisations should never lie, one can be sure that a single issue pressure group will uncover any untruths and then use the fact against the offending organisation. Such single issue groups are usually very tenacious and highly committed and will probe any and all messages put out by their opponents.

Professional and trade bodies

In terms of public relations, professional and trade bodies often act as a clearing house and co-ordinating centre for their members. By their very nature they are able to speak with a greater degree of authority than individuals or small organisations. They are also able to co-ordinate a response to any issue across a range of organisations. To do this, of course, they relay on receiving accurate, up-to-date information from their members. Membership of such a body brings many benefits to an organisation but if the organisation is consistently at fault there is the possibility of it being expelled, and it is likely that the professional/trade body will be able to use public relations more effectively than the organisation. The organisation will have to explain its expulsion whilst the professional/trade body can use it to show how concerned they are about maintaining standards.

The media

The media has been left until last, not because it is unimportant but because it encompasses much of what has gone before. The power of the press (the Fourth Estate), the television and radio companies and, increasingly, the INTERNET cannot be overestimated.

Much of the information people receive comes via the media and, however pure that information was, it is in some way transformed. The media have their own agendas and deal with stories accordingly.

Public relations and the media may be either proactive or reactive. It is proactive if the organisation initiates the story, it is reactive when the media initiate and then approach the organisation.

Newspapers and journals

Just as there are typologies of organisations there are also typologies of newspapers and journals. Newspapers fall into the following categories:

- Broadsheet nationals – daily, e.g. *The Times*
- Tabloid nationals – daily, e.g. *The Mirror*
- Broadsheet – Sunday, e.g. *The Observer*
- Tabloid – Sunday, e.g. *News of the World*
- Regional dailies, e.g. *Manchester Evening News*
- Regional weekly or bi-weekly, e.g. *Perth Advertiser*
- Local weeklies, e.g. *Strathearn Herald*
- Specialist dailies, e.g. *Financial Times/Racing Post*
- Specialist weeklies, e.g. *New Musical Express.*

Each type of newspaper has a particular type of reader. As a humorous comment in the book *Yes Minister* by Lynn & Jay (1987), and also a successful TV sitcom, remarks:

> '*The Times* is read by the people who run the country, the *Daily Mirror* is read by the people who think they run the country. *The Guardian* is read by people who think they ought to run the country etc.'

This is a very true, if humorous method of looking at the newspaper coverage. Suppliers of goods and services are normally fairly adept at knowing which newspapers are likely to be read by a particular target audience. Many of the questionnaires on lifestyles or even at the end of package holidays ask which newspapers the respondent reads. This is so that advertising, which is very expensive, can be properly targeted. It is unlikely that an expensive Mercedes car will be advertised in *The Mirror* but it may well feature in *The Times*.

Whilst all of the daily newspapers may carry the same story, the manner with which it will be treated varies according to the readership and the views of the newspaper. Newspapers often espouse a particular political viewpoint or may take up a campaigning stance on an issue, especially if that is likely to increase sales. The newspaper industry is an example of where the customer accumulator introduced in Chapter 1 is especially relevant; a reader gained is normally a reader lost to the main competitor.

Regional and local newspapers tend to concentrate on a narrower front but like the nationals they may well take up particular issues. There are also specialist newspapers covering a range of subjects from finance to music. The essential difference between newspapers and magazines lies in the word 'news'. Newspapers deal with the more ephemeral issues; a story that is page one today may be on page three tomorrow and forgotten by the end of the week. The articles in magazines usually have a longer shelf-life. All newspapers employ a considerable number of journalists and researchers. If they believe that there is a story then they will approach the organisation concerned, normally through the press officer or the public relations' department. Dealing with the press is a specialised skill and best left to the experts. A throw-away line by a member of staff could be a banner headline in a national paper.

Magazines tend to fall into two groups:

- special interest
- general interest.

Special interest magazines, e.g. *Autocar* and *Railway Modeller*, are targeted at particular interest groups whilst the general interest publications, e.g. *Woman*, *Esquire* etc., are designed to appeal to a wide range of readership, often gender specific.

TV and radio

It is salutary to consider that mass ownership of televisions did not commence until after World War II and that since then there has been such growth that few homes in developed countries are without at least one TV set and many have additional sets. Radio was developed earlier, in the 1920s, and by 1939 there was a mass market for radio sets. TV and radio are able to react much more quickly to news items than newspapers, as the latter have to await the printing of the next edition whereas TV and radio can break into a programme. Where newspapers have an advantage is in the depth of analysis they can provide and, as with all written material, there is the ability to scan pages and return to items of interest. TV can now accommodate teletext and there are large numbers of text pages available to the viewer.

Radio does not have this advantage but is able to produce analytical programmes related to the news with interviews of relevant personalities. Up to the 1970s an advantage that radio had over TV was the ease of outside broadcasting, with radio just needing a car as against the outside broadcast van required for television. The development of video cameras of increasing sophistication has led to the introduction of Electronic News Gathering (ENG) using lightweight cameras, allowing TV crews to gather news in more remote areas and to broadcast it back to base. Jefkins (1980) considers that radio has four special characteristics that should guarantee its survival alongside TV:

- the attractiveness of the human voice regardless of the appearance of the presenter who is, of course, not seen
- the speed with which material can be produced and the immediacy of interactive programmes such as 'phone ins'
- the low cost of personal radios
- the ability to broadcast in many different languages, thus allowing ethnic groups access to news etc. in their own languages.

To these four above should be added a fifth:

- the ability to listen to the radio whilst driving.

Television has become an important part of people's lives. There has been a growth in consumer related programmes where organisations have had their products and services put under the public spotlight, often unfavourably. In the late 1990s, organisations began to fight back. The holiday industry has complained that such programmes are actively seeking complainants and are thus a magnet for attention seekers who may have no real complaint but just wish to appear on television. It cannot be doubted however that programmes such as *That's Life* and *Watchdog* etc. have put companies on their mettle as regards the treatment of their customers.

How the media obtain their stories

Given the power of the press, it is useful to consider how they obtain their stories. There are eleven basic methods used by both newspapers, journals, TV and radio:

Reporters

Reporters are employed directly by the newspaper and may be specialists, e.g. sports, crime, science etc., or general reporters, which is the way most specialists start. The role of the reporter is to seek out information and, as such, they need to have excellent people skills as they are required to probe into stories and may have to interview people on sensitive or distressing issues.

Special correspondents

Employed by newspapers to provide in-depth coverage of their specialist subject, the special correspondent often has a world-wide brief. War correspondents are often attached to military forces. Of particular relevance to this book are those special correspondents who cover particular commercial sectors. A reporter may not have the in-depth knowledge of the special correspondent and, if contacted by the latter, it is as well to be aware that the correspondent has probably gained a considerable depth of knowledge about the subject.

Foreign correspondents

The larger newspapers station foreign correspondents in strategic locations abroad. An alternative to employing one's own staff is to make an arrangement with a local newspaper for the use of one of their staff (see stringers, below)

Stringers

Smaller newspapers cannot afford to have reporters all over a country and abroad and will use the services of a local journalist who will usually be employed by a local newspaper. One of the roles of a stringer is to feed local stories to the national press.

Feature writers

Newspapers employ feature writers to produce articles rather than news stories. Like special correspondents, they have a considerable depth of knowledge about their specialist field. They are often used to provide background material for news stories.

Contributors

Outside writers who are experts in their field may be commissioned to produce articles for the press. The newspaper usually approaches them as an expert and asks for so many words on a given topic, the contribution then being edited in-house.

Syndication and picture libraries

If a newspaper or magazine gains a 'scoop' they may sell the material, especially pictures, to other newspapers and magazines. Picture libraries collect photographs from a huge range of sources and then make them available to newspapers and magazines. Such libraries are often used to obtain pictures to accompany articles.

Wire and news services

Reuters, Associated Press etc. are well known companies which collect news items from whatever sources they can and then put these out to newspapers and magazines who subscribe to the service. The growth in INTERNET usage has also led to INTERNET news channels that provide up-to-the-minute news coverage, which is available to the public.

PR departments

Large organisations, trade bodies and governments usually have their own public relations' department who will respond to press enquiries, set up interviews and press conferences, supply background material and issue press releases. The PR officer needs to maintain active communications with the press whilst at the same time protecting the organisation when necessary.

The public

Although often forgotten in the texts on the subject, the public can be a valuable source of news items. Local groups can and do issue press statements and individuals often contact the press to inform them of a news event. Not all such events are actually newsworthy but occasionally a member of the public with a camera takes a picture that is of interest to the press, sometimes world-wide. Dissatisfied customers may use the press as a means to gain redress and many newspapers, magazines, television and radio stations have consumer affairs columns or programmes where the public are encouraged to come forward with 'horror' stories. Holidays companies seem to suffer considerable bad exposure in this way.

Complaints against the media

Complaints against the media tend to fall into three categories:

- complaints about accuracy
- complaints about intrusion
- complaints about bias.

Accuracy

Contrary to popular belief, reporters are very concerned about the accuracy of their stories and for good reason. The most reliable defence against a libel charge is the truth! In 1999 Jonathan Aitkin, who had been a government minister in the 1992–97 Conservative government, sued a UK newspaper for making a libellous statement about him. Not only was the statement proved to be true but the case bankrupted Mr Aitkin and led to him being given a prison sentence for perjury. Had the statement been false then he could well have received a considerable sum in damages.

Inaccuracies should always be pointed out to the publisher of the story. Court action is rare as even if the publisher has printed in error, few organisations wish for the publicity of a court case that will keep the issue in the public domain for some considerable time. Minor inaccuracies are normally corrected by a statement in the newspaper, magazine or by the TV/radio company. It must be said, however, that the corrections usually appear in smaller print than the original story.

Intrusion

There is a delicate balance between the privacy of the individual and the right of the public to have access to information. There have been a number of high profile instances of personalities complaining of undue intrusion into their lives, not least of which have been the complaints by the British Royal Family. The usual defence given by the media is 'public interest'. Whilst the UK had not enacted privacy legislation by 1999, there was a groundswell building in favour of such legislation. It is unlikely, however, that it will apply to organisations as opposed to individuals. Journalists, whilst having a great deal of influence are, of course, covered by laws of trespass etc. and may not commit offences in order to gain information.

Bias

Organisations and groups often complain about media bias. In many cases this is just because the media have not presented the organisation's view in the manner that the organisation would prefer. In recent years the BBC has been accused of bias against nearly every political party. If all the parties are complaining then perhaps the Corporation's claim that it is neutral is perfectly logical.

In a democracy there is theoretically freedom of the press. In practice, all governments reserve the right to suppress stories on the grounds of national interest and security. Such powers are normally used sparingly by democratic regimes. Non-democratic regimes control the media to a much higher degree.

The Press Complaints and the Broadcasting Standards Council are able to adjudicate on complaints made against the media, although they are only able to make reports. Further action is left to the complainant.

Marketing and corporate PR

It is possible to make a distinction between marketing public relations and corporate public relations. The former normally constitutes part of the wider promotion of the organisation and its products/services. As such, it is a form of active public relations in that it will be generated internally. Corporate public relations is more concerned with the image of the organisation as a whole and may well be a defensive reaction to an externally generated issue.

Marketing public relations is capable of being planned well in advance and may well form part of an advertising campaign. Sponsorship (see later) can be considered a form of marketing PR. Whilst corporate PR can be planned, as in the case of a major development, it also needs to contain contingency plans to cope with the unexpected. 'Be prepared' is not only a suitable motto for the S movement; it applies as much to PR. There is nothing more damaging to an organisation than a spokesperson who has been poorly briefed.

LICAL

In Chapter 5 the acronym LICAL – Lying, Ignorance, Complacency, Arrogance and Lethargy (Cartwright & Green, 1997) – was introduced. It was pointed out in Chapter 5 that these are the five worst things that any organisation can do to its customers. They are certainly the things that should never, ever happen in public relations.

In the developed world, with its enhanced communications and media systems, it is very difficult to keep anything secret. A free press is particularly adept at finding out the truth, especially if they believe that a cover up is going on. The *Washington Post* journalists', Bernstein & Woodward (1994), uncovering of the Watergate conspiracy in the USA caused the resignation of President Nixon – a classic example of the power of the media. As the story unfolds it can be seen that the White House staff committed every one of the LICAL sins, but to no avail as the full story was eventually revealed.

Techniques for public relations

Public relations does not just happen. Regardless of whether the issue requires reactive or proactive PR, there are a number of methods open to an organisation to put their message across, as detailed below:

Press releases

Speed may well be of the essence in ensuring that an organisation is able to put forward the message it wishes to. Whether it is response to an externally driven event or an internal one that the organisation wishes the public and the media to know about, a press release can be a very useful tool. A typical press release will be succinct, covering the main part of the issue only and not cluttered up by detail, and will state clearly who to approach for any additional information. The PR departments of larger organisations will have a list of media outlets that press releases should be sent to, and modern facsimile machines and email (see Chapter 7) can ensure that this is carried out in an effective and speedy manner. It is, of course, important that the contact name on a press release is thoroughly briefed, as a lack of knowledge when contacted could lead to a public relations' disaster.

If an organisation knows that there is likely to be public and media interest in one of its activities, products or services, it is best to be proactive and issue a press release prior to the media contacting the organisation.

Press conferences

Major issues often result in the need for the organisation to call the media together for a press conference. The advantage is that the organisation can make a statement once, rather than dealing with individuals from the media, and there is the option of allowing questions. The disadvantage is that the person or persons delivering the press conference cannot predict the nature, tone and direction of the questions. Again, thorough briefing is required.

Publicity stunts

Most people are well aware of 'stunts' that are arranged to promote a particular product or service. In many ways this is a form of advertising but, not being as controlled as commercial advertising, there is always the danger that the stunt can go wrong and thus produce the wrong image. If a publicity stunt is successful, it carries with it more credibility than advertising because the customers are well aware that advertising is both paid for and controlled.

Sponsorship

Sponsorship has become a major part of commercial operations. Sponsorship is based on the concept of association. An organisation that is linked to a successful football team comes to be associated with that success. Whilst there is a degree of altruism in sponsorship, the main aim of a sponsor is to ensure that their name is put before the public and thus reaches potential customers. As with publicity stunts, as mentioned above, there is always a danger of being associated with failure and sponsors do remove their sponsorship if they feel that they are receiving neither enough exposure or the wrong form of exposure. Sponsorship can be used as a subtle means of targeting customers in that the sponsor can choose events and activities that are likely to be enjoyed by their own particular customer base. There are huge ranges of sponsored activities from football to classical music. There is even sponsorship in academia with organisations sponsoring professorships and research positions within colleges and universities. The important requisite of successful sponsorship is that the organisation's name is always spoken or written in association with the event or activity. For a long time in the USA, and more recently in the UK, there has been the sponsorship of popular television programmes by commercial organisations. Whether viewers actually link *Coronation Street* (probably the most successful

UK TV soap opera) with its sponsor is a mute point but the sponsor obviously feels that it is money well spent. The term 'soap opera' derives from the fact that it was US soap manufacturers who first sponsored that particular form of serialised drama.

Trade shows etc.

Trade shows, county shows, military tattoos etc. all present an opportunity for organisations to meet their publics. Retailers and others in the value chain are an important public, and trade shows give an opportunity for organisations to meet them and to provide corporate hospitality. For many years banks have provided a mobile unit at major events. This provides a good public relations' opportunity even if it is actually a loss-making activity for the bank.

Charities

Many commercial organisations support named charities. Whilst there may be an altruistic element to charitable donations, it is also true that such donations can offer tax advantages and help to show the caring nature of the organisation.

Advertising

One could debate the question of where does public relations end and advertising begin for a long time. This section does not seek to be a treatise on advertising but to show how advertising can link to customer relations. Modern advertising is expensive and is thus carefully targeted. Advertising fits into the AIDA (Attention, Interest, Desire, Action) model introduced in Chapter 2. By using such devices as clever story lines, brash colours, romance, evocative music and images and even warnings etc., the advertiser seeks to attract the attention of a potential customer, interest them and create a desire for the product or service. The hope is that they will action this desire or, in the case of something that the organisation wants to prevent, e.g. smoking, curb the desire. There has been much debate about smoking, as at one time tobacco companies were advertising their brands whilst the health authorities were advertising for smokers to quit the habit. In the UK there are now considerable and growing restrictions on any form of tobacco advertising.

In addition to gaining new customers, the organisation will wish to use its advertising monies to remind existing customers of its products and services. As shown in Chapter 6, there are legal requirements relating to the truthfulness of advertising. From a customer relations' point of view, it is important that advertising does not have a negative effect on the customer. A famous cigarette advert that showed a cigarette smoking man alone on a bridge late at night with the caption 'You're never alone with a Strand (the brand name)' failed because consumers associated the cigarette with being lonely, and who wants to admit that!

A further danger is that promoting a brand also promotes the generic product. A successful coffee advertisement will stimulate sales for that brand but it may also stimulate the whole coffee market and thus provide increased sales for the competition.

It is important that advertisements do not mislead. Regardless of the legal consequences, disappointed customers are likely to become ex-customers. The lying part of LICAL can have very dramatic consequences for organisations.

Corporate identity

In Chapter 3 the importance of product branding was discussed. Corporate image is also a form of brand and is very important in respect of customer relations. A corporate image that is perceived by the customer to be customer centred and focused will aid customer relations. The opposite is, of course, also true.

Much public relations' activity is directed at showing the corporate body in a good light. There may well be problems with an individual product but it is important to the organisation that the problems are perceived as isolated to that product and not related to the organisation in general.

Summary

This chapter has examined the relationship of an organisation with its various publics and the need to ensure effective communication with them. The nature and role of the media were discussed, as was the difference between publicity and advertising. The importance of understanding the LICAL model was raised, together with the need to ensure a good corporate identity.

Terms introduced

- Advertising
- Corporate image
- Media
- Press releases
- Press statements
- Pressure groups
- Product recall
- Professional and trade bodies
- Public relations
- Publicity
- Publicity stunts
- Publics
- Stakeholders
- Trade shows

QUESTIONS

1. How would you define the difference between public relations and advertising? How do the differences manifest themselves through organisational behaviour?
2. Explain the importance of LICAL to the public relations' function of an organisation. What effects can a failure to avoid the LICAL terms have on potential and existing customers?
3. What do you understand by the term 'publics'? Using an organisation you are familiar with, explain its relationships with each of its publics.

☑ 10 Customer relations in action

Hal Malquardt (USA) – Scottish Prison Service (UK) – Princess Cruises (UK/USA) – Highland Distillers' Glenturret Distillery (UK) – Caledonian Cinemas (UK) – Roseanna Cunningham MP, MSP (UK)

Throughout this book there have been references to various organisations. This chapter provides details of the customer relations employed by a variety of organisations, large and small, in the UK and the USA, and in the public and the private sectors.

Hal Malquardt (USA)

The entertainment industry, especially the performing arts, has not received a great deal of attention by researchers into customer relations. In many ways this is a shame as the industry provides very speedy and demonstrable feedback between the supplier (the artiste) and the customer (the audience).

Live entertainment can be anything from a very intimate cabaret through to a huge rock concert. The former is much harder for the artiste as the customer is much closer and thus the body language cues will be much stronger. It is also much harder not to interact with a small, discrete group than with a huge audience.

Hal Malquardt is a larger-than-life USA-based comedy magician who is regularly booked to entertain on cruise ships catering for the US market. From the age of 19 when he worked as a classical magician he has developed an act, not dissimilar to that of the legendary UK-based Tommy Cooper, and sees himself as an entertainer first and a magician second.

Hal's product is a paradoxical one to sell. On one hand, rationality tells us that there is a logical explanation to all his illusions; on the other, we would, perhaps, all like to believe in magic.

Part of the true magic of Hal's act is that he has fun on stage himself. The problem with all entertainers in the cruise industry is that it is difficult to get away from the audience as they are living and eating on the same ship, and thus an entertainer is almost always on stage unless they are in their cabin. It is not unusual for Hal to be stopped on deck or in a bar and told a joke 'that would be great for your act' or asked how an illusion was carried out.

One thing that Hal has learnt, and it is something a lot of people find difficulty with, is how to take a compliment. Whilst on a cruise ship and watching a show the customers may be termed an audience, but they are still customers all the same.

On many of the cruises, Hal will have an audience that is predominantly from the USA, but more and more ships are carrying significant numbers of UK and Canadian citizens and the material that Hal uses needs to be relevant to them. This can be a problem as much humour is contextualised and a joke that can have a group of Britons rolling about may mean nothing to Americans.

Hal is fortunate that he has worked for Disney in the Magic Shop, and part of the Disney philosophy is that they should appeal to all nationalities.

In ensuring a good relationship with his customers, Hal stresses the need to know the audience and in the case of a performer this may mean making some very quick changes to the act. It certainly means researching the possible audience base on the ship when putting a particular show together. Hal makes the point that nine-tenths of the population enjoy magic and indeed would like to believe in the tooth fairy or the Easter bunny.

For one who deals in illusions Hal's comment that there is 'magic out there in the world' is interesting. He sees his role and indeed talent as bringing out the belief in a magical process that is inside every one of us. He does so in a way that is enjoyable and not too mentally taxing for the audience for, as he says: 'when people are on vacation, they check their brains in'.

One of the problems he has found is that people on vacation want more than just sound bites from acts such as Hal's. To the customer he is an integral part of their vacation and, thus, in this regard he is public property.

For Hal, the audience is everything and he appreciates that he is not there for himself, a true customer driven approach. If they don't laugh (which is rare), then he must carry on. As he says of the one occasion when this happened, 'at least they didn't leave'. At times like that he relies on body language and his own carefully developed senses of how people are feeling.

He feels comfortable on stage and has the ability to make each member of the audience feel that they are in a private show. His careful approach to the needs of his customers has paid off, especially as his six-year-old daughter is quoted as saying 'everything you do is fake'.

Selling something we all know to be impossible is not easy but Hal Malquardt manages it with aplomb.

Scottish Prison Service (SPS)

As has been shown earlier in this book, not all customers are willing and not all products are viewed with delight. At some time we all have to make 'grudge' purchases: those things we need but do not want. Dental treatment, politicians, insurance, defence, law and order, and even government may come under this heading.

It is relatively easy to consider customer relations in respect of retail operations, less easy when dealing with an area like the prison service. The Scottish Prison Service is responsible for the custodial care of offenders and those on remand awaiting trial throughout Scotland. The service employs over 5000 staff.

This case study looks at two particular aspects of customer relations. Prisoners are involved in commercial activities, making a variety of products from boats to garden sheds, and these are supplied to outside commercial operations; the first part of this case study looks at the quality aspects of this area of operations. The second part considers the operation of the Scottish Prison Service College which is responsible for training and development of staff, i.e. an internal supplier/customer relationship.

Are prisoners customers?

The mission statement of the Scottish Prison Service is as follows:

- To keep in custody those committed by the Courts
- To maintain good order in each prison
- To care for prisoners with humanity
- To provide prisoners with a range of opportunities to exercise personal responsibility and preparation for release.

For a time in the early 1990s, the word customers was used in respect of prisoners but current thinking has moved away from this concept. In the view of the author it is difficult to associate the word customer with somebody who has no choice. Even hostages as described in Chapter 4 have the choice not to use a particular product or service, whereas prisoners have no choice as to their sentence or where it will be served. They are able to request transfers to prisons nearer home and indeed there are transfers between Scottish prisons and those in the rest of the UK, but that is under the complete control of the authorities. Thus for the purposes of this book, prisoners are not considered customers as such, save for the last point of the SPS mission statement. The opportunities provided can be considered as products, and whilst prisoners have lost their freedom, they have not lost their right to high-quality products and services. This is recognised by the staff of the SPS and it can, and is, argued that the better opportunities a prisoner receives, especially in relation to education and development, the less likely he or she is to re-offend.

In respect of the training and learning activities, prisoners can be considered customers as they are able to chose which if any of these activities they undertake.

Prisons are a grudge purchase for the prisoners but they are also a grudge purchase for the rest of society. We know we need them but would rather not pay for them. There is often an outcry when a new prison is built with enhanced facilities for the inmates. However, those making the outcry have one vital commodity that the prisoner does not have – the right to go home at night.

For most people the nearest they will come to the Prison Service is through television dramas and documentaries. What these often fail to bring out is the considerable sensitivity displayed by officers of the service. SPS staff are dealing with inmates who may be violent, have a drug addiction or mental health problems and are often amongst the most inadequate in society, and they do so with authority but with a wish to respect the dignity of those in their custody.

Prisoner-made products

The prisoners at HM Prison Glenochil, situated between Stirling and Alloa, produce, amongst other products, fibreglass boats and garden sheds. Such activities are far removed from the traditional sewing of mailbags. These are items that are to be sold on the commercial market and thus quality is highly important. Prisoners receive a small sum of money for their work but it is only a token payment compared to remuneration in the normal world of work. Herzberg (1962), as covered in Chapter 2, and Deming's 14 Principles (see Chapter 3) stress the importance of achievement, recognition and pride in workmanship. Sensitive supervision by SPS workshop staff coupled by the very real sense of pride in a product being well-constructed seem to play an important part in the quality of the products produced at Glenochil and other prisons. Whilst it might be thought, superficially, that there is little that might motivate prisoners to produce quality products for customers they may never meet and who are considerably better off than the prisoners, pride and achievement seem to be the main motivators and reduce any tendency to deliver low-quality goods. This could be called 'The Bridge over the River Kwai' paradox. In the book and film of that name, a group of British prisoners of war were forced to build a bridge on the Burma 'death' railway by the Japanese. They could have built to the lowest standard but their commanding officer used the exercise to build morale by insisting on the highest standards. It is a paradox because in the story it is allied agents who cannot understand why the prisoners had not sabotaged the bridge, and then have to demolish it as it could have aided the Japanese war effort. Another motivating factor is the potential job opportunities using skills developed in prison upon release.

It is possible that those purchasing the sheds and boats built at HMP Glenochil have no idea that they are the result of work by prisoners but they can be assured of a quality product.

It is not just in commercial ventures that a quality approach is demonstrated. Prisoners throughout the UK have arranged charity events with a high degree of professionalism and the attitude to many of the training opportunities from basic literacy to Open University degrees is positive and thus very rewarding.

Internal customer service

There are many internal value chains within the SPS, divided as it is into a large number of establishments ranging from young offender centres to maximum-security prisons. One internal supplier that is common to all establishments, however, is the Prison Service College.

Within any large organisation such as the SPS there is a continual need for training and development of a consistent and high quality. The SPS College exists to both deliver and facilitate such training. The College provides its own in-house courses but also works with external providers to deliver external, qualification based programmes. Examples include the Higher National Certificate in Prison Studies and the Individual Management Development Programme. The College is a centre of the National Examining Board for Supervision and Management (NEBSM) in its own right.

In 1998 it was decided to acquire the services in a new purpose-built college facility for the SPS and to appoint a customer service manager. The new facility will be a partnership initiative with a large private sector provider. The new facility should provide for SPS's direct needs with the private sector provider retailing any surplus space etc. in the facility to third parties.

In 1999, companies were asked to tender for building and resourcing the ongoing facilities management of the new college. The intention is for the SPS to be responsible for the administration of the operation but to outsource the hotel aspects. With the contract intended to run for 15 years, the development of effective performance criteria is seen as critical.

One of the key problems that any training and development organisation has is to devise methods to evaluate training. Cartwright *et al.* (1998a) considered the differences between training, development and education. They concluded that:

- training referred to learning a set of specific job skills
- development was concerned with the individual achieving their potential
- education comprised a mixture of both job and life skills.

They also stated that learning should lead to a permanent change in behaviour.

If the training is for a simple task then evaluation may be fairly straightforward. Could the trainee carry out the task at the end of the training session, 'yes' or 'no'? If the answer is 'yes' then the training was effective, if 'no' then it is deficient in some way. Even this may be too simplistic; perhaps the test should be undertaken some time later to see if the trainee has retained the new skill. The more complex the task, the harder it is to evaluate the effect of the passage of time unless there are ways of receiving feedback from the trainees' work situations.

Evaluation has to take account of added value to the organisation both immediately and in the longer term, and this has to be measured.

Development is even harder to evaluate as the effects may not be seen for some time. Many training providers ask their participants to complete an evaluation sheet at the end of a session or programme. This tends to be completed as a 'happiness' sheet. It does not measure the effectiveness of the training/development process, only how the participant has perceived the experience. Research for this book provided an example of where a participant had not enjoyed a particular session at a college in England and had rated it very low. A number of years later this same person was saying that it was the most useful session they had ever attended. The reason for the low rating was that the session required a considerable degree of self-analysis which the participant found uncomfortable, hence the apparent unhappiness.

The SPS College intend to work very closely with the prison establishments to devise means of evaluating the effectiveness of the training product provided, especially to see how it has been contextualised into the workplace.

The aim of the customer service manager at the SPS College is to work closely with establishments. Governors of prisons have considerable autonomy in spending their training budgets and the College is able to assist them in gaining the best deal possible. However, for the College to obtain a larger slice of an establishment's training and development budgets it must be able to provide a high-quality, best-value service in every respect. It has to be accountable and demonstrate high-quality training delivery, as well as providing physical facilities that compare favourably to those in the rest of the training and development market outwith the SPS.

It is clear that the SPS College is listening to their customers and seeking ways to strengthen the relationship by recognising that individual establishments may have differing needs that the College can facilitate, and by devising an evaluation methodology that involves all the partners to the product, namely the College, the establishment and the individual participant.

Princess Cruises (USA/UK)

The world cruise industry carried nearly 7.8 million holidaymakers in 1998 compared with 5.4 million in 1992 (Ward, 1994, 1998, 1999), a fantastic growth rate that would be the envy of many industries. It is surprising that, despite the success of the industry in not only holding on to its customer base but in generating new customers, there have been only two texts that have considered it in depth. Dickinson & Vladimir (1997) is a text predominantly concerned with the US market whilst Cartwright & Baird (1999) looked at the world market.

As the latter have pointed out, cruise vacations are at the top end of any holiday price range and customers expect and demand superlative service. For many holidaymakers a cruise is the result of many years' saving, perhaps to celebrate a special anniversary. It is thus very important for the cruise companies to provide excellent service, especially as they wish to attract considerable customer loyalty (see Chapter 4) leading to high levels of repeat business. Cartwright & Green have reported levels of over 66% repeat business on particular cruises, indicating the high repeat business levels the successful companies in the industry generate.

Princess Cruises (mentioned in Chapter 3 of this book) form part of the P&O Group of companies. Princess is, in effect, the US arm of a very old established UK company.

P&O (the Peninsular and Oriental Steam Navigation Company) was founded as early as 1837 as the Peninsular Steam Navigation Company to serve Spain and Portugal (the Iberian Peninsular countries) from the UK. Indeed, their house flag/logo which can now be seen on cruise liners, container ships, car ferries, lorries and building sites is based on the colours of the ancient Royal Houses of Spain and Portugal. Today P&O operate cruise liners, container ships, car ferries, Rhine cruise boats, river barges, road transport, building concerns (Bovis) and even operated the prestigious exhibition centres of Olympia and Earls Court in London until their sale in September 1999.

P&O's cruising interests include US market cruises under the Princess brand (although these cruises have been attracting increasing numbers of UK cruisers in recent years), P&O Cruises in the UK, who operate the group's 69 000 GRT flagship, *Oriana*, which entered service in 1995, the specialist cruise operator Swan Hellenic and P&O Holidays based in Australia. Other shipping operations include P&O Containers, P&O Ferries operating in the English Channel, the North Sea, the Irish Sea and the North of Scotland, and a variety of freight and cruise operations on Europe's major rivers.

Princess Cruises of Los Angeles was a fairly small operator that was acquired by P&O in 1974 (see Chapter 3 on reforming in the Enhanced Porter Model). In 1988 P&O also acquired Sitmar Cruises which was incorporated into the Princess fleet giving P&O a major stake in the US market cruise industry and the honour of operating the original '*Love Boat*®' of the long running television series.

Princess Cruises operate in all of the world's major cruising areas including Alaska (where the company owns hotel and railroad interests), the Caribbean, Northern Europe, the Mediterranean, the West Coast of the USA and Transcanal cruising through the Panama Canal.

Cruising is not cheap and therefore value for money is very important. It is interesting to consider why increasing numbers of people undertake a cruise given the relatively high cost. What is the experience they are seeking? If the answer is connected to service then the attitudes of the crew will be a very important factor in customer perception and future choices.

Cruising has generally been perceived as very relaxing although the increase in what may be termed 'destination intensive' cruises, with one and sometimes two ports of call per day and perhaps only one full day at sea, may be making it less so. The food is normally excellent and international rather than local in character. Once on board, customers can travel from port to port without having to unpack as their hotel moves with them. Medical facilities are provided and the environment is very safe, a factor that Cartwright & Baird (1999) found appealed to the more elderly customers. The vast majority of cruises sail to where the sunshine is. Itineraries vary from the exotic – the Amazon, the adventurous – the Antarctic, the tropical – the Caribbean and the South Seas, the spectacular – Norway and Alaska to the cultural – much of the Mediterranean.

The disadvantages to customers are that they never spend very long in one place, although most companies now offer cruise and stay packages, and seas can be rough at times. As mentioned earlier, cruises are not cheap compared with comparable package holidays and on-board accommodation may well be smaller than found in hotels, although the vast majority of cabins/staterooms have private facilities (all Princess ships are so equipped) and standards are rising as more and more ships offer cabins with balconies.

Discussions with regular cruise customers suggest that there are certain intangibles that make this form of holiday special and therefore those involved in customer services on board need to understand the roots of these intangibles. As has already been shown earlier in this book it is often the supplementary, often intangible part of a product that is of great importance to the customer. Of all the intangibles and supplementaries, service is frequently the most important.

The excellent cruise companies provide their customers with the illusion that they are on their own personal vessel, with enough quiet places to be alone to support that illusion, and standards of service that are both high and personal. Cruise ships themselves are just so many thousand tons of steel, so the ship itself cannot be the deciding factor. The organisation is headquartered many miles away on shore and customers will rarely meet any staff from corporate headquarters so that the most important factor in achieving excellence and the personal illusion must be the people themselves, a fact that Tom Peters (1987) has stressed. The key to excellence must lie within the crew members on board the ship.

In a growing market it is, paradoxically, just as important to retain customer loyalty as in a shrinking market. The current growth rate of up to 10% in the cruise industry requires considerable expenditure to tap the potential new customers, and in 1999 P&O announced a major building programme that will keep the group at the forefront of the cruise industry for many years to come. Overall, in 1999 P&O were number three in the world cruise market in terms of market share. A successful company will not only generate a growth in new clients but will wish to build on its existing customer base as the existing customers carry far fewer marketing customers than new ones. In effect, existing customers, if satisfied, will perform part of the marketing function by promoting the company to their friends, relatives and colleagues (Cartwright & Green, 1997).

Whilst there is a highly complex organisational chart for a cruise ship, the ship almost appearing as a distinct organisation in its own right, from the customer point of view there are four main areas of operation that directly affect the experience of the customer, with the vessel's captain being in overall control of the first three.

Navigation/safety aspects connected with the ship

Under the direct control of the captain, the navigation, engineering, electrical etc. staffs ensure that the voyage is completed on schedule, in safety and with as little inconvenience to the customers as possible.

Hotel aspects

Up to 2500 customers (on the largest ships) need to be accommodated and fed. One can never complain about the quantity of food offered on a cruise. Eating can commence at 0600 and finish with a midnight buffet with any number of meals and snacks in between. Laundry facilities need to be provided; staterooms kept clean and made up; indeed a whole range of housekeeping activities. Customers need to obtain foreign currency and postage stamps; their accounts need to be kept up to date and they may need medical attention. Many of these roles are delegated by the captain to the purser's department which is a very busy department indeed.

Entertainment

Cruise ships provide a full range of entertainment and activities for customers, ranging from quizzes and deck games through to cabaret and full-scale production shows that would not be out of place in the West End of London, Las Vegas or Broadway. Indeed *Oriana* was the first cruise ship to provide customers with a proper West End style theatre at sea as opposed to the more traditional show-lounge found on older vessels.

There are show excursions to be planned and arranged, shops to be operated and photographic services to be provided as well as children to be entertained. Modern cruise ships carry a full entertainments team in addition to singers and dancers, a team that is under the control of the all-important cruise director who usually reports directly to the captain. The cruise director is one member of the senior team who customers will come to know very closely, as he or she is always around chatting to the customers as the day on board unfolds.

Pre and post cruise

Customers have to reach the ship and have to be transported home at the end of their cruise. Fly cruises have gained popularity in recent years and they are indeed the norm in the US market because of the large distances customers may need to travel to reach the ship. Not only must the customer be transported but so must their luggage, and any crew and entertainers who are joining or leaving the ship.

Travel to and from the ship for the vast majority of customers is arranged by Princess Cruises but is not under their direct control. In effect, Princess Cruises are customers of the airlines etc. When a customer who has travelled on two or three different airlines, say Denver to New York, then New York to London and London to Venice in order to join their cruise ship, finds that their luggage has not arrived at the same time as they have, they will approach the purser's department in order for something to be done. Princess Cruises cannot (and to their credit do not) say that this is not their problem. Every effort is made to track down the luggage and have it recovered prior to sailing. If it cannot be recovered by then and needs to be sent on to the next port of call, toiletries and clothing vouchers can be provided. There is always a problem for any organisation that has third parties servicing a particular need for their customers. An excellent organisation takes ownership of these issues on behalf of the customer.

It may not be Princess Cruises' fault that the luggage is lost but they owe it to their customer to find an acceptable solution. Most luggage does turn up although it can require considerable liaison between the ship and the airlines to track missing items down and deliver them to the quayside. The airlines are also concerned because it is their reputation and future business, not only with Princess Cruises but also the individual customer, that is at stake. Princess

Cruises are major customers of a number of airlines through the tickets that they book for their customers, and that valuable business could be lost if airline service adversely affected the quality of a holiday.

All of the organisations involved in transporting the customer to and from the ship and with their comfort when ashore – airlines, hotels and excursion companies – need to get it right first time, every time if the experience is to be both enjoyable and memorable for the right and not the wrong reasons. In the case of third party activities booked by the cruise company, no matter what the legal position is, they will be held accountable if things go wrong even when they are beyond their control.

The Princess Cruises CRUISE customer care programme

A major component of any cruise is the service provided by cabin stewards and catering staff. Traditionally these people have formed part of a low wage economy and there is much reliance in both the accommodation and catering industries (whether on land or at sea) on tipping. There are cultural differences on tipping, it being much more the norm in the USA to tip regardless of the standard of service than it is in the UK. Many of the cruise companies, including Princess, provide information and advice to their customers on the level of tipping expected. A number of cruise companies operating at the luxury end of the market discourage the practice of tipping and include gratuities in the holiday price. It remains a fact, however, that the majority of staff employed as stewards, stewardesses, waiters, bus boys (assistant waiters) and bar staff in the cruise industry relay on tips to supplement their salaries. Many of the companies include a gratuity on all bar bills as a matter of course.

It might be thought that this reliance on tips would in itself guarantee excellent service. The danger, however, as Ward (1999) has commented, is that customers can feel pressurised into giving gratuities regardless of whether the service is excellent or indifferent.

Princess Cruises suggest (and it must be noted that it is only a suggestion) a sum of between £5 and £6 per customer per day for tips (Princess Cruises Mediterranean and Scandinavian brochure, 1999, p. 50). On a 14-day cruise this can add £168 per couple to the cost of a holiday. Interestingly, the UK-based P&O Cruises, part of the same group, suggest £3.50 per customer per day on UK market cruises (P&O Cruises winter brochure, 1999–2000, p. 116). This bears out the difference in tipping norms between the US and the UK commented on by Cartwright & Baird (1999).

Given that US customers will probably tip regardless, tipping does not, in fact, add to the service standard. The very high rates of repeat business achieved by Princess Cruises (and P&O Cruises in the UK) suggest that their service is of a very high standard. This is due very much to a comprehensive customer care programme named CRUISE.

CRUISE is an acronym standing for:

Courtesy, Respect, Unfailing, In, Service, Excellence

The CRUISE programme has a cornerstone statement of:

> 'At one point in every day, one of our customers will come into contact with one of us, the Princess employees and at that moment in time we will be Princess Cruises. Our entire reputation as a company will be in our hands and we will make an impression. The impression will either be good or it will be bad and we will have spoken to our customer more loudly than all our community involvement, all our advertising and all our public relations put together'.
>
> (*Source*: Princess Cruises CRUISE Programme, information to customers)

The above is a very powerful statement that recognises that the success of the organisation is ultimately in the hands of those who interface directly with the customer. It is an illustration of the concept of the 'Moments of Truth' covered in Chapter 8 of this book. The statement is not just for internal consumption; it is placed in every stateroom on every Princess ship for the customer to read. In being so public, Princess Cruises is drawing attention to the programme and, in effect, inviting customers to judge the performance of the company against strict criteria.

The 10 points of the Princess Service Credo as included in the documentation provided for customers are:

1. **We strive to be the very best.** We do the best job we are capable of all the time in every part of the ship. We are proud of what we do.
2. **We react** quickly to resolve passenger problems immediately. We do everything possible to please our passengers.
3. **We smile; we are on stage.** We always maintain positive eye contact and use our service vocabulary. We greet our passengers: we tell them 'certainly' and 'I will be happy to do so' and 'it will be a pleasure'.
4. **We are friendly, helpful and courteous.** It is the Princess way. We treat our fellow passengers and crew members as we would like to be treated ourselves [*author's note*: an excellent example of looking after the internal customer].
5. **We are ambassadors of our cruise ship** when at work and at play. We always speak positively and never make negative comments.
6. **Our uniforms are immaculate.** We wear proper and safe footwear that is clean and polished and we wear our nametags. We take pride and care in our personal grooming.
7. **We are positive.** We always find a way to get it done. We always try to make it happen. We never, never give up.
8. **We use proper telephone etiquette.** We always try to answer within three rings and with a smile in our voice [*author's note*: see Chapter 8]. If necessary we always ask if we may place callers on hold, and we eliminate call transfers whenever possible.
9. **We are knowledgeable** about all cruise ship information and always recommend the shipboard services.
10. **We never say 'no'.** We say, 'I will be pleased to check and see'. We suggest

alternatives. We call our supervisor or manager if we feel we cannot satisfy our passenger's needs.

(*Source*: Princess Cruises CRUISE Programme, information to customers)

Many of the points in the above credo can be related to the topics covered in this book: the care for the internal as well as the external customer, 'Moments of Truth', image, body language, Organisational Body Language etc.

Customers are asked to nominate staff who have provided them with outstanding service. It is the nature of things that the majority of such nominations are given to stateroom (all Princess accommodation is described as a stateroom, unlike the UK P&O Cruises where the term cabin is still used, staterooms being midway in price between cabins and suites – another US–UK difference) staff, dining room staff or bar staff. However, Princess have a parallel scheme in operation whereby those staff in the front line are able to nominate colleagues who rarely come into contact with the paying customer but who provided their internal customer with outstanding service. This removes one of the major disadvantages of customer nomination schemes, namely the exclusion of staff not in the front line.

Each ship in the Princess fleet has a CRUISE committee, made up from the heads of department on the ship, that considers both CRUISE nominations and suggestions from crew members for service improvements. Cash incentives can be awarded and there is the award of CRUISE badges and an 'Employee of the Month'. Discussions with crew members whilst researching this study indicated that the badges were highly valued and that the scheme, giving as it did recognition, was an excellent motivator as described by Herzberg (see Chapter 2).

The CRUISE programme is supported by regular training sessions. The nature of maritime employment is that there is a constant turnaround of staff and it is important that new crew members become familiar with the high standards of service expected of them as quickly as possible.

There is no doubt that the CRUISE programme exemplifies many of the concepts covered in this book and that the high level of customer service provided by Princess Cruises accounts for their continuing success and high levels of repeat business.

Highland Distillers' Glenturret Distillery (UK)

Hard against the banks of the River Tay is the corporate headquarters of the Highland Distillers Group whose brands include Famous Grouse, The Macallan (note The Macallan, not Macallan), Highland Park (all whiskies), Remy Martin, Finlandia Vodka, Gloag's Gin etc.

Whisky is a major source of income to the Scottish economy, not only through world-wide sales but also through its role in the tourist industry. Visitors to Scotland comprise both whisky connoisseurs and those whose knowledge of the drink may well be very limited. The interest in the national drink has spawned a thriving tourist sector for the distilling industry with a number of distilleries operating guided tours. Different areas of Scotland produce their own single and double malts, the taste reflecting the nature of the countryside in the area. There are in fact over three hundred different Scottish whiskies. There is also whiskey (note the different spelling) produced in Ireland and even Japan. A visit to a distillery is almost obligatory for the visitor to Scotland.

Highland Distillers, as one of the major players in the whisky market, operate two very distinctive tourist attractions, one for the connoisseur and the other, the subject of this case study, for the general tourist market.

The Macallan Distillery, situated high above the River Spey, can be visited by connoisseurs of whisky by appointment, whilst the Glenturret Distillery caters for the general visitor. Other visitor attractions in the group are at the Highland Park distillery in Orkney and the Bunnahabhain distillery in Islay. The tourism aspect and its spin-off connections to the core drinks business are considered as a very important part of the Highland Distillers' operation; each attraction has a tourism manager and there is an overall Director of Group Tourism. In order to ensure that the customers would receive the best service possible, when the tourism manager at Glenturret was due to retire, the successor was brought in to work alongside her for a period of months, ensuring that there would be no gaps in provision and that she could pass on her knowledge. Whilst this may have caused slightly increased costs and needs to be handled with sensitivity, its benefits in ensuring consistency of service far outweigh these and it is to be regretted that other organisations do not often adopt this approach to the replacement of personnel.

The Glenturret Distillery, with its distinctive tartan reflecting the nature of the area and its history, was founded in 1775 and claims the title of the oldest distillery in Scotland. The distillery lies just outwith the ancient market town of Crieff in Strathearn on the road from Perth to Oban (the Road to the Isles). It is situated on the banks of the quick flowing Turret Burn, which rises on Benchonzie, flows into Loch Turret and thence to the River Earn just a few miles below the distillery. Whisky distilling requires a good supply of clean water and the Turret Burn provides that.

From an organisational body language point of view, the location of the distillery, set as it is amongst woods with the soothing sounds of both water and birds nearby, is superb. Clean, whitewashed buildings greet the visitor, a pair of waterwheels, good signage and a large car park, extended in 1998. The parking for coaches is separate from the car park and there is separate staff parking.

Visitors come from all over the world; a clue to this is the 'Drive on the left' sign clearly visible to drivers leaving the car park. The sign is written in English, German, French, Italian and Flemish with Spanish recently (1999) being added.

The customer base includes not only those using their own or hire cars but also a considerable number of coach parties, and Glenturret have made it an important priority to have an excellent relationship with the tour companies. Most customers on an organised tour are hostages (see Chapter 4) to the extent that the tour company normally chooses their itinerary. Glenturret staff are well aware, however, of the need to treat these visitors just as well as they do for those who use their own transport. They all have friends and are thus able to spread the word about an enjoyable trip.

Guided tours are provided with knowledgeable local guides and the visitor is able to see (and smell) the whole whisky-making process. The restaurant (Smugglers) provides a wide variety of local and international dishes, and there is a well-stocked shop selling a huge range of Glenturret merchandise plus, of course, a variety of Glenturret whiskies and liqueurs. The Glenturret operation is consistently within the top ten most visited attractions in Scotland, receiving over 200 000 visitors annually. Part of the success is the mixture of a good micro location and a macro location that is easily reached from the Glasgow, Edinburgh and Loch Lomond areas on a day trip.

Whilst the Glenturret operation is based around distilling, the core product is actually a tourist experience and not the drink *per se*. The majority of the day visitors to Glenturret are not connoisseurs of whisky but people who want to experience a particular aspect of Scotland. To that end the audio-visual production at Glenturret includes Scottish history in addition to an explanation of the whisky process. Glenturret does receive visits from connoisseurs however, particularly at the specially arranged evening functions.

It is unusual for one of the unique selling points (USPs) of an organisation to be a cat but Glenturret has always had a working cat and one of the previous holders of the post, Towser, lived for 24 years in the still house and appears in the *Guinness Book of Records*; it has been calculated that Towser caught a world record 28 899 mice during her lifetime. There is a statue commemorating Towser at the distillery and a line of Towser merchandise for children.

Local inhabitants are not forgotten by the Glenturret operation which is open all year round (albeit with reduced opening hours in winter), with the exception of Christmas and New Year. There are regular themed evenings and the restaurant is used by locals on a regular basis. This provides valuable income during the 'shoulder business' times on either side of the spring/summer peak.

The staff are well trained in customer care, Highland Distillers operating a vocational qualification in customer service through a local college plus their own in-house training. There is a corporate uniform based on the Glenturret tartan and this adds to the air of professionalism that pervades the operation.

As an exemplar of good customer relations, Glenturret scores highly because of:

- smart, well-trained and knowledgeable staff
- excellent presentations throughout the facility
- well-kept facilities
- good merchandising, not cheap but of high quality and well displayed
- good food and beverage operations
- thought given to the types and nationalities of visitors
- separation of coaches and private cars
- location both macro and micro
- the linking of the whisky aspects of the operation to a general Scottish theme
- good relations with the local community.

Recognising that they are part of the tourist industry, Glenturret are involved in the sponsorship of the Scottish Thistle Awards for tourism through the area tourism initiative. It is not enough to be an excellent tourist attraction as there is a need for other attractions nearby to make a visit worth while for tourists, and suggestions for other attractions to visit are provided at Glenturret.

In 1998, a conference suite equipped with video conferencing facilities, presentation technology and designed to accommodate up to 40 delegates was opened. This facility, which can be hired by outside bodies, has brought a useful facility to businesses in the Strathearn area.

Whilst not every operation can have the physical location of Glenturret with all its advantages, the care that the organisation takes of its customers and its assessment and meeting of their needs can be replicated elsewhere.

Caledonian Cinemas (UK)

From the outside, the Playhouse Cinema in Perth, the ancient capital of Scotland, has the appearance of the typical 1930s Art Deco cinema design that was to be found in towns and cities throughout the UK well into the 1970s. In its original single-screen design the cinema held 1700 people and was the largest cinema in Perthshire and the flagship of the owning company, Caledonian Associated Cinemas.

Designed by Colonel Cattenach, a local architect, the cinema was completed in 1933, its construction taking an amazingly short ten weeks.

In 1991 the Art Deco design was recognised as being of important architectural significance and was listed as a category B building, preserving the frontage for future generations.

Cinema audiences in the UK began to decline in the late 1950s as television ownership grew, many cinemas being converted into bingo halls. The Perth Playhouse survived as a cinema but in 1978 it was converted into a three-screen operation, allowing greater flexibility in the product that could be offered to the customer.

By 1999, Caledonian Cinemas had an 11% share of the Scottish market. They are an independent group and not tied to any of the major film distributors.

In 1997, Caledonian Cinemas was part of Taylor Clark Leisure, which included Caledonian Nightclubs and Littlejohn Restaurants. And the decision was made to convert the Perth Playhouse to Caledonian Cinema's first 'Multiplex' cinema with seven screens, the conversion being a £2.1 million investment.

Prior to the redevelopment of the Perth operation, Caledonian Cinema's Operations Manager, Gavin Sharp, had already begun a process of customer care training with managers from all of the group's cinemas (Perth, Stirling, Elgin, Inverness and Glasgow West End). This training also included team-building exercises and introduced managers to the Hostage, Mercenary etc. model (see Chapter 4) and Organisational Body Language (see Chapter 8). It was at the unreconstructed Perth Playhouse that the technique highlighted the lack of toilet facilities for children and such facilities have been incorporated into the new development. Another direct result of the training was the improvements to signage at the box office and foyer lighting.

The redevelopment of the Perth Playhouse

As soon as it had been decided to redevelop the cinema into a multiplex operation, plans were drawn up, displayed and discussed with customers. The management of the cinema were well used to 'managing by wandering around' (Peters, 1987) and thus customers were used to being asked their views. Societies catering for the disabled were also contacted and became involved in the planning process, and indeed a consultant was appointed to co-ordinate the process of ensuring that the cinema was accessible to as wide a customer base as possible.

The whole philosophy of the design process centred on providing a better service to customers with more choice and improved facilities.

Disabled facilities

The facilities provided for the disabled include:

- Two sets of disabled toilets as opposed to the one set normally found in this size of facility
- Low counters at both the ticket desk and food counter
- Infra-red system for the hard of hearing
- Wheelchair spaces in all but two of the cinema halls (it was not possible to incorporate wheelchair spaces in two of the halls for design reasons)
- Disabled parking facilities
- Ramp access and electric door (to be fitted in the near future).

It is hoped to put a cine-tracker for the visually impaired into two of the screens in the near future. This device will provide a verbal description of the film for those whose sight is impaired.

Whilst the budget did not allow for the fitting of all the devices in stage 1, the design was drawn up with them in mind and thus retro-fitting will be relatively simple as the wiring etc. is already in place.

Family entertainment

Caledonian cinemas are aware that the business they are in is mainly the family entertainment business and thus they are in competition not only with television companies and video rental outlets but also with theme parks, leisure centres and other visitor attractions. Caledonian Cinemas have ensured that a family of four can have an evening out for £12.

The company was lucky in that there was waste ground to the rear of the original cinema and thus they were able to expand towards the rear.

The key features of the new multiplex from the point of view of customer relations are:

- One screen is branded as a luxury product with seating similar to that used in airline business class products. This hall, known as 'The Screening Room', is the smallest commercial screen in Scotland to utilise Dolby® Digital sound and yet costs only 50p extra per person.

- Cinema 1 is the main hall, with some luxury seating; interestingly, these seats tend to sell out first.
- Improved vending facilities include not only the traditional ice creams and popcorn but also vegetarian and vegan options.
- There is a Kids Saturday Fun Time every Saturday at 11.00 am with sing-alongs, quizzes etc. The cost is £1.00 per child. This is not commercial but is seen as a loss leader. Fun Time includes fairly recent film releases.
- All chairs are fitted with cup holders.
- Every seat has a good view. This has been achieved by not filling the halls to their maximum capacity.
- Auto ticketing machines for use with credit cards are available. At present, these are only used for the collection of tickets because of concerns about youngsters being able to buy tickets for films with 12, 15 or R classifications.
- There is the ability to use 'interlocking', i.e. to show the same film on more than one screen at once. This is useful for highly popular films and makes use of a totally new, state-of-the-art projection system.

Mystery shopper

The Perth Playhouse receives regular visits from a mystery customer (see mystery shoppers in Chapter 3) and the reports are analysed by the staff to see where improvements can be made. Senior staff make a point of talking to customers to ascertain their degree of satisfaction with the product.

The modern film industry has seen a resurgence in recent times. A trip to the cinema is no longer purely to see a film; it is a family event and may include a meal out. A trip to the cinema is much more of a total experience and Caledonian Cinemas are aware of the need to delight the customer with a total package that includes ease of access, a choice of films (there is always at least one family film on the bill) and attractive food and drinks to support the package. The redevelopment of the Perth Playhouse has been planned and accomplished with the customer clearly at the centre of the operation.

Roseanna Cunningham MP, MSP (UK)

Whilst politicians may come in for much criticism from their electorate, there are few people in the world who ascribe to a system of complete anarchy. It is difficult to conceive of any society that could prosper under a system where there is no government whatsoever, and in the Western democracies it is hard for people to accept the notion of a totalitarian dictatorship. We have politicians because we need them, and the political process is certainly as old as recorded history and probably has its roots in the organisation of primate societies, as recent studies with other primates, especially the great apes, seem to suggest.

This section is not centred around the political process *per se* but with the relationship that exists between the politician and the customer. In Chapter 2, a customer was defined as 'one for whom you satisfy a need'. The concept of a grudge purchase has also already been introduced and politicians might well fall into this category, regardless of how good, bad or indifferent they are as a politician. The need for laws, lawmakers and government is hard to dispute, and thus some form of political process is a human need. Maslow's hierarchy of needs introduced in Chapter 2 showed belonging as a middle-level human need and, in order to belong, a person has to obey the rules and the rules have to be made by either the group (if it is small) or representatives of the group if it is a large group; when this occurs with regional or national groups we call these rule (or law) makers, politicians. Unfortunately whilst most people recognise this process, they also begrudge paying for it and, because of the electoral processes used, there will always be those who are represented by somebody they did not vote for and did not want in the first place.

A good politician is aware of the problem that under the first past the post system used for British general and local elections a large majority of the electorate may well have voted for somebody else or, because of apathy, not voted at all.

It is not difficult to imagine the following result being declared by the returning officer for a constituency on the south coast of England:

Jones Marjorie (Conservative)	14 324
Brown Alan (Liberal Democrat)	12 657
Smith Ella (Labour)	6 369
Michaels Peter (Stop the bypass)	456
Rowe June (Independent)	318
Spoilt papers	60
Turnout	77%

Jones' majority is 1667 and Jones is duly elected. (Please note that the figures are purely illustrative and do not necessarily reflect the political leanings of the author!)

However of the votes cast, Jones received 14 324 out of 34 184, i.e. only 41%, meaning that 59% of those who voted did not want Jones. As the number of registered voters (if the turnout was 77%) was 44 500, then only 32% of those eligible to choose a Member of Parliament actually voted for Jones; 68% either wanted somebody else or didn't bother to vote.

There has been a history of smaller political parties in the UK campaigning for a system of proportional representation to redress the situation brought about by the above system. Such systems are widely used in other parts of the European Union (EU) and in the late 1990s were introduced in Northern Ireland. In 1999 a proportional representation system was implemented for the elections to the Scottish Parliament and in accordance with EU regulations for the election of UK members to the European Parliament. It is likely that proportional representation will be extended to at least Scottish and perhaps all UK local elections in the near future.

The interest in politicians in respect of this book is to examine how a politician manages the relationship with those customers who are in fact very reluctant customers (hostages in the terms of Chapter 4) – those who have that politician as their representative despite the fact they would have preferred somebody else. Politicians, as stated earlier, are aware of this problem. One result of the 1996 UK general election was the fact that no conservative members were elected in either Scotland or Wales but this did not mean that those two countries had no conservatives in them. They had a fair number but the vagaries of the first past the post system meant that they had no members elected. One of the points that will be made about politicians who have thought about the relationship with the customers is a realisation that once elected they represent everybody in their constituency and not just those who have voted for them!

In 1995 Roseanna Cunningham produced a famous by-election victory for the Scottish National Party (SNP) when she won the election for the once safe Conservative seat of Perth and Kinross. Her achievement was made all the greater in 1997 when, despite boundary changes, she won the newly formed Perth constituency in the General Election of that year, being the first SNP member to hold a seat won at a by-election. In 1999 she won the seat for a third time, becoming a member of the newly formed Scottish Parliament. Thus she was both the Member of Parliament (MP) and the Member of the Scottish Parliament (MSP) for Perth, although she announced during the campaign for the Scottish Parliament that she would not stand as an MP at the next UK General Election. In 1999 she was appointed as the Shadow Minister for Justice, Equality and Land Reform in the Scottish Parliament.

Interestingly, much of Roseanna's early life was spent not in Perth (Scotland) but in Perth (Western Australia) as her family emigrated there in 1960, Roseanna studying politics at the University in Western Australia. She returned to Scotland in 1976 where having worked full time for the SNP she undertook a law degree, becoming an advocate in 1990.

Roseanna Cunningham is one of those politicians who is accorded a considerable degree of respect even by those who would not, in most circumstances, vote for her. As a member of the SNP she is a believer in Scottish independence and she is also known for her deeply held republican views, a stance that can generate considerable passion from those on both sides of the argument.

Interviewing Roseanna for this book with the emphasis on her views on her relationship with her customers – the electorate – it was interesting to gain her impressions of how the relationship politicians have with the electorate has changed over the years.

Prior to and just after World War II, indeed until the advent of television, politicians were often regarded as remote and having a purely representational role. The only contact most people would have with their elected representatives would be through press comment, which was normally restrained and respectful, although at public meetings the atmosphere could become somewhat boisterous. The local MP was probably unknown to the vast majority of the electorate.

Today we live in an age of soundbites and media that are no respecter of reputations. Interviewers pursue even the most senior of politicians and do not hesitate to be challenging even to the point of rudeness if they feel it necessary.

Televising of parliamentary debates has brought a small part of the workings of the democratic process into people's homes, but all most people see is only what the media cover and that is not always complimentary.

Roseanna makes the point that much of the work of a politician is behind the scenes, in committees or around the country finding things out or working with constituents. The debates that appear as part of the television news are only the tip of a very large iceberg and in no way show the complexity of the law-making process. Unfortunately the customers of a politician are both unaware and probably disinterested in the long hours behind the scenes; their issue is what effects them and that is what they want resolved.

As a constituency MP/MSP (a dual role), Roseanna Cunningham maintains an office in Perth with a full-time staff and holds regular surgeries around what is a fairly rural constituency. Surgeries are where she meets her customers face to face and they tend to fall into two categories. There are those who come to lobby and those who come with a personal problem. In dealing with the former, Roseanna makes the point that she would rather they set up a private meeting with her so that she can be properly briefed on the issue and, importantly, valuable surgery time that could be used for people with more personal problems will not be wasted.

Surgeries are very important to Roseanna as she believes that the role of an MP/MSP is no longer merely to represent constituents but at times to use the power of the title to deliver answers that are held up in the bureaucratic process. An MP has more chance of receiving an informed and speedy reply to a query, be it from the public or the private sector, than most other individuals. MPs/MSPs have the right to raise issues with the benefit of privilege and are listened to eagerly by journalists, and this can and does produce results.

Whether it is a person lobbying or coming with a very personal problem, Roseanna has the art of listening and empathising. The ability to empathise was covered in Chapter 8 and means that she does not have to agree with what she is being told but she can put herself in the person's position and understand where they are coming from.

Roseanna was asked how she deals with a request to do something for a constituent that she fundamentally disagrees with. She replied that for matters of conscience (she is an opponent of capital punishment) she is completely honest and will say that she cannot help but, and this is an important point, she will put the person in contact with somebody who shares their views if at all possible. There are other times, and she gave the example of the sale of council houses, where she disagreed with the scheme as a matter of principle; but once it became law she helped people whose applications to buy their council house were being held up. As a lawmaker she has the view that once a law is made, it is for parliamentarians to uphold it and seek to change it only through the political process.

Many times there is nothing that she can do, although constituents do not seem to mind too much – it is enough that she tried and Roseanna Cunningham has a reputation for trying very hard.

The Cunningham family has been involved in politics at various levels in the UK and Australia, and Roseanna believes that one reason she became interested in politics was that she saw early on in life that in her experience it was something that ordinary people can do. Like many of the politicians from all parties who command wide respect, Roseanna can be seen in local café's (not electioneering but having a coffee) and on the streets of the constituency talking to people. It is this link with constituents and an ability to listen and act that makes her customer relations worthy of mention.

During the 1999 Scottish election campaign a lady called a local council candidate to her door to discuss a particular burning local issue. As Roseanna was going to be in that part of the constituency the next day, the candidate offered to bring her round to talk about the issue. 'Good', the candidate was told, 'I'm not going to vote for her because I've always been a (another party) supporter, but when she's elected she'll get some action'. That is praise indeed from a customer who is actually going to give his or her business to somebody else.

In politics, customer care begins from realising that the person who is bringing an issue or a problem to you may well be making a 'grudge purchase', they may well wish that somebody else were sitting in front of them. However, they are your customer and they deserve the best that the MP/MSP or local councillor can do for them. Politicians lose potential customers and repeat business for a number of reasons (national issues often obscuring local ones) but if they lose a vote because they have failed to empathise with a constituent or failed to try to help, then they deserve to lose it because they have shown poor customer care. Roseanna Cunningham is one of a growing number of politicians who have realised that the relationship with the customer is a vital area of study for those in politics because those customers are voters and, as has been stressed in this book, nobody is more important than the customer.

☑ ▮▮ Developing a customer relations' strategy

What is strategy? – Mission – Strategy determinants – Internal analysis – BACK analysis – Culture – SWOT analysis – 7S analysis – External analysis – PESTLE – Stakeholder/publics – Competitor analysis – Supplier analysis – Customer analysis – OBL audit – Evaluating the results – Customer relations' analysis

A common assessment for students undertaking a customer care/service/relations unit or module is 'develop a customer care strategy for a given organisation'. Such assessments use either a real organisation that can be visited by the student or are based around a case study on an imaginary or real organisation examined using case study material.

Whether one is considering the development of a customer relations' strategy in order to pass an assignment or as part of a job role, a systematic analytical approach will produce the most implementable strategy.

What is strategy?

Johnson & Scholes (1993) have deflned strategy as:

> '... the direction and scope of an organisation over the long term: ideally, which matches its resources to its changing environment, and in particular its markets, customers or clients so as to meet stakeholder expectations'.

It follows, therefore, that in order to plan strategically, you need to have analysed the organisation in terms of:

- the environment
- the available resources
- customers and clients
- stakeholders.

4 elements of a strategic plan

Johnson & Scholes point out that strategic planning is thus likely to be concerned with:

- the scope of an organisation's activities, i.e. it is broad based
- matching the activities of the organisation to its environment
- matching the organisation's activities to its resource capability

- the values and expectations of those who hold power within the organisation
- the long-term direction of the organisation.

Strategic planning is planning for the long term; strategic decisions are those long-term decisions from which the day-to-day operational decisions flow. To be effective, operational (or tactical) decisions need to be firmly rooted within the strategic framework of the organisation.

Whereas operational decisions are mainly routine, specific, involve small-scale changes and are resource driven, strategic decisions must take account of ambiguity and complexity, the work of the whole organisation, the implications of significant changes and are likely to be driven by the environment within which the organisation operates. *and these changing customer needs impact the external environment e ultimately the*

The mission of the organisation *organisations operations. which back to adopt to the evolving environment.*

All decisions and plans, operation or strategic, flow from the mission of the organisation. As we shall see later, the mission of the organisation has strong links both with the external environment and the culture of the organisation. Every decision or plan should be capable of definition in terms of the mission of the organisation, i.e. it should be directly traceable to the stated objectives of the organisation.

Every organisation is different and every customer has their individual needs, and thus there is not a single generic strategy that can be adopted by all organisations. The aim of this chapter is to provide a series of analytical models that can be applied to each and every unique organisational situation.

The model shown in Figure 11.1 is designed to show the factors that determine the most effective strategy an organisation can develop to build and enhance its relationship with its customers.

The circle represents the organisation. The model requires four internal and three external analyses to be carried out. The results of these analyses will then

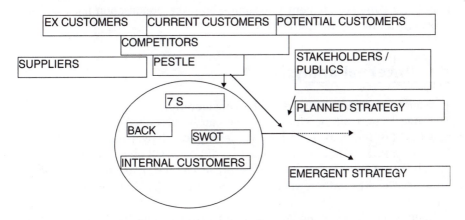

Figure 11.1   Customer service strategy determinants.

allow a desired strategy to be derived and implemented. It must be remembered however that the eventual strategy is unlikely to be as planned because, whilst the organisation may have considerable control over internal factors, planning and implementation take time and the external factors that influenced the plan may change and thus exert new influences over the implementation.

At the end of this chapter the full series of analytical questions required are laid out and numbered corresponding to the explanatory sections that follow. There is a military maxim that no plan ever survives the first encounter with the enemy. Plans provide a guide to the way forward but an effective plan has sufficient flexibility built in to enable a series of contingencies to be dealt with.

All plans, and one definition of strategy is that it is a plan designed to move the organisation in a desired direction, should be built around clearly understood aims and objectives.

Organisations should have clearly defined aims and objectives that set out in C-SMART (see Chapter 1) terms what it is the organisation is wishing to achieve. There will doubtless be financial considerations and many aims and objectives may be written in financial terms. These can, however, often be related to customers. For example, if a 15% return on investment is a stated objective of an organisation, then this could be achieved by selling X% more product to the current number of customers, or Y amount of product to an increased number of customers, or Z amount of product to the current number of customers but at an increased price, and so on.

The vast majority of organisations will wish to either grow or at least stay the same. Not-for-profit organisations will wish to increase or maintain service levels. In times of cost reduction they will wish to maximise cost reduction whilst minimising the effect on service delivery. Few organisations will wish to decrease their customer base, although this may be an objective for the law and order and health sectors.

As stated earlier, no analysis can feature every facet of every organisation and those using the following techniques should adapt them as necessary to suit the particular organisational circumstances pertaining at the particular time. The analytical framework is split into two main sections, **INTERNAL** and **EXTERNAL**, representing the requirement to examine both the organisation itself and the wider environment within which it operates.

A) Internal analysis

1. What type of organisation is under consideration?
The organisation will be either one that can be described as FOR PROFIT or one that fits the NOT FOR PROFIT description. It will also be a PRIVATE SECTOR, a PUBLIC SECTOR or a VOLUNTARY SECTOR organisation. The aims, objectives and mission statement of the organisation should reflect its particular typology. The organisation will either be primarily PRODUCT based or SERVICE based.

Traditionally it has been private sector organisations that have led in the development of customer relations, although the public and voluntary sectors have been catching up rapidly. If the organisation is in the voluntary sector it may well have a part of the operation that mirrors the private sector and part that is more akin to the public sector. Charity shops are run on private sector, for profit lines, whilst the operations that use the monies generated by the shops may be more like those of the public sector.

2. Is the organisation CONCENTRATED or DIFFUSE?

A concentrated organisation will be located and operates in a small geographical area. A diffuse organisation may have branches and operations stretching over a wide, even global area. Consistency across the organisation is obviously easier for a concentrated organisation.

By answering questions 1 and 2, the organisation will have been fitted into a particular typology and this will allow for comparison with other organisations that 'look' the same.

3. Is the organisation: GROWING, STATIONARY or CONTRACTING?

A growing organisation will be concerned to expand its customer base; one that is at a standstill may wish to grow if the circumstances allow but is certainly likely to wish to protect its customer base. A contracting organisation may be doing so through choice but, for whatever reason it is contracting, it will wish to protect the relationship with its remaining customers; and if the contraction is not through choice it will wish to take steps to halt and hopefully reverse the decline.

4. What are the core and supplementary products/services of the organisation?

When thinking about this section, consider the question from the point of view of both the organisation and the customer. The organisation may feel that its product is motor cars, to the customer the real product is personal transportation.

5. What are the current strategic objectives of the organisation?

Not only should the current objectives be listed, but they should be translated into C-SMART criteria if they are not already in that format. The impact of the objectives on the customer is of vital importance when drawing up a strategy for effective customer relations.

6. BACK ANALYSIS

This is a recently devised analysis by Cartwright et al. (1994) designed to provide an analytical picture of an organisation. The letters stand for: BAGGAGE, ASPIRATIONS, CULTURE and KNOWLEDGE.

BAGGAGE

Imagine a person, with suitcases and hand baggage and souvenirs trying to exit a hotel through a set of revolving doors. In order to make progress they are going to have to put down one or more pieces of baggage. So it is with both organisational and personal life. 'Baggage' is collected as the organisation or individual moves through life. Life also presents a series of revolving doors which, being fixed in time, means that unlike the holidaymaker above, baggage once set down may not always be retrieved. Often it is the case that some baggage must be relinquished in order to make progress. The problem with baggage is that both individuals and organisations become very attached to it even when it no longer serves a practical purpose. How many lofts, garages and garden sheds are filled with those things that people cannot bear to throw away, just in case they might be useful! In organisational terms, baggage can include procedures that were once relevant but are no longer needed, or the imposition of procedures that do not match the need of the customer. A true case illustrates this well.

On moving to another part of the country a lady decided to replace her original kitchen appliances and to fit out her new house with new appliances. She visited a local retailer and ordered a new cooker, refrigerator, washing machine and tumble dryer at a total cost of over £2000. She asked for delivery in eight weeks' time and then made out a cheque for the whole amount and presented it with her cheque guarantee card. To her astonishment she was asked for further identification as company procedures demanded two sets of identification when a purchase was over £200. That is understandable when the customer is taking the goods with them but in this case the lady did not want delivery until eight weeks had passed. As the lady did not have a second form of identification with her, the sales person refused to process the order 'as it would be against company policy'. Despite the fact that it was the customer who was actually taking the risk that the company could go bankrupt in the time before delivery, and the company was, in effect, receiving an interest free loan of £2000, the sales person still refused to take the order. Result – a solid £2000 sale lost and, even worse, remembering the customer accumulator introduced early in this book, a gain of one customer by a competitor who was much more sensible. Baggage can cost money.

Procedures, policies, rules and even products themselves all need to be looked at when considering baggage. Much baggage is necessary but organisations should review it on a regular basis if they are still doing things that at best are of no practical use and at worse actually impede the relationship with the customer as shown above. Surplus baggage always consumes organisational energy and should be dropped as soon as possible. The best way to ascertain the baggage that an organisation carries with it is to talk to members of staff, not only about what they do but why they do it. If they don't know the answer to the second question, then this may indicate a piece of baggage that should be dropped.

ASPIRATIONS

If baggage is about where the organisation has been, then Aspirations is about where it wants to go. In conducting a BACK analysis, it is useful to ask staff at various levels within the organisation as to what they see as the main aspirations.

Aspirations can only be realised if they are unhindered by baggage, fit into the culture of the organisation and if the organisation possesses the necessary knowledge. This shows the interlocking nature of the four components of the BACK analysis. It is important that an organisation has an idea of its aspirations and that they are realistic, since it is only if one knows where one wants to go that proper plans can be made and implemented.

CULTURE

Culture, when referring to organisations, is a function of 'the way we do things around here'. As in definitions of national cultures, it is made up of a set of underlying values, assumptions and beliefs.

At its simplest, the organisation will lie on a continuum of 'Putting the Customer First' at one end and 'Putting the Organisation First' at the other, i.e. customer led or product driven (see Chapter 1).

It is possible to write whole books about organisational culture, as has indeed been done. Charles Handy (1976, 1978) has produced a simple-to-understand but highly effective descriptive method for illustrating organisational cultures. Handy has identified four types of organisational cultures each with its own distinctive behaviours.

ROLE CULTURE: This, which Handy depicted as a Greek temple (Figure 11.2), represents the typical bureaucratic organisation.

Such organisations have a plethora of rules and regulations with departmental boundaries clearly defined. They are often slow to change, seeing in stability their means of survival. The ROLE culture places great emphasis on stating what a person's job title is, rather than what the person actually does. In terms of customer relations, a ROLE culture can present a minefield for the customer, as there is little inter-departmental communication across the pillars of the temple. Communication tends to be up and down individual pillars. Such a structure is typical of many large organisations and has often been identified with the traditional public sector/governmental organisations. As concern for the customers becomes more and more important, even traditional organisations are trying to move away from the inflexibility that such a structure produces. Handy ascribes the god Apollo to this type of culture, as Apollo was the Greek god of order and rules.

CLUB/POWER: The god Zeus is ascribed by Handy to the spider's web of the CLUB/POWER culture (Figure 11.3). Power rests in the centre, often with a single

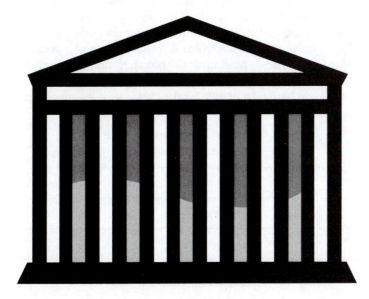

Figure 11.2   Role culture.

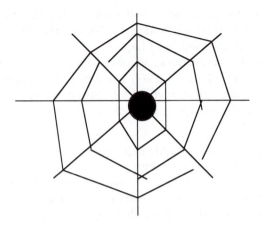

Figure 11.3   Club/Power culture.

individual with a strong personality. It is not unusual for that person to be the founder of the organisation. Power flows outwards from the centre. This is a culture that suits the entrepreneur who can keep an eye on operations. From the customer relations' standpoint, if the customer can get to the central power base, things will happen very quickly. CLUB cultures can move very quickly but only in the direction personally favoured by those at the centre. The UK based Virgin Group with Richard Branson in the centre became a byword for entrepreneurship in the 1990s, with operations that included an airline, music, personal finance and publishing – all interests of Mr Branson.

TASK CULTURE: In the 1980s and 1990s many larger organisations began to adopt a TASK culture approach. The TASK culture described by Handy is ascribed to Athena, the goddess of craftsmen and pioneering captains. Power in a TASK culture lies in expertise and creativity. Handy represents TASK cultures as a matrix (Figure 11.4). Whilst in a ROLE culture, promotion and advancement are regulated by rules relating to position in the hierarchy and time served; for those in a TASK culture advancement is purely on ability. TASK cultures actively break down departmental barriers and thus for the customer it is a much easier task to

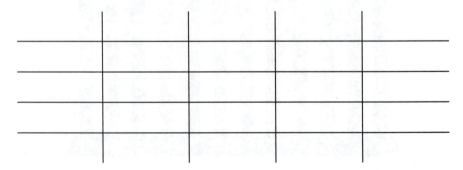

Figure 11.4   TASK culture.

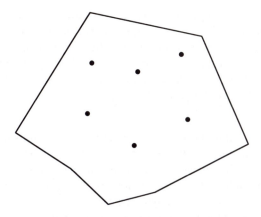

Figure 11.5   EXISTENTIAL culture.

make contact with the right person, who can then involve others. A customer is more likely to be perceived of as an integral part of the organisation in a TASK culture.

EXISTENTIAL CULTURE: Represented in Handy's work by the god Dionysus, the god of wine and song, Handy (1978) points out that the ROLE, POWER/CLUB and TASK cultures all have one thing in common: the individual employee is there to serve the organisation (it might be argued that this does not apply to the individual or the small group at the centre of a POWER/CLUB culture). In the EXISTENTIAL culture (Figure 11.5), the organisation exists to serve the needs of those in it. A partnership of doctors, architects, lawyers etc. is an example of an EXISTENTIAL culture. Such organisations suit professionals who may well appoint a manager to see to the day-to-day running but the professionals themselves operate on the basis that they are all equal. The lack of rules and procedures may actually make it difficult for the customer but they will not have to negotiate a bureaucracy in order to communicate.

It is interesting to observe what happens when two cultures interact in either a competitor situation or a customer/supplier relationship. In the 1980s and 1990s the rivalry between British Airways and Virgin Atlantic led to a series of court actions (Gregory, 1994). In terms of organisation, what was actually happening was that a ROLE culture (as BA was at the time) was competing with a POWER/CLUB culture, with interesting results.

It is not difficult to imagine the frustration a ROLE culture might experience if it becomes the customer of an EXISTENTIAL supplier; the former's rules may well be alien to the latter. One can look at the possibilities of a whole range of combinations. What is important when considering relationships with the customer is that:

The customer should not have to adapt their culture to the organisation; it is the organisation that must adapt if it wishes to gain and retain that customer.

There is a useful concept from George Bernard Shaw and used by Handy in 1989: Shaw remarked that all progress depends on unreasonable people. Reasonable people adapt themselves to the world whilst those who are unreasonable persist in trying to adapt the world to themselves. A successful organisation will attempt to adapt itself to the customers and not force customers to adapt to its methods and procedures.

KNOWLEDGE

It is common sense that certain things cannot be accomplished without prior knowledge. If an organisation wishes to pursue a particular strategy or set of goals it needs people with the relevant knowledge. This is one area where consultancy has grown, as that allows the organisation to obtain the knowledge and skills when needed without long-term payroll costs.

Organisations that value the knowledge held by their people and which have the development of people as a clear part of their overall strategy can be termed 'Learning Organisations'. An organisation that develops its staff also acquires organisational knowledge, which permeates through to organisation. As part of the BACK analysis it is important to consider those aspects of organisational knowledge that can form entries in the SWOT analysis, details of which follow this section.

7. SWOT ANALYSIS

A SWOT analysis is a two-part analysis: the first part looks at the strengths and weaknesses of the organisation and is thus an INTERNAL analysis, while the second part considers the threats and opportunities facing the organisation from the external environment, many of which may be derived from the EXTERNAL PESTLE analysis that is covered later.

The STRENGTHS of an organisation are those things it does particularly well, especially when viewed against the operations of its competitors, whereas its WEAKNESSES are areas in which it is less strong than the competition.

OPPORTUNITIES are those external factors where the organisation can use its STRENGTHS to outclass the competition and THREATS are those factors from

STRENGTHS	WEAKNESSES
OPPORTUNITIES	THREATS

Figure 11.6   SWOT quadrant.

the external environment from which the organisation may suffer because of its WEAKNESSES.

The goal should always be to aim for strategies that build on STRENGTHS, minimise WEAKNESSES, exploit OPPORTUNITIES and defend against THREATS.

A SWOT analysis is usually displayed as a quadrant, as shown in Figure 11.6.

Items may appear in more than one quadrant. The large size of an organisation may be seen as a strength when it comes to economies of scale but a weakness in respect of communications. It is perfectly legitimate to place it in both quadrants.

8. 7S ANALYSIS

As part of their seminal work on excellence, Peters & Waterman (1982) developed a model of the internal factors that affect an organisation. This has become known as the McKinsey 7S Model (Figure 11.7) after the consulting firm who sponsored their research.

Whilst originally designed as a model to aid an understanding of those factors leading to excellence, the model is also useful when considering the nature of organisations and change scenarios.

At the centre of the model are SHARED VALUES, part of the culture of the organisation. These are the values that all who work within the organisation are expected to share; if they do not then something is wrong. Often it is that the organisation has not disseminated its values effectively enough. These values change very slowly over time and are reflected in the culture of the organisation.

Around the outside and all interlinked are the other key 'Ss':

STRUCTURE
How has the organisation structured itself, is it very hierarchical or centred around one or two powerful individuals or departments, or is there a matrix structure in place? Very often the structure reflects the underlying culture of the organisation, with an old-fashioned hierarchy often having a very clear layered structure, and a task culture organisation being much more diffuse in its structure.

SYSTEM
What system has the organisation in place to control and monitor its operations? Linked to this will be the amount of freedom given to subordinates to make decisions and the degree to which initiative is allowed and tolerated.

STYLE
What is the main style of management used in the organisation? Are managers free to innovate and to deal with customer issues without recourse to higher authority, or does the culture and organisation constrain their responses?

STAFF
What type of people does the organisation employ and how readily will they respond to change? Whilst SKILLS relates to the actual tasks people carry out, STAFF is concerned with their attitudes.

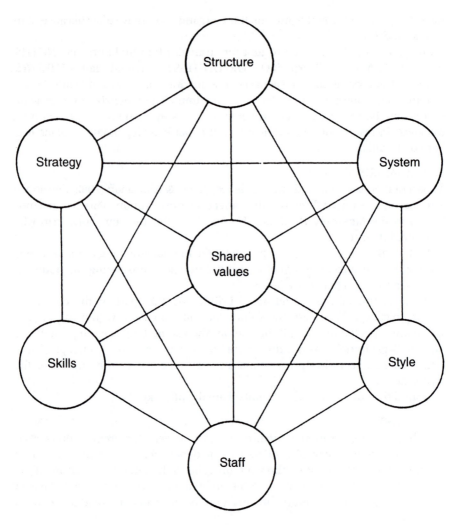

Figure 11.7   The McKinsey 7S Model.

SKILLS
Are the skills required to move forward present in the organisation or will they need to be developed and maybe brought in?

STRATEGY
Where does the organisation want to go and how easy will this be given the implications of the other Ss?

The key point about this model is that the Ss are interlinked and that a change to one will require changes to the others. It is also important that the organisation tries to keep either the centre or the rim stable. If the six outer Ss are being changed then it is helpful to keep the shared values constant; if a cultural change is required, try to have as few changes as possible in the rim.

To show the model can be used, consider the following example. Without wishing to change its values of care for customers and quality etc., an organisation decides to introduce a new computerised ordering system, i.e. a change to SYSTEM. However such a change will also require new SKILLS and maybe STAFF with different aptitudes and abilities. Perhaps the new IT system will allow for changes in the way the organisation communicates (email etc.) and this may allow for a change in STRUCTURE to a more decentralised form. This may well lead to a change in STYLE and with new methods of working in place and a (hopefully) more effective communications system, it may be that new STRATEGIES are possible.

9. INTERNAL CUSTOMERS

The importance of the internal customer has been stressed throughout this book. A series of value chains for the organisation showing the links between internal customers should be constructed.

B) External analysis

10. PESTLE ANALYSIS

Originally known as a PEST (Political, Economic, Social and Technological) analysis, this has recently been refined to PESTLE by the addition of Environmental and Legal considerations. This model provides a framework with which to consider the key EXTERNAL factors that will affect your organisation.

Each of the six components will be taken in turn although it should be noted that they do not form rigid pigeonholes. For instance, Interest rates may be seen as an Economic or a Political factor, for whilst the Bank of England has sole responsibility for setting rates, they are influenced heavily by the government. It matters less where something is placed as long as it is considered.

The items that you would consider under each heading vary from organisation to organisation. If you are a manager in a major airline, oil prices and exchange rates are key considerations under the Economic heading; they may be less important to a public sector, service based organisation.

POLITICAL

Political factors include government policy, and the policy of international organisations if relevant, for example the EU and the UN. The Public Sector Borrowing Requirement (PSBR) may be placed here or under the Economic heading for public sector organisations. Relationships between government and staff associations and unions may be relevant.

ECONOMIC

Every organisation needs money to function. Public sector organisations receive the vast majority of their operating cash from the public purse. How much is available and what other calls are there on the public purse? If the organisation needs to borrow money, how will changes in interest rates affect the raising of capital? Shareholders need to respond to changes in economic circumstances and the availability of disposable income to customers will be a major consideration.

SOCIAL

What does society want from the organisation and how will social trends affect it? The move towards ethical considerations may affect the relationship between an organisation and its customers.

TECHNOLOGICAL

What is happening in the fast moving world of technology that will affect your organisation? Chapter 7 considered the impact of technology on customer service and provided examples that may be relevant to this part of the analysis.

LEGAL

Chapter 6 considered the legal issues that affect the relationship between an organisation and its customers. Which of them are important to the organisation in question?

ENVIRONMENTAL

This has recently been added as a separate heading to reflect the growing public awareness of the environment. How will environmental concerns affect the way the organisation operates? As not only chemical but also noise and even visual pollution enter the public consciousness, may these have implications for the organisation?

11. STAKEHOLDERS/PUBLICS

The next step is to list the major stakeholders/publics who interface with the organisation (see Chapter 9) and consider their particular needs. The following list provides an idea of the groups to be considered but there may be others depending on the nature of the organisation: Customers, Employees, Shareholders, Local taxpayers, National taxpayers, Trade Unions, Local and National Government, Suppliers and the Media.

12. COMPETITOR ANALYSIS

List the current major competitors and complete a SWOT analysis on each of them. This will allow for a direct comparison between the organisation and its current competitors to see if there are any competitors whose strengths outweigh the organisation or whose weaknesses are less than those of the organisation.

It is also important to consider what are the barriers to any other competitors entering the market and whether there are any possible competitors who could enter the market by acquiring another organisation (re-forming) or who could re-enter the market, together with the likelihood of there being substitute products/services.

13. SUPPLIERS

Suppliers are obviously very important as they form part of the value chain that leads to the external customer. Consider whether the organisation has a large or a small number of key suppliers. What happens if a major supplier fails in its customer care?

14. CUSTOMER ANALYSIS

There are three types of customers to consider:

a) Ex Customers, who are they and why are they no longer customers?
b) Current Customers, who are they and what do they value about the organisation? Are there any hostages?
c) Potential Customers, i.e. are there any groups that could become customers and what steps can the organisation take to gain their custom?

And not forgetting:

d) Are there any existing or potential customers that the organisation DOES NOT want to be associated with? It might be that there are particular groups or types of customers that might cause a public relations' problem or who might be just too demanding.

15. OBL AUDIT

Based on the information provided in Chapter 8, an Organisational Body Language audit should be undertaken.

For the part of the organisation under consideration or the whole organisation if required, consider the following points and rate them as either EXCELLENT (E), SATISFACTORY (S) or NOT SATISFACTORY (N). For excellent ratings, comment on why that particular facet of OBL is so good. For SATISFACTORY or NOT SATISFACTORY ratings, suggest how improvements could be made.

Facet	E	S	N	Comment
LOCATION / BUILDINGS				
Easy to find				
Attractive				
Gardens etc.				
Maintenance				
Cleanliness				
SECURITY				
Well lit				
Security of access				
Internal security				
CONVENIENCE				
Car parking				

(*continued on page 220*)

(*continued*)

Toilets				
Children's facilities				
Disabled facilities				
COMMUNICATIONS				
Signs				
General information				
Correspondence				
Telephone techniques				
AMBIENCE				
Reception				
Waiting areas				
Drinks etc.				
Staff attitudes				

The above is a basic OBL audit. When carrying out such an audit, you should devise your own form. There is no reason why scores should not be allocated in order to compare similar organisations or different parts of the operation within the same organisation. This can be especially useful when dealing with a branch network, as there can be a degree of objectivity in comparing the branches.

Evaluation of data

Carrying out the various analyses will provide a vast amount of data. It will be possible to provide a clear picture of both the organisation and the needs and wants of its customers. The data can then be used to derive effective strategies for customer relations.

The final step will be to look at any costs associated with the chosen strategy. If the costs required to meet the needs of the customer are acceptable to the organisation and the customer, then all well and good; if not, then the strategy might be an excellent one for the customer but a poor one for the organisation.

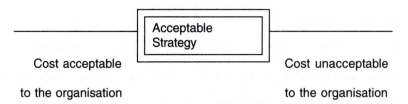

Price/quality unacceptable   Price/quality acceptable

to the customer   to the customer

Acceptable Strategy

Cost acceptable   Cost unacceptable

to the organisation   to the organisation

Figure 11.8   Acceptable strategy.

For an organisation that measures success in terms of profit, the acceptable strategy will be linked to whether the organisation deals in high volumes with a low margin or low volumes with a high margin, i.e. pile 'em high and sell 'em cheap or vice versa.

The acceptable strategy will meet the needs of both organisation and customer (Figure 11.8) in that it delivers mutually acceptable quality at a cost the organisation can accept and at a price the customer is willing to pay. Such a strategy can only be derived through a careful study of the customer.

The full analysis follows.

CUSTOMER RELATIONS' ANALYSIS

A)   INTERNAL ANALYSIS

1. What type of organisation is under consideration?

FOR PROFIT   NOT FOR PROFIT

PRIVATE SECTOR   PUBLIC SECTOR   VOLUNTARY SECTOR

2. Is the organisation: CONCENTRATED   DIFFUSE?

3. Is the organisation: GROWING   STATIONARY   CONTRACTING?

4.

a) What are the core products/services of the organisation? List these in terms of what the organisation believes they are and what it is that the customer actually wants.

Organisation's view of what the product is	Customer's actual need/want

(*continued on page 222*)

(*continued*)

b) What are the supplementary products/services of the organisation?

5. What are the current strategic objectives of the organisation?

6. BACK ANALYSIS:
BAGGAGE

ASPIRATIONS

CULTURE

KNOWLEDGE

7. SWOT ANALYSIS

STRENGTHS	WEAKNESSES
OPPORTUNITIES	THREATS

You should give each item under each heading a score out of 10. Add up the scores and put them below:

Strengths _____   Weaknesses: _____

Opportunities: _____   Threats: _____

(these scores will be used in question 8)

8. 7S ANALYSIS

a) What are the Shared Values of the organisation?

b) Consider the organisation in terms of the strengths and weaknesses for each of the 6 remaining 7S components:

COMPONENT	STRENGTHS	WEAKNESSES
STAFF		
STRUCTURES		
SYSTEMS		
SKILLS		
STYLE		
STRATEGY		

9. INTERNAL CUSTOMERS

Draw up a series of value chains for the organisation showing the links between internal customers.

B) EXTERNAL ANALYSIS

10. PESTLE ANALYSIS

POLITICAL

ECONOMIC

SOCIAL

TECHNOLOGICAL

LEGAL

ENVIRONMENTAL

11. STAKEHOLDERS/PUBLICS

List the major stakeholders/publics who interface with the organisation and consider their particular needs.

Stakeholder/Public	Needs
Customers	
Employees	
Shareholders (if appropriate)	
Taxpayers (local & national if appropriate)	
Trade Unions	
Government (local and national)	
Government –pan-national, e.g. EU (if appropriate)	
Suppliers	
Media	
Others	

12. COMPETITOR ANALYSIS

a) List the current major competitors:

b) Complete a SWOT analysis for each of them, highlighting any differences between the competitors and the organisation in question:

Competitor name: _____

STRENGTHS	WEAKNESSES
OPPORTUNITIES	THREATS

Score each item under each heading out of 10.

c) Complete the following table using the scores from the organisation in question and all the competitors you considered:

	Strengths	Weaknesses	Opportunities	Threats
Organisation				
Competitor A				
Competitor B				
Competitor C				
Competitor D				

Continue with other competitors if necessary.

d) Are there any competitors whose strengths outweigh the organisation or whose weaknesses are fewer than those of the organisation? What steps can be taken to rectify the situation?

e) What are the barriers to any other competitors entering the market?

f) Are there any possible competitors who could enter the market by acquiring another organisation (re-forming)?

g) Are there any organisations that could re-enter the market?

h) What are the likelihood of there being substitute products/services?

13. SUPPLIERS

a) Has the organisation a large or a small number of key suppliers?

b) How effective is the customer service relationship between the key suppliers and the organisation?

14. CUSTOMER ANALYSIS

a) Ex-Customers

List, putting into groups where appropriate, ex-customers together with the reason why they are no longer customers.

Customer Group   Reason for leaving

b) Current Customers

List the current groups of customers and state why it is believed they use the organisation. Be on the lookout for any 'hostages'.

Customer Group   Reason

c) Potential Customers
Are there any groups that could become customers and what steps can the organisation take to gain their custom?

Customer Group	Steps to gain custom

d) Are there any existing or potential customers that the organisation DOES NOT want to be associated with?

15. ORGANISATIONAL BODY LANGUAGE AUDIT

For the part of the organisation under consideration or the whole organisation if required, consider the following points and rate them as either EXCELLENT (E), SATISFACTORY (S) or NOT SATISFACTORY (N). For excellent ratings, comment on why that particular facet of OBL is so good. For SATISFACTORY or NOT SATISFACTORY ratings, suggest how improvements could be made.

Facet	E	S	N	Comment
LOCATION / BUILDINGS				
Easy to find				
Attractive				
Gardens etc.				
Maintenance				
Cleanliness				
SECURITY				
Well lit				
Security of access				
Internal security				
CONVENIENCE				
Car parking				
Toilets				
Children's facilities				
Disabled facilities				
COMMUNICATIONS				
Signs				
General information				
Correspondence				
Telephone techniques				
AMBIENCE				
Reception				

(*continued on page 232*)

(continued)

Waiting areas				
Drinks etc.				
Staff attitudes				

The above is a basic OBL audit. When carrying out such an audit, you should devise your own form. There is no reason why scores should not be allocated in order to compare similar organisations or different parts of the operation within the same organisation. This can be especially useful when dealing with a branch network, as there can be a degree of objectivity in comparing the branches.

▼ Bibliography

Adler E (1969) *Lectures in Market Research*, Crosby Lockwood, London
Allen R E (ed) (1990) *The Concise Oxford Dictionary*, Oxford University Press
Alsop R (1989) 'Brand Loyalty is Rarely Blind Loyalty', *Wall Street Journal*, 19 October, p. 1
Benjamin W (1973) 'The Work of Art in the Age of Mechanical Reproduction', in *Illuminations*, Fontana
Berne E (1964) *Games People Play*, André Deutsch
Bernstein C & Woodward B (1994) *All the Presidents Men*, Touchstone
Brassington F & Pettitt S (1997) *Principles of Marketing*, Financial Times/Pitman
Cartwright R & Baird C (1999) *The Development and Growth of the Cruise Industry*, Butterworth Heinemann
Cartwright R & Green G (1997) *In Charge of Customer Satisfaction*, Blackwell
Cartwright R, Collins M, Green G & Candy A (1994) *In Charge – Managing Yourself*, Blackwell
Cartwright R, Collins M, Green G & Candy A (1998a) *In Charge – Managing People*, Blackwell
Cartwright R, Collins M, Green G & Candy A (1998b) *In Charge – Managing Resources and Information*, Blackwell
Casserley H C (1980) *The Observer's Directory of British Steam Locomotives*, Warne
Celsi T (1991) *Ralph Nader – The Consumer Revolution*, Millbrook
Churchill D (1999) 'Can I have my change in Air Miles please?' *British Airways Business Life*, July/August, pp. 83–6
Clutterbuck D & Goldsmith W (1983) *The Winning Streak*, Orion
Clutterbuck D & Goldsmith W (1997) *The Winning Streak Mark II*, Orion
Clutterbuck D, Clark G & Armistead C (1993) *Inspired Customer Service*, Kogan Page
Cobb R (1995) 'Testing the Ties', *Marketing*, 6 April, p. 18
Crosby P B (1979) *Quality is Free*, New American Library
Davie M (1986) *Titanic – The Full Story of a Tragedy*, Bodley Head
Dawkins R (1976) *The Selfish Gene*, Oxford University Press
de Jonge P (1999) whiteknuckleride@amazon.com, *Daily Telegraph Magazine*, 21 August, pp. 38–46
Deming W E (1988) *Out of Crisis*, Cambridge University Press
Dickinson R & Vladimir A (1997) *Selling the Sea*, Wiley
Eddy P, Potter E & Page B (1976) *Destination Disaster*, Hart-Davis
Fayol H (1916) *General and Industrial Administration*, translated from the French by C Storrs (1949) Pitman
Fenton J (1984) *How to Sell Against Competition*, Heinemann

Green W, Swanborough G & Mowinski J (1987) *Modern Commercial Aircraft*, Salamander

Gregory M (1994) *Dirty Tricks – British Airway's Secret War against Virgin Atlantic*, Little, Brown & Co

Handy C (1976) *Understanding Organisations*, Penguin

Handy C (1978) *Gods of Management*, Souvenir Press

Handy C (1989) *The Age of Unreason*, Business Books Ltd

Harris T A (1970) *I'm OK, You're OK* (first published as *The Book Of Choice*), Jonathan Cape

Hastings M & Jenkins S (1983) *The Battle for the Falklands*, Michael Joseph

Herzberg F (1962) *Work and the Nature of Man*, World Publishing

HM Government (1973) *Fair Trading Act 1973*, HMSO

HM Government (1974) *Consumer Credit Act 1974*, HMSO

HM Government (1974) *Health and Safety at Work Act 1974*, HMSO

HM Government (1982) *Supply of Goods and Service Act 1982*, HMSO

HM Government (1994) *Sale and Supply of Gods Act 1994*, HMSO

HM Government (1997) *Consumer Protection Act 1997*, HMSO

Irving C (1993) *Wide Body, the Making of the Boeing 747*, Hodder & Stoughton

Jefkins F (1980) *Public Relations*, Macdonald & Evans

Johnson G & Scholes K (1993) *Exploring Corporate Strategy*, 3rd edn, Prentice Hall

Jones T O & Strasser W E Jnr (1995) 'Why Satisfied Customers Defect', *Harvard Business Review*, Nov–Dec, pp. 88–99

Juran J (1964) *Managerial Breakthrough*, McGraw-Hill

Juran J (1989) *Juran on Leadership*, Macmillan

Kotler P (1980) *Marketing Management*, Prentice Hall

Lewin K (1951) *Field Theory in Social Science*, Harper

Lorenz K (1963) *On Aggression*, Methuen

Lynn J & Jay W (1987) *Yes Prime Minister*, BBC

Maslow A (1970) *Motivation and Personality*, Harper & Row

McCannell D (1973) 'Staged Authenticity: Arrangements of Social Space in Tourist Settings', *Journal of Sociology*, Vol. 79, pp. 589–603

MacDonald J & Piggott J (1990) *Global Quality – The New Management Culture*, Mercury

Marston J E (1979) *Modern Public Relations*, McGraw-Hill

Mechanical Engineering EDC (1971) *Market Research in Action – a Guide for Company Management*, HMSO

Mitchell A (1995) 'Preaching the Loyalty Message', *Marketing Week*, 1 December, pp. 26–7

Montague J (1987) *Business Law*, Chambers

Nader R (1965) *Unsafe at any Speed*, Grossman

Neave H (1990) *The Deming Dimension*, SPC Press

Pascale R T & Athos A G (1981) *The Art of Japanese Management*, Simon & Schuster

Peters T (1987) *Thriving on Chaos*, Alfred A Knopf

Peters T & Waterman R (1982) *In Search of Excellence*, Harper & Row

Porter M (1980) *Competitive Advantage*, Free Press

Porter M (1985) *Competitive Strategy*, Free Press

Sabbach K (1995) *21ˢᵗ Century Jet – the Making of the Boeing 777*, Macmillan

Sampson A (1984) *Empires of the Skies*, Hodder & Stoughton

Stewart S (1986*) Air Disasters*, Ian Allan

Taylor F W (1911) *Principles of Scientific Management*, Harper

Tice L (1989) *Investing in Excellence* (Multimedia), Pacific Institute

Trompenaars F (1993) *Riding the Waves of Culture*, Economist Books

Trudgill P (1975) *Accent, Dialect and the School*, Arnold

Vroom V H (1964) *Work and Motivation*, Wiley

Ward D (1994, 1998, 1999) *Berlitz Guide to Cruising and Cruise Ships – 1994, 1998, 1999*, Berlitz

Wille E (1992) *Quality – Achieving Excellence*, Century Business

Wilmshurst J (1978) *The Fundamentals and Practice of Marketing*, Heinemann

Wind J (1982) *Product, Policy and Concepts, Methods and Strategy*, Addison-Wesley

Winder D (1999) 'On Line Banking', in *PC Pro*, issue 57, July, pp. 206–18

Wotherspoon K R (1995) 'The Sale and Supply of Goods Act 1994', *Journal of the Law Society of Scotland*, March, pp. 88–91, Law Society of Scotland

Zdarek I (1988) *How Animals Communicate*, Hamlyn

⚎ Index